CHARLES DICKENS

A CRITICAL STUDY

BY

G. K. CHESTERTON

Author of Varied Types, Heretics, Etc.

NEW YORK
DODD MEAD & COMPANY
1907

First Edition Published in September, 1906

To

RHODA BASTABLE

CONTENTS

CONTENTS

CHAPTER I

THE DICKENS PERIOD

MUCH of our modern difficulty, in religion and other things, arises merely from this, that we confuse the word "indefinable" with the word "vague." If some one speaks of a spiritual fact as "indefinable" we promptly picture something misty, a cloud with indeterminate edges. But this is an error even in common-place logic. The thing that cannot be defined is the first thing; the primary fact. It is our arms and legs, our pots and pans, that are indefinable. The indefinable is the indisputable. The man next door is indefinable, because he is too actual to be defined. And there are some to whom spiritual things have the same fierce and practical proximity; some to whom God is too actual to be defined.

But there is a third class of primary terms. There are popular expressions which every one uses and no one can explain; which the wise man will accept and reverence, as he reverences desire or darkness or any elemental thing. The prigs of the debating club will demand that he should define his terms. And being a wise man he will flatly refuse. This first inexplicable term is the most important term of all. The word that has no definition is the word that has no substitute. If a man falls back again and again on some such word as "vulgar" or "manly" do not suppose that the word means nothing because he cannot say what it means. If he could say what the word means he would say what it means instead of saying the word. When the Game Chicken (that fine thinker) kept on saying to Mr. Toots, "It's mean. That's what it is—it's mean," he was using language in the wisest possible way. For what else could he say? There is no word for mean except mean. A man must be very mean himself before he comes to defining meanness. Precisely because the word is indefinable, the word is indispensable.

In everyday talk, or in any of our journals, we may find the loose but important phrase, "Why have we no great men to-day? Why have we no great men like Thackeray, or Carlyle, or Dickens?" Do not let us dismiss this expression, because it appears loose or arbitrary. "Great" does mean something, and the test of its actuality is to be found by noting how instinctively and decisively we do apply it to some men and not to others; above all how instinctively and decisively we do apply it to four or five men in the Victorian era, four or five men of whom Dickens was not the least. The term is found to fit a definite thing. Whatever the word " great " means, Dickens was what it means. Even the fastidious and unhappy who cannot read his books without a continuous critical exasperation, would use the word of him without stopping to think. They feel that Dickens is a great writer even if he is not a good writer. He is treated as a classic; that is, as a king who may now be deserted, but who cannot now be dethroned. The atmosphere of this word clings to him; and the curious thing is that we cannot get it to cling to any of the men of our own generation. " Great " is the first adjective which the most supercilious modern critic would apply to Dickens. And " great " is the last adjective that the most supercilious modern critic would apply to himself. We dare not claim to be great men, even when we claim to be superior to them.

Is there, then, any vital meaning in this idea of " greatness " or in our laments over its absence in our own time? Some people say, indeed, that this sense of mass is but a mirage of distance, and that men always think dead men great and live men small. They seem to think that the law of perspective in the mental world is the precise opposite to the law of perspective in the physical world. They think that figures grow larger as they walk away. But this theory cannot be made to correspond with the facts. We do not lack great men in our own day because we decline to look for them in our own day; on the contrary, we are looking for them all day long. We are not, as a matter of fact, mere examples of those who stone the prophets and leave it to their posterity to build their sepulchres. If the world would only produce our perfect prophet, solemn, searching, universal, nothing would give us keener pleasure than to build his sepulchre. In our eagerness we might even bury him alive. Nor is it true that the great men of the Victorian era were not called great in their own time. By many they were called great from the first. Charlotte Brontë held this heroic language about Thackeray. Ruskin held it about Carlyle. A definite school regarded Dickens as a great man from the first days of his fame: Dickens certainly belonged to this school.

In reply to this question, "Why have we no great men to-day?" many modern explanations are offered. Advertisement, cigarette-smoking, the decay of religion, the decay of agriculture, too much humanitarianism, too little humanitarianism, the fact that people are educated insufficiently, the fact that they are educated at all, all these are reasons given. If I give my own explanation, it is not for its intrinsic value; it is because my answer to the question, " Why have we no great men? " is a short way of stating the deepest and most catastrophic difference between the age in which we live and the early nineteenth century; the age under the shadow of the French Revolution, the age in which Dickens was born.

The soundest of the Dickens critics, a man of genius, Mr. George Gissing, opens his criticism by remarking that the world in which Dickens grew up was a hard and cruel world. He notes its gross feeding, its fierce sports, its fighting and foul humour, and all this he summarizes in the words hard and cruel. It is curious how different are the impressions of men. To me this old English world seems infinitely less hard and cruel than the world described in Gissing's own novels. Coarse external customs are merely relative, and easily assimilated. A man soon learnt to harden his hands and harden his head. Faced with the world of Gissing, he can do little but harden his heart. But the fundamental difference between the beginning of the nineteenth century and the end of it is a difference simple but enormous. The first period was full of evil things, but it was full of hope. The second period, the *fin de siècle,* was even full (in some sense) of good things. But it was occupied in asking what was the good of good things. Joy itself became joyless; and the fighting of Cobbett was happier than the feasting of Walter Pater. The men of Cobbett's day were sturdy enough to endure and inflict brutality; but they were also sturdy enough to alter it. This "hard and cruel" age was, after all, the age of reform. The gibbet stood up black above them; but it was black against the dawn.

This dawn, against which the gibbet and all the old cruelties stood out so black and clear, was the developing idea of liberalism, the French Revolution. It was a clear and a happy philosophy. And only against such philosophies do evils appear evident at all. The optimist is a better reformer than the pessimist; and the man who believes life to be excellent is the man who alters it most. It seems a paradox, yet the reason of it is very plain. The pessimist can be enraged at evil. But only the optimist can be surprised at it. From the reformer is required a simplicity of surprise. He must have the faculty of a violent and virgin astonishment. It is not enough that he should think injustice distressing; he must think injustice *absurd,* an anomaly in existence, a matter less for tears than for a shattering laughter. On the other hand, the pessimists at the end of the century could hardly curse even the blackest thing; for they could hardly see it against its black and eternal background. Nothing was bad, because everything was bad. Life in prison was infamous—like life anywhere else. The fires of persecution were vile—like the stars. We perpetually find this paradox of a contented discontent. Dr. Johnson takes too sad a view of humanity, but he is also too satisfied a Conservative. Rousseau takes too rosy a view of humanity, but he causes a revolution. Swift is angry, but a Tory. Shelley is happy, and a rebel. Dickens, the optimist, satirizes the Fleet, and the Fleet is gone. Gissing, the pessimist, satirizes Suburbia, and Suburbia remains.

Mr. Gissing's error, then, about the early Dickens period we may put thus: in calling it hard and cruel he omits the wind of hope and humanity that was blowing through it. It may have been full of inhuman institutions, but it was full of humanitarian people. And this humanitarianism was very much the better (in my view) because it was a rough and even rowdy humanitarianism.

It was free from all the faults that cling to the name. It was, if you will, a coarse humanitarianism. It was a shouting, fighting, drinking philanthropy—a noble thing. But, in any case, this atmosphere was the atmosphere of the Revolution; and its main idea was the idea of human equality. I am not concerned here to defend the egalitarian idea against the solemn and babyish attacks made upon it by the rich and learned of to-day. I am merely concerned to state one of its practical consequences. One of the actual and certain consequences of the idea that all men are equal is immediately to produce very great men. I would say superior men, only that the hero thinks of himself as great, but not as superior. This has been hidden from us of late by a foolish worship of sinister and exceptional men, men without comradeship, or any infectious virtue. This type of Cæsar does exist. There is a great man who makes every man feel small. But the real great man is the man who makes every man feel great.

The spirit of the early century produced great men, because it believed that men were great. It made strong men by encouraging weak men. Its education, its public habits, its rhetoric, were all addressed towards encouraging the greatness in everybody. And by encouraging the greatness in everybody, it naturally encouraged superlative greatness in some. Superiority came out of the high rapture of equality. It is precisely in this sort of passionate unconsciousness and bewildering community of thought that men do become more than themselves. No man by taking thought can add one cubit to his stature; but a man may add many cubits to his stature by not taking thought. The best men of the Revolution were simply common men at their best. This is why our age can never understand Napoleon. Because he was something great and triumphant, we suppose that he must have been something extraordinary, something inhuman. Some say he was the Devil; some say he was the Superhuman. Was he a very, very bad man? Was he a good man with some greater moral code? We strive in vain to invent the mysteries behind that immortal mask of brass. The modern world with all its subtleness will never guess his strange secret; for his strange secret was that he was very like other people.

And almost without exception all the great men have come out of this atmosphere of equality. Great men may make despotisms; but democracies make great men. The other main factory of heroes besides a revolution is a religion. And a religion again, is a thing which, by its nature, does not think of men as more or less valuable, but of men as all intensely and painfully valuable, a democracy of eternal danger. For religion all men are equal, as all pennies are equal, because the only value in any of them is that they bear the image of the King. This fact has been quite insufficiently observed in the study of religious heroes. Piety produces intellectual greatness precisely because piety in itself is quite indifferent to intellectual greatness. The strength of Cromwell was that he cared for religion. But the strength of religion was that it did not care for Cromwell; did not care for him, that is, any more than for anybody else. He and his footman were equally welcomed to warm places in the hospitality of hell. It has often been said, very truly, that religion is the thing that makes the ordinary man feel extraordinary; it is an equally important truth that religion is the thing that makes the extraordinary man feel ordinary.

Carlyle killed the heroes; there have been none since his time. He killed the heroic (which he sincerely loved) by forcing upon each man this question: "Am I strong or weak?" To which the answer from any honest man whatever (yes, from Cæsar or Bismarck) would certainly be "weak." He asked for candidates for a definite aristocracy, for men who should hold themselves consciously above their fellows. He advertised for them, so to speak; he promised them glory; he promised them omnipotence. They have not appeared yet. They never will. For the real heroes of whom he wrote had appeared out of an ecstacy of the ordinary. I have already instanced such a case as Cromwell. But there is no need to go through all the great men of Carlyle. Carlyle himself was as great as any of them; and if ever there was a typical child of the French Revolution, it was he. He began with the wildest hopes from the Reform Bill, and although he soured afterwards, he had been made and moulded by those hopes. He was disappointed with Equality; but Equality was not disappointed with him. Equality is justified of all her children.

But we, in the post-Carlylean period, have become fastidious about great men. Every man examines himself, every man examines his neighbours, to see whether they or he quite come up to the exact line of greatness. The answer is, naturally, "No." And many a man calls himself contentedly "a minor poet" who would then have been inspired to be a major prophet. We are hard to please and of little faith. We can hardly believe that there is such a thing as a great man.

They could hardly believe there was such a thing as a small one. But we are always praying that our eyes may behold greatness, instead of praying that our hearts may be filled with it. Thus, for instance, the Liberal party (to which I belong) was, in its period of exile, always saying, "O for a Gladstone!" and such things. We were always asking that it might be strengthened from above, instead of ourselves strengthening it from below, with our hope and our anger and our youth. Every man was waiting for a leader. Every man ought to be waiting for a chance to lead. If a god does come upon the earth, he will descend at the sight of the brave. Our protestations and litanies are of no avail; our new moons and our sabbaths are an abomination. The great man will come when all of us are feeling great, not when all of us are feeling small. He will ride in at some splendid moment when we all feel that we could do without him.

We are then able to answer in some manner the question, "Why have we no great men?" We have no great men chiefly because we are always looking for them. We are connoisseurs of greatness, and connoisseurs can never be great; we are fastidious, that is, we are small. When Diogenes went about with a lantern looking for an honest man, I am afraid he had very little time to be honest himself. And when anybody goes about on his hands and knees looking for a great man to worship, he is making sure that one man at any rate shall not be great. Now, the error of Diogenes is evident. The error of Diogenes lay in the fact that he omitted to notice that every man is both an honest man and a dishonest man. Diogenes looked for his honest man inside every crypt and cavern; but he never thought of looking inside the thief. And that is where the Founder of Christianity found the honest man; He found him on a gibbet and promised him Paradise. Just as Christianity looked for the honest man inside the thief, democracy looked for the wise man inside the fool. It encouraged the fool to be wise. We can call this thing sometimes optimism, sometimes equality; the nearest name for it is encouragement. It had its exaggerations—failure to understand original sin, notions that education would make all men good, the childlike yet pedantic philosophies of human perfectibility. But the whole was full of a faith in the infinity of human souls, which is in itself not only Christian but orthodox; and this we have lost amid the limitations of a pessimistic science. Christianity said that any man could be a saint if he chose; democracy, that any man could be a citizen if he chose. The note of the last few decades in art and ethics has been that a man is stamped with an irrevocable psychology, and is cramped for perpetuity in the prison of his skull. It was a world that expected everything of everybody. It was a world that encouraged anybody to be anything. And in England and literature its living expression was Dickens.

We shall consider Dickens in many other capacities, but let us put this one first. He was the voice in England of this humane intoxication and expansion, this encouraging of anybody to be anything. His best books are a carnival of liberty, and there is more of the real spirit of the French Revolution in " Nicholas Nickleby " than in " The Tale of Two Cities." His work has the great glory of the Revolution, the bidding of every man to be himself; it has also the revolutionary deficiency; it seems to think that this mere emancipation is enough. No man *encouraged* his characters so much as Dickens. " I am an affectionate father," he says, " to every child of my fancy." He was not only an affectionate father, he was an everindulgent father. The children of his fancy are spoilt children. They shake the house like heavy and shouting schoolboys; they smash the story to pieces like so much furniture. When we moderns write stories our characters are better controlled. But, alas! our characters are rather easier to control. We are in no danger from the gigantic gambols of creatures like Mantalini and Micawber. We are in no danger of giving our readers too much Weller or Wegg. We have not got it to give. When we experience the ungovernable sense of life which goes along with the old Dickens sense of liberty, we experience the best of the revolution. We are filled with the first of all democratic doctrines, that all men are interesting; Dickens tried to make some of his people appear dull people, but he could not keep them dull. He could not make a monotonous man. The bores in his books are brighter than the wits in other books.

I have put this position first for a defined reason. It is useless for us to attempt to imagine Dickens and his life unless we are able at least to imagine this old atmosphere of a democratic optimism—a confidence in common men. Dickens depends upon such a comprehension in a rather unusual manner, a manner worth explanation, or at least remark.

The disadvantage under which Dickens has fallen, both as an artist and a moralist, is very plain. His misfortune is that neither of the two last movements in literary criticism has done him any good. He has suffered alike from his enemies, and from the enemies of his enemies. The facts to which I refer are familiar. When the world first awoke from the mere hypnotism of Dickens, from the direct tyranny of his temperament, there was, of course, a reaction. At the head of it came the Realists, with their documents, like Miss Flite. They declared that scenes and types in Dickens were wholly impossible (in which they were perfectly right), and on this rather paradoxical ground objected to them as literature. They were not "like life," and there, they thought, was an end of the matter. The Realist for a time prevailed. But Realists did not enjoy their victory (if they enjoyed anything) very long. A more symbolic school of criticism soon arose. Men saw that it was necessary to give a much deeper and more delicate meaning to the expression "like life." Streets are not life, cities and civilizations are not life, faces even and voices are not life itself. Life is within, and no man hath seen it at any time. As for our meals, and our manners, and our daily dress, these are things exactly like sonnets; they are random symbols of the soul. One man tries to express himself in books, another in boots; both probably fail. Our solid houses and square meals are in the strict sense fiction. They are things made up to typify our thoughts. The coat a man wears may be wholly fictitious; the movement of his hands may be quite unlike life.

This much the intelligence of men soon perceived. And by this much Dickens's fame should have greatly profited. For Dickens is "like life" in the truer sense, in the sense that he is akin to the living principle in us and in the universe; he is like life, at least in this detail, that he is alive. His art is like life, because, like life, it cares for nothing outside itself, and goes on its way rejoicing. Both produce monsters with a kind of carelessness, like enormous by-products; life producing the rhinoceros, and art Mr. Bunsby. Art indeed copies life in not copying life, for life copies nothing. Dickens's art is like life because, like life, it is irresponsible, because, like life, it is incredible.

Yet the return of this realization has not greatly profited Dickens, the return of romance has been almost useless to this great romantic. He has gained as little from the fall of the Realists as from their triumph; there has been a revolution, there has been a counter revolution, there has been no restoration. And the reason of this brings us back to that atmosphere of popular optimism of which I spoke. And the shortest way of expressing the more recent neglect of Dickens is to say that for our time and taste he exaggerates the wrong thing.

Exaggeration is the definition of Art. That both Dickens and the moderns understood Art is, in its inmost nature, fantastic. Time brings queer revenges, and while the Realists were yet living, the art of Dickens was justified by Aubrey Beardsley. But men like Aubrey Beardsley were allowed to be fantastic, because the mood which they overstrained and overstated was a mood which their period understood. Dickens overstrains and overstates a mood our period does not understand. The truth he exaggerates is exactly this old Revolution sense of infinite opportunity and boisterous brotherhood. And we resent his undue sense of it, because we ourselves have not even a due sense of it. We feel troubled with too much where we have too little; we wish he would keep it within bounds. For we are all exact and scientific on the subjects we do not care about. We all immediately detect exaggeration in an exposition of Mormonism or a patriotic speech from Paraguay. We all require sobriety on the subject of the sea serpent. But the moment we begin to believe a thing ourselves, that moment we begin easily to overstate it; and the moment our souls become serious, our words become a little wild. And certain moderns are thus placed towards exaggeration. They permit any writer to emphasize doubts, for instance, for doubts are their religion, but they permit no man to emphasize dogmas. If a man be the mildest Christian, they smell "cant"; but he can be a raving windmill of pessimism, and they call it "temperament." If a moralist paints a wild picture of immorality, they doubt its truth, they say that devils are not so black as they are painted. But if a pessimist paints a wild picture of melancholy, they accept the whole horrible psychology, and they never ask if devils are as blue as they are painted.

It is evident, in short, why even those who admire exaggeration do not admire Dickens. He is exaggerating the wrong thing. They know what it is to feel a sadness so strange and deep that only impossible characters can express it: they do not know what it is to feel a joy so vital and violent that only impossible characters can express that. They know that the soul can be so sad as to dream naturally of the blue faces of the corpses of Baudelaire: they do not know that the soul can be so cheerful as to dream naturally of the blue face of Major Bagstock.

They know that there is a point of depression at which one believes in Tintagiles: they do not know that there is a point of exhilaration at which one believes in Mr. Wegg. To them the impossibilities of Dickens seem much more impossible than they really are, because they are already attuned to the opposite impossibilities of Maeterlinck. For every mood there is an appropriate impossibility—a decent and tactful impossibility—fitted to the frame of mind. Every train of thought may end in an ecstasy, and all roads lead to Elfland. But few now walk far enough along the street of Dickens to find the place where the cockney villas grow so comic that they become poetical. People do not know how far mere good spirits will go. For instance, we never think (as the old folk-lore did) of good spirits reaching to the spiritual world. We see this in the complete absence from modern, popular supernaturalism of the old popular mirth. We hear plenty to-day of the wisdom of the spiritual world; but we do not hear, as our fathers did, of the folly of the spiritual world, of the tricks of the gods, and the jokes of the patron saints. Our popular tales tell us of a man who is so wise that he touches the supernatural, like Dr. Nikola; but they never tell us (like the popular tales of the past) of a man who was so silly that he touched the supernatural, like Bottom the Weaver. We do not understand the dark and transcendental sympathy between fairies and fools. We understand a devout occultism, an evil occultism, a tragic occultism, but a farcical occultism is beyond us. Yet a farcical occultism is the very essence of "The Midsummer Night's Dream." It is also the right and credible essence of "The Christmas Carol." Whether we understand it depends upon whether we can understand that exhilaration is not a physical accident, but a mystical fact; that exhilaration can be infinite, like sorrow; that a joke can be so big that it breaks the roof of the stars. By simply going on being absurd, a thing can become godlike; there is but one step from the ridiculous to the sublime.

Dickens was great because he was immoderately possessed with all this; if we are to understand him at all we must also be moderately possessed with it. We must understand this old limitless hilarity and human confidence, at least enough to be able to endure it when it is pushed a great deal too far. For Dickens did push it too far; he did push the hilarity to the point of incredible character-drawing; he did push the human confidence to the point of an unconvincing sentimentalism. You can trace, if you will, the revolutionary joy till it reaches the incredible Sapsea epitaph; you can trace the revolutionary hope till it reaches the repentance of Dombey. There is plenty to carp at in this man if you are inclined to carp; you may easily find him vulgar if you cannot see that he is divine; and if you cannot laugh with Dickens, undoubtedly you can laugh at him.

I believe myself that this braver world of his will certainly return; for I believe that it is bound up with realities, like morning and the spring. But for those who beyond remedy regard it as an error, I put this appeal before any other observations on Dickens. First let us sympathize, if only for an instant, with the hopes of the Dickens period, with that cheerful trouble of change. If democracy has disappointed you, do not think of it as a burst bubble, but at least as a broken heart, an old love-affair. Do not sneer at the time when the creed of humanity was on its honeymoon; treat it with the dreadful reverence that is due to youth. For you, perhaps, a drearier philosophy has covered and eclipsed the earth. The fierce poet of the Middle Ages wrote, "Abandon hope all ye who enter here" over the gates of the lower world. The emancipated poets of to-day have written it over the gates of this world. But if we are to understand the story which follows, we must erase that apocalyptic writing, if only for an hour. We must recreate the faith of our fathers, if only as an artistic atmosphere. If, then, you are a pessimist, in reading this story, forego for a little the pleasures of pessimism. Dream for one mad moment that the grass is green. Unlearn that sinister learning that you think so clear; deny that deadly knowledge that you think you know. Surrender the very flower of your culture; give up the very jewel of your pride; abandon hopelessness, all ye who enter here.

CHAPTER II

THE BOYHOOD OF DICKENS

CHARLES DICKENS was born at Landport, in Portsea, on February 7, 1812. His father was a clerk in the Navy Pay-office, and was temporarily on duty in the neighbourhood. Very soon after the birth of Charles Dickens, however, the family moved for a short period to Norfolk Street, Bloomsbury, and then for a long period to Chatham, which thus became the real home, and for all serious purposes, the native place of Dickens. The whole story of his life moves like a Canterbury pilgrimage along the great roads of Kent.

John Dickens, his father, was, as stated, a clerk; but such mere terms of trade tell us little of the tone or status of a family. Browning's father (to take an instance at random) would also be described as a clerk and a man of the middle class; but the Browning family and the Dickens family have the colour of two different civilizations. The difference cannot be conveyed merely by saying that Browning stood many strata above Dickens. It must also be conveyed that Browning belonged to that section of the middle class which tends (in the small social sense) to rise; the Dickenses to that section which tends in the same sense to fall. If Browning had not been a poet, he would have been a better clerk than his father, and his son probably a better and richer clerk than he. But if they had not been lifted in the air by the enormous accident of a man of genius, the Dickenses, I fancy would have appeared in poorer and poorer places, as inventory clerks, as caretakers, as addressers of envelopes, until they melted into the masses of the poor.

Yet at the time of Dickens's birth and childhood this weakness in their worldly destiny was in no way apparent; especially it was not apparent to the little Charles himself. He was born and grew up in a paradise of small prosperity. He fell into the family, so to speak, during one of its comfortable periods, and he never in those early days thought of himself as anything but as a comfortable middle-class child, the son of a comfortable middle-class man. The father whom he found provided for him, was one from whom comfort drew forth his most pleasant and reassuring qualities, though not perhaps his most interesting and peculiar. John Dickens seemed, most probably, a hearty and kindly character, a little florid of speech, a little careless of duty in some details, notably in the detail of education. His neglect of his son's mental training in later and more trying times was a piece of unconscious selfishness which remained a little acrimoniously in his son's mind through life. But even in this earlier and easier period what records there are of John Dickens give out the air of a somewhat idle and irresponsible fatherhood. He exhibited towards his son that contradiction in conduct which is always shown by the too thoughtless parent to the too thoughtful child. He contrived at once to neglect his mind, and also to over-stimulate it.

There are many recorded tales and traits of the author's infancy, but one small fact seems to me more than any other to strike the note and give the key to his whole strange character. His father found it more amusing to be an audience than to be an instructor; and instead of giving the child intellectual pleasure, called upon him, almost before he was out of petticoats, to provide it. Some of the earliest glimpses we have of Charles Dickens show him to us perched on some chair or table singing comic songs in an atmosphere of perpetual applause. So, almost as soon as he can toddle, he steps into the glare of the footlights. He never stepped out of it until he died. He was a good man, as men go in this bewildering world of ours, brave, transparent, tender-hearted, scrupulously independent and honourable; he was not a man whose weaknesses should be spoken of without some delicacy and doubt. But there did mingle with his merits all his life this theatrical quality, this atmosphere of being shown off—a sort of hilarious self-consciousness. His literary life was a triumphal procession; he died drunken with glory. And behind all this nine years' wonder that filled the world, behind his gigantic tours and his ten thousand editions, the crowded lectures and the crashing brass, behind all the thing we really see is the flushed face of a little boy singing music-hall songs to a circle of aunts and uncles. And this precocious pleasure explains much, too, in the moral way. Dickens had all his life the faults of the little boy who is kept up too late at night. The boy in such a case exhibits a psychological paradox; he is a little too irritable because he is a little too happy. Dickens was always a little too irritable because he was a little too happy. Like the over-wrought child in society, he was splendidly sociable, and yet suddenly quarrelsome. In all the practical relations of his life he was what the child is in the last hours of an evening party, genuinely delighted, genuinely delightful, genuinely affectionate and happy, and yet in some strange way fundamentally exasperated and dangerously close to tears.

There was another touch about the boy which made his case more peculiar, and perhaps his intelligence more fervid; the touch of ill-health. It could not be called more than a touch, for he suffered from no formidable malady and could always through life endure a great degree of exertion even if it was only the exertion of walking violently all night. Still the streak of sickness was sufficient to take him out of the common unconscious life of the community of boys; and for good or evil that withdrawal is always a matter of deadly importance to the mind. He was thrown back perpetually upon the pleasures of the intelligence, and these began to burn in his head like a pent and painful furnace. In his own unvaryingly vivid way he has described how he crawled up into an unconsidered garret, and there found, in a dusty heap, the undying literature of England. The books he mentions chiefly are "Humphrey Clinker" and "Tom Jones." When he opened those two books in the garret he caught hold of the only past with which he is at all connected, the great comic writers of England of whom he was destined to be the last.

It must be remembered (as I have suggested before) that there was something about the county in which he lived, and the great roads along which he travelled that sympathized with and stimulated his pleasure in this old picaresque literature. The groups that came along the road, that passed through his town and out of it, were of the motley laughable type that tumbled into ditches or beat down the doors of taverns under the escort of Smollett and Fielding. In our time the main roads of Kent have upon them very often a perpetual procession of tramps and tinkers unknown on the quiet hills of Sussex; and it may have been so also in Dickens's boyhood. In his neighbourhood were definite memorials of yet older and yet greater English comedy. From the height of Gad's-hill at which he stared unceasingly there looked down upon him the monstrous ghost of Falstaff, Falstaff who might well have been the spiritual father of all Dickens's adorable knaves, Falstaff the great mountain of English laughter and English sentimentalism, the great, healthy, humane English humbug, not to be matched among the nations.

At this eminence of Gad's-hill Dickens used to stare even as a boy with the steady purpose of some day making it his own. It is characteristic of the consistency which underlies the superficially erratic career of Dickens that he actually did live to make it his own. The truth is that he was a precocious child, precocious not only on the more poetical but on the more prosaic side of life. He was ambitious as well as enthusiastic. No one can ever know what visions they were that crowded into the head of the clever little brat as he ran about the streets of Chatham or stood glowering at Gad's-hill. But I think that quite mundane visions had a very considerable share in the matter. He longed to go to school (a strange wish), to go to college, to make a name, nor did he merely aspire to these things; the great number of them he also expected. He regarded himself as a child of good position just about to enter on a life of good luck. He thought his home and family a very good spring-board or jumping-off place from which to fling himself to the positions which he desired to reach. And almost as he was about to spring the whole structure broke under him, and he and all that belonged to him disappeared into a darkness far below.

Everything had been struck down as with the finality of a thunder-bolt. His lordly father was a bankrupt, and in the Marshalsea prison. His mother was in a mean home in the north of London, wildly proclaiming herself the principal of a girl's school, a girl's school to which nobody would go. And he himself, the conqueror of the world and the prospective purchaser of Gads-hill, passed some distracted and bewildering days in pawning the household necessities to Fagins in foul shops, and then found himself somehow or other one of a row of ragged boys in a great dreary factory, pasting the same kinds of labels on to the same kinds of blacking bottles from morning till night.

Although it seemed sudden enough to him, the disintegration had, as a matter of fact, of course, been going on for a long time. He had only heard from his father dark and melodramatic allusions to a "deed" which, from the way it was mentioned, might have been a claim to the crown or a compact with the devil, but which was in truth an unsuccessful documentary attempt on the part of John Dickens to come to a composition with his creditors. And now, in the lurid light of his sunset, the character of John Dickens began to take on those purple colours which have made him under another name absurd and immortal. It required a tragedy to bring out this man's comedy. So long as John Dickens was in easy circumstances, he seemed only an easy man, a little long and luxuriant in his phrases, a little careless in his business routine. He seemed only a wordy man, who lived on bread and beef like his neighbours; but as bread and beef were successively taken away from him, it was discovered that he lived on words. For him to be involved in a calamity only meant to be cast for the first part in a tragedy. For him blank ruin was only a subject for blank verse. Henceforth we feel scarcely inclined to call him John Dickens at all; we feel inclined to call him by the name through which his son celebrated this preposterous and sublime victory of the human spirit over circumstances. Dickens, in "David Copperfield," called him Wilkins Micawber. In his personal correspondence he called him the Prodigal Father.

Young Charles had been hurriedly flung into the factory by the more or less careless good-nature of James Lamert, a relation of his mother's; it was a blacking factory, supposed to be run as a rival to Warren's by another and "original" Warren, both practically conducted by another of the Lamerts. It was situated near Hungerford Market. Dickens worked there drearily, like one stunned with disappointment. To a child excessively intellectualized, and at this time, I fear, excessively egotistical, the coarseness of the whole thing—the work, the rooms, the boys, the language—was a sort of bestial nightmare. Not only did he scarcely speak of it then, but he scarcely spoke of it afterwards. Years later, in the fulness of his fame, he heard from Forster that a man had spoken of knowing him. On hearing the name, he somewhat curtly acknowledged it, and spoke of having seen the man once. Forster, in his innocence, answered that the man said he had seen Dickens many times in a factory by Hungerford Market. Dickens was suddenly struck with a long and extraordinary silence. Then he invited Forster, as his best friend, to a particular interview, and, with every appearance of difficulty and distress, told him the whole story for the first and the last time. A long while after that he told the world some part of the matter in the account of Murdstone and Grinby's in "David Copperfield." He never spoke of the whole experience except once or twice, and he never spoke of it otherwise than as a man might speak of hell.

It need not be suggested, I think, that this agony in the child was exaggerated by the man. It is true that he was not incapable of the vice of exaggeration, if it be a vice. There was about him much vanity and a certain virulence in his version of many things. Upon the whole, indeed, it would hardly be too much to say that he would have exaggerated any sorrow he talked about. But this was a sorrow with a very strange position in Dickens's life; it was a sorrow he did not talk about. Upon this particular dark spot he kept a sort of deadly silence for twenty years. An accident revealed part of the truth to the dearest of all his friends. He then told the whole truth to the dearest of all his friends. He never told anybody else. I do not think that this arose from any social sense of disgrace; if he had it slightly at the time, he was far too self-satisfied a man to have taken it seriously in after life. I really think that his pain at this time was so real and ugly that the thought of it filled him with that sort of impersonal but unbearable shame with which we are filled, for instance, by the notion of physical torture, of something that humiliates humanity. He felt that such agony was something obscene. Moreover there are two other good reasons for thinking that his sense of hopelessness was very genuine. First of all, this starless outlook is common in the calamities of boyhood. The bitterness of boyish distresses does not lie in the fact that they are large; it lies in the fact that we do not know that they are small. About any early disaster there is a dreadful finality; a lost child can suffer like a lost soul.

It is currently said that hope goes with youth, and lends to youth its wings of a butterfly; but I fancy that hope is the last gift given to man, and the only gift not given to youth. Youth is preeminently the period in which a man can be lyric, fanatical, poetic; but youth is the period in which a man can be hopeless. The end of every episode is the end of the world. But the power of hoping through everything, the knowledge that the soul survives its adventures, that great inspiration comes to the middle-aged; God has kept that good wine until now. It is from the backs of the elderly gentlemen that the wings of the butterfly should burst. There is nothing that so much mystifies the young as the consistent frivolity of the old. They have discovered their indestructibility. They are in their second and clearer childhood, and there is a meaning in the merriment of their eyes. They have seen the end of the End of the World.

First, then, the desolate finality of Dickens's childish mood makes me think it was a real one. And there is another thing to be remembered. Dickens was not a saintly child after the style of Little Dorrit or Little Nell. He had not, at this time at any rate, set his heart wholly upon higher things, even upon things such as personal tenderness or loyalty. He had been, and was, unless I am very much mistaken, sincerely, stubbornly, bitterly ambitious. He had, I fancy, a fairly clear idea previous to the downfall of all his family's hopes of what he wanted to do in the world, and of the mark that he meant to make there. In no dishonourable sense, but still in a definite sense he might, in early life, be called worldly; and the children of this world are in their generation infinitely more sensitive than the children of light. A saint after repentance will forgive himself for a sin; a man about town will never forgive himself for a *faux pas*. There are ways of getting absolved for murder; there are no ways of getting absolved for upsetting the soup. This thin-skinned quality in all very mundane people is a thing too little remembered; and it must not be wholly forgotten in connection with a clever, restless lad who dreamed of a destiny. That part of his distress which concerned himself and his social standing was among the other parts of it the least noble; but perhaps it was the most painful. For pride is not only (as the modern world fails to understand) a sin to be condemned; it is also (as it understands even less) a weakness to be very much commiserated. A very vitalizing touch is given in one of his own reminiscences. His most unendurable moment did not come in any bullying in the factory or any famine in the streets. It came when he went to see his sister Fanny take a prize at the Royal Academy of Music. "I could not bear to think of myself—beyond the reach of all such honourable emulation and success. The tears ran down my face. I felt as if my heart were rent. I prayed when I went to bed that night to be lifted out of the humiliation and neglect in which I was. I never had suffered so much before. There was no envy in this." I do not think that there was, though the poor little wretch could hardly have been blamed if there had been. There was only a furious sense of frustration; a spirit like a wild beast in a cage. It was only a small matter in the external and obvious sense; it was only Dickens prevented from being Dickens.

If we put these facts together, that the tragedy seemed final, and that the tragedy was concerned with the supersensitive matters of the ego and the gentleman, I think we can imagine a pretty genuine case of internal depression. And when we add to the case of the internal depression the case of the external oppression, the case of the material circumstances by which he was surrounded, we have reached a sort of midnight. All day he worked on insufficient food at a factory. It is sufficient to say that it afterwards appeared in his works as Murdstone and Grinby's. At night he returned disconsolately to a lodging-house for such lads, kept by an old lady. It is sufficient to say that she appeared afterwards as Mrs. Pipchin. Once a week only he saw anybody for whom he cared a straw; that was when he went to the Marshalsea prison, and that gave his juvenile pride, half manly and half snobbish, bitter annoyance of another kind. Add to this, finally, that physically he was always very weak and never very well. Once he was struck down in the middle of his work with sudden bodily pain. The boy who worked next to him, a coarse and heavy lad named Bob Fagin, who had often attacked Dickens on the not unreasonable ground of his being a "gentleman," suddenly showed that enduring sanity of compassion which Dickens was destined to show so often in the characters of the common and unclean. Fagin made a bed for his sick companion out of the straw in the workroom, and filled empty blacking bottles with hot water all day. When the evening came, and Dickens was somewhat recovered, Bob Fagin insisted on escorting the boy home to his father. The situation was as poignant as a sort of tragic farce. Fagin in his wooden-headed chivalry would have died in order to take Dickens to his family; Dickens in his bitter gentility would have died rather than let Fagin know that his family were in the Marshalsea. So these two young idiots tramped the tedious streets, both stubborn, both suffering for an idea. The advantage certainly was with Fagin, who was suffering for a Christian compassion, while Dickens was suffering for a pagan pride. At last Dickens flung off his friend with desperate farewell and thanks, and dashed up the steps of a strange house on the Surrey side. He knocked and rang as Bob Fagin, his benefactor and his incubus, disappeared round the corner. And when the servant came to open the door, he asked, apparently with gravity, whether Mr. Robert Fagin lived there. It is a strange touch. The immortal Dickens woke in him for an instant in that last wild joke of that weary evening. Next morning, however, he was again well enough to make himself ill again, and the wheels of the great factory went on. They manufactured a number of bottles of Warren's Blacking, and in the course of the process they manufactured also the greatest optimist of the nineteenth century.

This boy who dropped down groaning at his work, who was hungry four or five times a week, whose best feelings and worst feelings were alike flayed alive, was the man on whom two generations of comfortable critics have visited the complaint that his view of life was too rosy to be anything but unreal. Afterwards, and in its proper place, I shall speak of what is called the optimism of Dickens, and of whether it was really too cheerful or too smooth. But this boyhood of his may be recorded now as a mere fact. If he was too happy, this was where he learnt it. If his school of thought was a vulgar optimism, this is where he went to school. If he learnt to whitewash the universe, it was in a blacking factory that he learnt it.

As a fact, there is no shred of evidence to show that those who have had sad experiences tend to have a sad philosophy. There are numberless points upon which Dickens is spiritually at one with the poor, that is, with the great mass of mankind. But there is no point in which he is more perfectly at one with them than in showing that there is no kind of connection between a man being unhappy and a man being pessimistic. Sorrow and pessimism are indeed, in a sense, opposite things, since sorrow is founded on the value of something, and pessimism upon the value of nothing. And in practice we find that those poets or political leaders who come from the people, and whose experiences have really been searching and cruel, are the most sanguine people in the world. These men out of the old agony are always optimists; they are sometimes offensive optimists. A man like Robert Burns, whose father (like Dickens's father) goes bankrupt, whose whole life is a struggle against miserable external powers and internal weaknesses yet more miserable—a man whose life begins grey and ends black—Burns does not merely sing about the goodness of life, he positively rants and cants about it. Rousseau, whom all his friends and acquaintances treated almost as badly as he treated them—Rousseau does not grow merely eloquent, he grows gushing and sentimental, about the inherent goodness of human nature. Charles Dickens, who was most miserable at the receptive age when most people are most happy, is afterwards happy when all men weep. Circumstances break men's bones; it has never been shown that they break men's optimism. These great popular leaders do all kinds of desperate things under the immediate scourge of tragedy. They become drunkards; they become demagogues; they become morpho-maniacs. They never become pessimists. Most unquestionably there are ragged and unhappy men whom we could easily understand being pessimists. But as a matter of fact they are not pessimists. Most unquestionably there are whole dim hordes of humanity whom we should promptly pardon if they cursed God. But they don't. The pessimists are aristocrats like Byron; the men who curse God are aristocrats like Swinburne. But when those who starve and suffer speak for a moment, they do not profess merely an optimism, they profess a cheap optimism; they are too poor to afford a dear one. They cannot indulge in any detailed or merely logical defence of life; that would be to delay the enjoyment of it. These higher optimists, of whom Dickens was one, do not approve of the universe; they do not even admire the universe; they fall in love with it. They embrace life too closely to criticize or even to see it. Existence to such men has the wild beauty of a woman, and those love her with most intensity who love her with least cause.

CHAPTER III

THE YOUTH OF DICKENS

THERE are popular phrases so picturesque that even when they are intentionally funny they are unintentionally poetical. I remember, to take one instance out of many, hearing a heated Secularist in Hyde Park apply to some parson or other the exquisite expression, "a sky-pilot." Subsequent inquiry has taught me that the term is intended to be comic and even contemptuous; but in that first freshness of it I went home repeating it to myself like a new poem. Few of the pious legends have conceived so strange and yet celestial a picture as this of the pilot in the sky, leaning on his helm above the empty heavens, and carrying his cargo of souls higher than the loneliest cloud. The phrase is like a lyric of Shelley. Or, to take another instance from another language, the French have an incomparable idiom for a boy playing truant: "Il fait l'école buissonnière"—he goes to the bushy school, or the school among the bushes. How admirably this accidental expression, "the bushy school" (not to be lightly confounded with the Art School at Bushey)—how admirably this "bushy school" expresses half the modern notions of a more natural education! The two words express the whole poetry of Wordsworth, the whole philosophy of Thoreau, and are quite as good literature as either.

Now, among a million of such scraps of inspired slang there is one which describes a certain side of Dickens better than pages of explanation. The phrase, appropriately enough, occurs at least once in his works, and that on a fitting occasion. When Job Trotter is sent by Sam on a wild chase after Mr. Perker, the solicitor, Mr. Perker's clerk condoles with Job upon the lateness of the hour, and the fact that all habitable places are shut up. "My friend," says Mr. Perker's clerk, "you've got the key of the street." Mr. Perker's clerk, who was a flippant and scornful young man, may perhaps be pardoned if he used this expression in a flippant and scornful sense; but let us hope that Dickens did not. Let us hope that Dickens saw the strange, yet satisfying, imaginative justice of the words; for Dickens himself had, in the most sacred and serious sense of the term, the key of the street. When we shut out anything, we are shut out of that thing. When we shut out the street, we are shut out of the street. Few of us understand the street. Even when we step into it, we step into it doubtfully, as into a house or room of strangers. Few of us see through the shining riddle of the street, the strange folk that belong to the street only—the street-walker or the street arab, the nomads who, generation after generation, have kept their ancient secrets in the full blaze of the sun. Of the street at night many of us know even less. The street at night is a great house locked up. But Dickens had, if ever man had, the key of the street. His earth was the stones of the street; his stars were the lamps of the street; his hero was the man in the street. He could open the inmost door of his house—the door that leads into that secret passage which is lined with houses and roofed with stars.

This silent transformation into a citizen of the street took place during those dark days of boyhood, when Dickens was drudging at the factory. Whenever he had done drudging, he had no other resource but drifting, and he drifted over half London. He was a dreamy child, thinking mostly of his own dreary prospects. Yet he saw and remembered much of the streets and squares he passed. Indeed, as a matter of fact, he went the right way to work unconsciously to do so. He did not go in for "observation," a priggish habit;

he did not look at Charing Cross to improve his mind or count the lamp-posts in Holborn to practise his arithmetic. But unconsciously he made all these places the scenes of the monstrous drama in his miserable little soul. He walked in darkness under the lamps of Holborn, and was crucified at Charing Cross. So for him ever afterwards these places had the beauty that only belongs to battlefields. For our memory never fixes the facts which we have merely observed. The only way to remember a place for ever is to live in the place for an hour; and the only way to live in the place for an hour is to forget the place for an hour. The undying scenes we can all see if we shut our eyes are not the scenes that we have stared at under the direction of guide-books; the scenes we see are the scenes at which we did not look at all—the scenes in which we walked when we were thinking about something else—about a sin, or a love affair, or some childish sorrow. We can see the background now because we did not see it then. So Dickens did not stamp these places on his mind; he stamped his mind on these places. For him ever afterwards these streets were mortally romantic; they were dipped in the purple dyes of youth and its tragedy, and rich with irrevocable sunsets.

Herein is the whole secret of that eerie realism with which Dickens could always vitalize some dark or dull corner of London. There are details in the Dickens descriptions—a window, or a railing, or the keyhole of a door—which he endows with demoniac life. The things seem more actual than things really are. Indeed, that degree of realism does not exist in reality: it is the unbearable realism of a dream. And this kind of realism can only be gained by walking dreamily in a place; it cannot be gained by walking observantly. Dickens himself has given a perfect instance of how these nightmare minutiæ grew upon him in his trance of abstraction. He mentions among the coffee-shops into which he crept in those wretched days " one in St. Martin's Lane, of which I only recollect that it stood near the church, and that in the door there was an oval glass plate with 'COFFEE ROOM' painted on it, addressed towards the street. If I ever find myself in a very different kind of coffee-room now, but where there is such an inscription on glass, and read it backwards on the wrong side, MOOR EEFFOC (as I often used to do then in a dismal reverie), a shock goes through my blood." That wild word, " Moor Eeffoc," is the motto of all effective realism! it is the masterpiece of the good realistic principle—the principle that the most fantastic thing of all is often the precise fact. And that elvish kind of realism Dickens adopted everywhere. His world was alive with inanimate objects. The date on the door danced over Mr. Grewgius, the knocker grinned at Mr. Scrooge, the Roman on the ceiling pointed down at Mr. Tulkinghorn, the elderly armchair leered at Tom Smart—these are all *moor eeffocish* things. A man sees them because he does not look at them.

And so the little Dickens Dickensized London. He prepared the way for all his personages. Into whatever cranny of our city his characters might crawl, Dickens had been there before them. However wild were the events he narrated as outside him, they could not be wilder than the things that had gone on within. However queer a character of Dickens might be, he could hardly be queerer than Dickens was. The whole secret of his after-writings is sealed up in those silent years of which no written word remains. Those years did him harm perhaps, as his biographer, Forster, has thoughtfully suggested, by sharpening a certain fierce individualism in him which once or twice during his genial life flashed like a half-hidden knife. He was always generous; but things had gone too hardly with him for him to be always easy-going. He was always kind-hearted; he was not always good-humoured. Those years may also, in their strange mixture of morbidity and reality, have increased in him his tendency to exaggeration. But we can scarcely lament this in a literary sense; exaggeration is almost the definition of art—and it is entirely the definition of Dickens's art. Those years may have given him many moral and mental wounds, from which he never recovered. But they gave him the key of the street.

There is a weird contradiction in the soul of the born optimist. He can be happy and unhappy at the same time. With Dickens the practical depression of his life at this time did nothing to prevent him from laying up those hilarious memories of which all his books are made. No doubt he was genuinely unhappy in the poor place where his mother kept school. Nevertheless it was there that he noticed the unfathomable quaintness of the little servant whom he made into the Marchioness. No doubt he was comfortless enough at the boarding-house of Mrs. Roylance; but he perceived with a dreadful joy that Mrs. Roylance's name was Pipchin. There seems to be no incompatibility between taking in tragedy and giving out comedy; they are able to run parallel in the same personality. One incident which he described in his unfinished "autobiography," and which he afterwards transferred almost verbatim to David Copperfield, was peculiarly rich and impressive. It was the inauguration of a petition to the King for a bounty, drawn up by a committee of the prisoners in the Marshalsea, a committee of which Dickens's father was the president, no doubt in virtue of his oratory, and also the scribe, no doubt in virtue of his genuine love of literary flights.

"As many of the principal officers of this body as could be got into a small room without filling it up, supported him in front of the petition; and my old friend, Captain Porter (who had washed himself to do honour to so solemn an occasion), stationed himself close to it, to read it to all who were unacquainted with its contents. The door was then thrown open, and they began to come in in a long file; several waiting on the landing outside, while one entered, affixed his signature, and went out. To everybody in succession Captain Porter said, 'Would you like to hear it read'? If he weakly showed the least disposition to hear it, Captain Porter in a loud, sonorous voice gave him every word of it. I remember a certain luscious roll he gave to such words as 'Majesty—Gracious Majesty—Your Gracious Majesty's unfortunate subjects—Your Majesty's well-known munificence,' as if the words were something real in his mouth and delicious to taste: my poor father meanwhile listening with a little of an author's vanity and contemplating (not severely) the spike on the opposite wall. Whatever was comical or pathetic in this scene, I sincerely believe I perceived in my corner, whether I demonstrated it or not, quite as well as I should perceive it now. I made out my own little character and story for every man who put his name to the sheet of paper."

Here we see very plainly that Dickens did not merely look back in after days and see that these humours had been delightful. He was delighted at the same moment that he was desperate. The two opposite things existed in him simultaneously, and each in its full strength. His soul was not a mixed colour like grey and purple, caused by no component colour being quite itself. His soul was like a shot silk of black and crimson, a shot silk of misery and joy.

Seen from the outside, his little pleasures and extravagances seem more pathetic than his grief. Once the solemn little figure went into a public-house in Parliament Street, and addressed the man behind the bar in the following terms—" What is your very best—the VERY *best* ale a glass?" The man replied, "Twopence." "Then," said the infant, "just draw me a glass of that, if you please, with a good head to it." "The landlord," says Dickens, in telling the story, "looked at me in return over the bar from head to foot with a strange smile on his face; instead of drawing the beer looked round the screen and said something to his wife, who came out from behind it with her work in her hand and joined him in surveying me. . . . They asked me a good many questions as to what my name was, how old I was, where I lived, how I was employed, etc., etc. To all of which, that I might commit nobody, I invented appropriate answers. They served me with the ale, though I suspect it was not the strongest on the premises; and the landlord's wife, opening the little half-door, and bending down, gave me a kiss." Here he touches that other side of common life which he was chiefly to champion; he was to show that there is no ale like the ale of a poor man's festival, and no pleasures like the pleasures of the poor. At other places of refreshment he was yet more majestic. "I remember," he says, "tucking my own bread (which I had brought from home in the morning) under my arm, wrapt up in a piece of paper like a book, and going into the best dining-room in Johnson's Alamode Beef House in Clare Court, Drury Lane, and magnificently ordering a small plate of *à-la-mode* beef to eat with it. What the waiter thought of such a strange little apparition coming in all alone I don't know; but I can see him now staring at me as I ate my dinner, and bringing up the other waiter to look. I gave him a halfpenny, and I wish, now, that he hadn't taken it."

For the boy individually the prospect seemed to be growing drearier and drearier. This phrase indeed hardly expresses the fact; for, as he felt it, it was not so much a run of worsening luck as the closing in of a certain and quiet calamity like the coming on of twilight and dark. He felt that he would die and be buried in blacking. Through all this he does not seem to have said much to his parents of his distress. They who were in prison had certainly a much jollier time than he who was free. But of all the strange ways in which the human being proves that he is not a rational being, whatever else he is, no case is so mysterious and unaccountable as the secrecy of childhood. We learn of the cruelty of some school or child-factory from journalists; we learn it from inspectors, we learn it from doctors, we learn it even from shame-stricken schoolmasters and repentant sweaters; but we never learn it from the children; we never learn it from the victims. It would seem as if a living creature had to be taught, like an art of culture, the art of crying out when it is hurt. It would seem as if patience were the natural thing; it would seem as if impatience were an accomplishment like whist. However this may be, it is wholly certain that Dickens might have drudged and died drudging, and buried the unborn Pickwick, but for an external accident.

He was, as has been said, in the habit of visiting his father at the Marshalsea every week. The talks between the two must have been a comedy, at once more cruel and more delicate than Dickens ever described. Meredith might picture the comparison between the child whose troubles were so childish, but who felt them like a damned spirit, and the middle-aged man whose trouble was final ruin, and who felt it no more than a baby. Once, it would appear, the boy broke down altogether—perhaps under the unbearable buoyancy of his oratorical papa—and implored to be freed from the factory—implored it, I fear, with a precocious and almost horrible eloquence. The old optimist was astounded—too much astounded to do anything in particular. Whether the incident had really anything to do with what followed cannot be decided, but ostensibly it had not. Ostensibly the cause of Charles's ultimate liberation was a quarrel between his father and Lamert, the head of the factory. Dickens the elder (who had at last left the Marshalsea) could no doubt conduct a quarrel with the magnificence of Micawber; the result of this talent, at any rate, was to leave Mr. Lamert in a towering rage. He had a stormy interview with Charles, in which he tried to be good-tempered to the boy, but could hardly master his tongue about the boy's father. Finally he told him he must go, and with every observance the little creature was solemnly expelled from hell.

His mother, with a touch of strange harshness, was for patching up the quarrel and sending him back. Perhaps, with the fierce feminine responsibility, she felt that the first necessity was to keep the family out of debt. But old John Dickens put his foot down here—put his foot down with that ringing but very rare decision with which (once in ten years, and often on some trivial matter) the weakest man will overwhelm the strongest woman. The boy was miserable; the boy was clever; the boy should go to school. The boy went to school; he went to the Wellington House Academy, Mornington Place. It was an odd experience for any one to go from the world to a school, instead of going from school to the world. Dickens, we may say, had his boyhood after his youth. He had seen life at its coarsest before he began his training for it, and knew the worst words in the English language probably before the best. This odd chronology, it will be remembered, he retained in his semi-autobiographical account of the adventures of David Copperfield, who went into the business of Murdstone and Grinby's before he went to the school kept by Dr. Strong. David Copperfield, also, went to be carefully prepared for a world that he had seen already. Outside David Copperfield, the records of Dickens at this time reduce themselves to a few glimpses provided by accidental companions of his schooldays, and little can be deduced from them about his personality beyond a general impression of sharpness and, perhaps, of bravado, of bright eyes and bright speeches. Probably the young creature was recuperating himself for his misfortunes, was making the most of his liberty, was flapping the wings of that wild spirit that had just not been broken. We hear of things that sound suddenly juvenile after his maturer troubles, of a secret language sounding like mere gibberish, and of a small theatre, with paint and red fire, such as that which Stevenson loved. It was not an accident that

Dickens and Stevenson loved it. It is a stage unsuited for psychological realism; the cardboard characters cannot analyze each other with any effect. But it is a stage almost divinely suited for making surroundings, for making that situation and background which belong peculiarly to romance. A toy theatre, in fact, is the opposite of private theatricals. In the latter you can do anything with the people if you do not ask much from the scenery; in the former you can do anything in scenery if you do not ask much from the people. In a toy theatre you could hardly manage a modern dialogue on marriage, but the Day of Judgment would be quite easy.

After leaving school, Dickens found employment as a clerk to Mr. Blackmore, a solicitor, as one of those inconspicuous under-clerks whom he afterwards turned to many grotesque uses. Here, no doubt, he met Lowten and Swiveller, Chuckster and Wobbler, in so far as such sacred creatures ever had embodiments on this lower earth. But it is typical of him that he had no fancy at all to remain a solicitor's clerk. The resolution to rise which had glowed in him even as a dawdling boy, when he gazed at Gad's-hill, which had been darkened but not quite destroyed by his fall into the factory routine, which had been released again by his return to normal boyhood and the boundaries of school, was not likely to content itself now with the copying out of agreements. He set to work, without any advice or help, to learn to be a reporter. He worked all day at law, and then all night at shorthand. It is an art which can only be effected by time, and he had to effect it by overtime. But learning the thing under every disadvantage, without a teacher, without the possibility of concentration or complete mental force, without ordinary human sleep, he made himself one of the most rapid reporters then alive. There is a curious contrast between the casualness of the mental training to which his parents and others subjected him and the savage seriousness of the training to which he subjected himself. Somebody once asked old John Dickens where his son Charles was educated. "Well, really," said the great creature, in his spacious way, "he may be said—ah—to have educated himself." He might indeed.

This practical intensity of Dickens is worth our dwelling on, because it illustrates an elementary antithesis in his character, or what appears as an antithesis in our modern popular psychology. We are always talking about strong men against weak men; but Dickens was not only both a weak man and a strong man, he was a very weak man and also a very strong man. He was everything that we currently call a weak man; he was a man hung on wires; he was a man who might at any moment cry like a child; he was so sensitive to criticism that one may say that he lacked a skin; he was so nervous that he allowed great tragedies in his life to arise only out of nerves. But in the matter where all ordinary strong men are miserably weak —in the matter of concentrated toil and clear purpose and unconquerable worldly courage—he was like a straight sword. Mrs. Carlyle, who in her human epithets often hit the right nail so that it rang, said of him once, " He has a face made of steel." This was probably felt in a flash when she saw, in some social crowd, the clear, eager face of Dickens cutting through those near him like a knife. Any people who had met him from year to year would each year have found a man weakly troubled about his worldly decline; and each year they would have found him higher up in the world. His was a character very hard for any man of slow and placable temperament to understand; he was the character whom anybody can hurt and nobody can kill.

When he began to report in the House of Commons he was still only nineteen. His father, who had been released from his prison a short time before Charles had been released from his, had also become, among many other things, a reporter. But old John Dickens could enjoy doing anything without any particular aspiration after doing it well. But Charles was of a very different temper. He was, as I have said, consumed with an enduring and almost angry thirst to excel. He learnt shorthand with a dark self-devotion as if it were a sacred hieroglyph. Of this self-instruction, as of everything else, he has left humorous and illuminating phrases. He describes how, after he had learnt the whole exact alphabet, " there then appeared a procession of new horrors, called arbitrary characters—the most despotic characters I have ever known; who insisted, for instance, that a thing like the beginning of a cobweb meant ' expectation,' and that a pen-and-ink skyrocket stood for ' disadvantageous.' " He concludes, " It was almost heartbreaking." But it is significant that somebody else, a colleague of his, concluded, " There never *was* such a shorthand writer."

Dickens succeeded in becoming a shorthand writer; succeeded in becoming a reporter; succeeded ultimately in becoming a highly effective journalist. He was appointed as a reporter of the speeches in Parliament, first by *The True Sun,* then by *The Mirror of Parliament,* and last by *The*

Morning Chronicle. He reported the speeches very well, and if we must analyze his internal opinions, much better than they deserved. For it must be remembered that this lad went into the reporter's gallery full of the triumphant Radicalism which was then the rising tide of the world. He was, it must be confessed, very little overpowered by the dignity of the Mother of Parliaments: he regarded the House of Commons much as he regarded the House of Lords, as a sort of venerable joke. It was, perhaps, while he watched, pale with weariness from the reporter's gallery, that there sank into him a thing that never left him, his unfathomable contempt for the British Constitution. Then perhaps he heard from the Government benches the immortal apologies of the Circumlocution Office. "Then would the noble lord or right honourable gentleman, in whose department it was to defend the Circumlocution Office, put an orange in his pocket, and make a regular field-day of the occasion. Then would he come down to that house with a slap upon the table and meet the honourable gentleman foot to foot. Then would he be there to tell that honourable gentleman that the Circumlocution Office was not only blameless in this matter, but was commendable in this matter, was extollable to the skies in this matter. Then would he be there to tell that honourable gentleman that although the Circumlocution Office was invariably right, and wholly right, it never was so right as in this matter. Then would he be there to tell the honourable gentleman that it would have been more to his honour, more to his credit, more to his good taste, more to his good sense, more to half the dictionary of common-places if he had left the Circumlocution Office alone and never approached this matter. Then would he keep one eye upon a coach or crammer from the Circumlocution Office below the bar, and smash the honourable gentleman with the Circumlocution Office account of this matter. And although one of two things always happened; namely, either that the Circumlocution Office had nothing to say, and said it, or that it had something to say of which the noble lord or right honourable gentleman blundered one half and forgot the other; the Circumlocution Office was always voted immaculate by an accommodating majority." We are now generally told that Dickens has destroyed these abuses, and that this is no longer a true picture of public life. Such, at any rate, is the Circumlocution Office account of this matter. But Dickens as a good Radical would, I fancy, much prefer that we should continue his battle than that we should celebrate his triumph; especially when it has not come. England is still ruled by the great Barnacle family. Parliament is still ruled by the great Barnacle trinity—the solemn old Barnacle, who knew that the Circumlocution Office was a protection, the sprightly young Barnacle who knew that it was a fraud, and the bewildered young Barnacle who knew nothing about it. From these three types our Cabinets are still exclusively recruited. People talk of the tyrannies and anomalies which Dickens denounced as things of the past like the Star Chamber. They believe that the days of the old stupid optimism and the old brutal indifference are gone for ever. In truth, this very belief is only the continuance of the old stupid optimism and the old brutal indifference. We believe in a free England and a pure England, because we still believe in the Circumlocution Office account of this matter. Undoubtedly our serenity is wide-spread. We believe that England is really reformed, we believe that England is really democratic, we believe that English politics are free from corruption. But this general satisfaction of ours does not show that Dickens has beaten the Barnacles. It only shows that the Barnacles have beaten Dickens.

It cannot be too often said, then, that we must

read into young Dickens and his works this old Radical tone towards institutions. That tone was a sort of happy impatience. And when Dickens had to listen for hours to the speech of the noble lord in defence of the Circumlocution Office, when, that is, he had to listen to what he regarded as the last vaporings of a vanishing oligarchy, the impatience rather predominated over the happiness. His incurably restless nature found more pleasure in the wandering side of journalism. He went about wildly in post-chaises to report political meetings for the *Morning Chronicle*. "And what gentlemen they were to serve," he exclaimed, "in such things at the old *Morning Chronicle*. Great or small it did not matter. I have had to charge for half a dozen breakdowns in half a dozen times as many miles. I have had to charge for the damage of a great-coat from the drippings of a blazing wax candle, in writing through the smallest hours of the night in a swift flying carriage and pair." And again, "I have often transcribed for the printer from my shorthand notes important public speeches in which the strictest accuracy was required, and a mistake in which would have been to a young man severely compromising, writing on the palm of my hand, by the light of a dark lantern, in a post-chaise and four, galloping through a wild country and through the dead of the night, at the then surprising rate of fifteen miles an hour." The whole of Dickens's life goes with the throb of that nocturnal gallop. All its real wildness shot through with an imaginative wickedness he afterwards uttered in the drive of Jonas Chuzzlewit through the storm.

All this time, and indeed from a time of which no measure can be taken, the creative part of his mind had been in a stir or even a fever. While still a small boy he had written for his own amusement some sketches of queer people he had met; notably, one of his uncle's barber, whose principal hobby was pointing out what Napoleon ought to have done in the matter of military tactics. He had a note-book full of such sketches. He had sketches not only of persons, but of places which were to him almost more personal than persons. In the December of 1833 he published one of these fragments in the *Old Monthly Magazine*. This was followed by nine others in the same paper, and when the paper (which was a romantically Radical venture, run by a veteran soldier of Bolivar) itself collapsed, Dickens continued the series in the *Evening Chronicle*, an off-shoot of the morning paper of the same name. These were the pieces afterwards published and known as the "Sketches by Boz "; and with them Dickens enters literature. He also enters many other things about this time; he enters manhood, and among other things marriage. A friend of his on the *Chronicle*, George Hogarth, had several daughters. With all of them Dickens appears to have been on terms of great affection. This sketch is wholly literary, and I do not feel it necessary to do more than touch upon such incidents as his marriage, just as I shall do no more than touch upon the tragedy that ultimately overtook it. But it may be suggested here that the final misfortunes were in some degree due to the circumstances attending the original action. A very young man fighting his way, and excessively poor, with no memories for years past that were not monotonous and mean, and with his strongest and most personal memories quite ignominious and unendurable, was suddenly thrown into the society of a whole family of girls. I think it does not overstate his weakness, and I think it partly constitutes his excuse, to say that he fell in love with all of them. As sometimes happens in the undeveloped youth, an abstract femininity simply intoxicated him. And again, I think we shall not be mistakenly accused of harshness if we put the point in this way; that by a kind of accident he got hold of the wrong sister. In what came afterwards he was enormously to blame. But I do not think that his was a case of cold division from a woman whom he had once seriously and singly loved. He had been bewildered in a burning haze, I will not say even of first love, but of first flirtations. His wife's sisters stimulated him before he fell in love with his wife; and they continued to stimulate him long after he had quarrelled with her for ever. This view is strikingly supported by all the details of his attitude towards all the other members of the sacred house of Hogarth. One of the sisters remained, of course, his dearest friend till death. Another who had died, he worshipped as a saint, and he always asked to be buried in her grave. He was married on April 2, 1836. Forster remarks that a few days before the announcement of their marriage in the *Times,* the same paper contained another announcement that on the 31st would be published the first number of a work called "The Posthumous Papers of the Pickwick Club." It is the beginning of his career.

The "Sketches," apart from splendid splashes of humour here and there, are not manifestations of the man of genius. We might almost say that this book is one of the few books by Dickens which would not, standing alone, have made his fame.

And yet standing alone it did make his fame. His contemporaries could see a new spirit in it, where we, familiar with the larger fruits of that spirit, can only see a continuation of the prosaic and almost wooden wit of the comic books of that day. But in any case we should hardly look in the man's first book for the fulness of his contribution to letters. Youth is almost everything else, but it is hardly ever original. We read of young men bursting on the old world with a new message. But youth in actual experience is the period of imitation and even obedience. Subjectively its emotions may be furious and headlong; but its only external outcome is a furious imitation and a headlong obedience. As we grow older we learn the special thing we have to do. As a man goes on towards the grave he discovers gradually a philosophy he can really call fresh, a style he can really call his own, and as he becomes an older man he becomes a newer writer. Ibsen, in his youth, wrote almost classic plays about vikings; it was in his old age that he began to break windows and throw fireworks. The only fault, it was said, of Browning's first poems was that they had "too much beauty of imagery, and too little wealth of thought." The only fault, that is, of Browning's first poems, was that they were not Browning's.

In one way, however, the "Sketches by Boz" do stand out very symbolically in the life of Dickens. They constitute in a manner the dedication of him to his especial task; the sympathetic and yet exaggerated painting of the poorer middle-class. He was to make men feel that this dull middle-class was actually a kind of elf-land. But here, again, the work is rude and undeveloped; and this is shown in the fact that it is a great deal more exaggerative than it is sympathetic. We are not, of course, concerned with the kind of people who say that they wish that Dickens was more refined. If those people are ever refined it will be by fire. But there is in this earliest work, an element which almost vanished in the later ones, an element which is typical of the middle-classes in England, and which is in a more real sense to be called vulgar. I mean that in these little farces there is a trace, in the author as well as in the characters, of that petty sense of social precedence, that hub-hub of little unheard-of oligarchies, which is the only serious sin of the bourgeoisie of Britain. It may seem pragmatical, for example, to instance such a rowdy farce as the story of Horatio Sparkins, which tells how a tuft-hunting family entertained a rhetorical youth thinking he was a lord, and found he was a draper's assistant. No doubt they were very snobbish in thinking that a lord must be eloquent; but we cannot help feeling that Dickens is almost equally snobbish in feeling it so very funny that a draper's assistant should be eloquent. A free man, one would think, would despise the family quite as much if Horatio had been a peer. Here, and here only, there is just a touch of the vulgarity, of the only vulgarity of the world out of which Dickens came. For the only element of lowness that there really is in our populace is exactly that they are full of superiorities and very conscious of class. Shades, imperceptible to the eyes of others, but as hard and haughty as a Brahmin caste, separate one kind of charwoman from another kind of charwoman. Dickens was destined to show with inspired symbolism all the immense virtues of the democracy. He was to show them as the most humorous part of our civilization; which they certainly are. He was to show them as the most promptly and practically compassionate part of our civilization; which they certainly are. The democracy has a hundred exuberant good qualities; the democracy has only one outstanding sin—it is not democratic.

CHAPTER IV

"THE PICKWICK PAPERS"

ROUND the birth of "Pickwick" broke one of those literary quarrels that were too common in the life of Dickens. Such quarrels indeed generally arose from some definite mistake or misdemeanour on the part of somebody else; but they were also made possible by an indefinite touchiness and susceptibility in Dickens himself. He was so sensitive on points of personal authorship and responsibility that even his sacred sense of humour deserted him. He turned people into mortal enemies whom he might have turned very easily into immortal jokes. It was not that he was lawless: in a sense it was that he was too legal; but he did not understand the principle of *de minimis non curat lex*. Anybody could draw him; any fool could make a fool of him. Any obscure madman who chose to say that he had written the whole of "Martin Chuzzlewit"; any penny-a-liner who chose to say that Dickens wore no shirt collar could call forth the most passionate and public denials as of a man pleading "not guilty" to witchcraft or high treason. Hence the letters of Dickens are filled with a certain singular type of quarrels and complaints, quarrels and complaints in which one cannot say that he was on the wrong side, but merely that even in being on the right side he was in the wrong place. He was not only a generous man, he was even a just man; to have made against anybody a charge or claim which was unfair would have been insupportable to him. His weakness was that he found the unfair claim or charge, however small, equally insupportable when brought against himself. No one can say of him that he was often wrong; we can only say of him as of many pugnacious people, that he was too often right.

The incidents attending the inauguration of the "Pickwick Papers" are not, perhaps, a perfect example of this trait, because Dickens was here a hand-to-mouth journalist, and the blow might possibly have been more disabling than those struck at him in his days of triumph. But all through those days of triumph, and to the day of his death, Dickens took this old tea-cup tempest with the most terrible gravity, drew up declarations, called witnesses, preserved pulverizing documents, and handed on to his children the forgotten folly as if it had been a Highland feud. Yet the unjust claim made on him was so much more ridiculous even than it was unjust, that it seems strange that he should have remembered it for a month except for his amusement. The facts are simple and familiar to most people. The publishers—Chapman & Hall—wished to produce some kind of serial with comic illustrations by a popular caricaturist named Seymour. This artist was chiefly famous for his rendering of the farcical side of sport, and to suit this specialty it was very vaguely suggested to Dickens by the publishers that he should write about a Nimrod Club, or some such thing, a club of amateur sportsmen, foredoomed to perpetual ignominies. Dickens objected in substance upon two very sensible grounds—first, that sporting sketches were stale; and second, that he knew nothing about sport. He changed the idea to that of a general club for travel and investigation, the Pickwick Club, and only retained one fated sportsman, Mr. Winkle, the melancholy remnant of the Nimrod Club that never was. The first seven pictures appeared with the signature of Seymour and the letterpress of Dickens, and in them Winkle and his woes were fairly, but not extraordinarily prominent. Before the eighth picture appeared Seymour had blown his brains out. After a brief interval of the employment of a man named Buss, Dickens obtained the assistance of Hoblot K. Brown whom we all call "Phiz," and may almost, in a certain sense, be said to have gone into partnership with him. They were as suited to each other and to the common creation of a unique thing as Gilbert and Sullivan. No other illustrator ever created the true Dickens characters with the precise and correct quantum of exaggeration. No other illustrator ever breathed the true Dickens atmosphere, in which clerks are clerks and yet at the same time elves.

To the tame mind the above affair does not seem to offer anything very promising in the way of a row. But Seymour's widow managed to evolve out of it the proposition that somehow or other her husband had written "Pickwick," or, at least, had been responsible for the genius and success of it. It does not appear that she had anything at all resembling a reason for this opinion except the unquestionable fact that the publishers had started with the idea of employing Seymour. This was quite true, and Dickens (who over and above his honesty was far too quarrelsome a man not to try to keep in the right, and who showed a sort of fierce carefulness in telling the truth in such cases) never denied it or attempted to conceal it. It was quite true, that at the beginning, instead of Seymour being employed to illustrate Dickens, Dickens may be said to have been employed to illustrate Seymour. But that Seymour invented anything in the letter-press large or small, that he invented either the outline of Mr. Pickwick's character or the number of Mr. Pickwick's cabman, that he invented either the story, or so much as a semi-colon in the story was not only never proved, but was never very lucidly alleged. Dickens fills his letters with all that there is to be said against Mrs. Seymour's idea; it is not very clear whether there was ever anything definitely said for it.

Upon the mere superficial fact and law of the affair, Dickens ought to have been superior to this silly business. But in a much deeper and a much more real sense he ought to have been superior to it. It did not really touch him or his greatness at all, even as an abstract allegation. If Seymour had started the story, had provided Dickens with his puppets, Tupman or Jingle, Dickens would have still have been Dickens and Seymour only Seymour. As a matter of fact, it happened to be a contemptible lie, but it would have been an equally contemptible truth. For the fact is that the greatness of Dickens and especially the greatness of Pickwick is not of a kind that could be affected by somebody else suggesting the first idea. It could not be affected by somebody else writing the first chapter. If it could be shown that another man had suggested to Hawthorne (let us say) the primary conception of the "Scarlet Letter," Hawthorne who worked it out would still be an exquisite workman; but he would be by so much less a creator. But in a case like Pickwick there is a simple test. If Seymour gave Dickens the main idea of Pickwick, what was it? There is no primary conception of Pickwick for any one to suggest. Dickens not only did not get the general plan from Seymour, he did not get it at all. In Pickwick, and, indeed, in Dickens, generally it is in the details that the author is creative, it is in the details that he is vast. The power of the book lies in the perpetual torrent of ingenious and inventive treatment; the theme (at least at the beginning) simply does not exist. The idea of Tupman, the fat lady-killer, is in itself quite dreary and vulgar; it is the detailed Tupman, as he is developed, who is unexpectedly amusing. The idea of Winkle, the clumsy sportsman, is in itself quite stale; it is as he goes on repeating himself that he becomes original. We hear of men whose imagination can touch with magic the dull facts of our life, but Dickens's yet more indomitable fancy could touch with magic even our dull fiction. Before we are halfway through the book the stock characters of dead and damned farces astonish us like splendid strangers.

Seymour's claim, then, viewed symbolically was even a compliment. It was true in spirit that Dickens obtained (or might have obtained) the start of Pickwick from somebody else, from anybody else. For he had a more gigantic energy than the energy of the intense artist, the energy which is prepared to write something. He had the energy which is prepared to write anything. He could have finished any man's tale. He could have breathed a mad life into any man's characters. If it had been true that Seymour had planned out Pickwick, if Seymour had fixed the chapters and named and numbered the characters, his slave would have shown even in these shackles such a freedom as would have shaken the world. If Dickens had been forced to make his incidents out of a chapter in a child's reading-book, or the names in a scrap of newspaper, he would have turned them in ten pages into creatures of his own. Seymour, as I say, was in a manner right in spirit. Dickens would at this time get his materials from anywhere, in the sense that he cared little what materials they were. He would not have stolen; but if he had stolen he would never have imitated.

The power which he proceeded at once to exhibit was the one power in letters which literally cannot be imitated, the primary inexhaustible creative energy, the enormous prodigality of genius which no one but another genius could parody. To claim to have originated an idea of Dickens is like claiming to have contributed a glass of water to Niagara. Wherever this stream or that stream started the colossal cataract of absurdity went roaring night and day. The volume of his invention overwhelmed all doubt of his inventiveness; Dickens was evidently a great man; unless he was a thousand men.

The actual circumstances of the writing and publishing of " Pickwick " show that while Seymour's specific claim was absurd, Dickens's indignant exactitude about every jot and tittle of authorship was also inappropriate and misleading. "The Pickwick Papers," when all is said and done, did emerge out of a haze of suggestions and proposals in which more than one person was involved. The publishers failed to base the story on a Nimrod Club, but they succeeded in basing it on a club. Seymour, by virtue of his idiosyncrasy, if he did not create, brought about the creation of Mr. Winkle. Seymour sketched Mr. Pickwick as a tall, thin man. Mr. Chapman (apparently without any word from Dickens boldly turned him into a short, fat man. Chapman took the type from a corpulent old dandy named Foster, who wore tights and gaiters and lived at Richmond. In this sense were we affected by this idle aspect of the thing we might call Chapman the real originator of "Pickwick." But as I have suggested, originating "Pickwick" is not the point. It was quite easy to originate "Pickwick." The difficulty was to write it.

However such things may be, there can be no question of the result of this chaos. In "The Pickwick Papers" Dickens sprang suddenly from a comparatively low level to a very high one. To the level of "Sketches by Boz" he never afterwards descended. To the level of "The Pickwick Papers" it is doubtful if he ever afterwards rose. "Pickwick," indeed, is not a good novel; but it is not a bad novel, for it is not a novel at all. In one sense, indeed, it is something nobler than a novel, for no novel with a plot and a proper termination could emit that sense of everlasting youth—a sense as of the gods gone wandering in England. This is not a novel, for all novels have an end; and "Pickwick," properly speaking, has no end—he is equal unto the angels. The point at which, as a fact, we find the printed matter terminates is not an end in any artistic sense of the word. Even as a boy I believed there were some more pages that were torn out of my copy, and I am looking for them still. The book might have been cut short anywhere else. It might have been cut short after Mr. Pickwick was released by Mr. Nupkins, or after Mr. Pickwick was fished out of the water, or at a hundred other places. And we should still have known that this was not really the story's end. We should have known that Mr. Pickwick was still having the same high adventures on the same high roads. As it happens, the book ends after Mr. Pickwick has taken a house in the neighbourhood of Dulwich. But we know he did not stop there. We know he broke out, that he took again the road of the high adventures; we know that if we take it ourselves in any acre of England, we may come suddenly upon him in a lane.

But this relation of "Pickwick" to the strict form of fiction demands a further word, which should indeed be said in any case before the consideration of any or all of the Dickens tales. Dickens's work is not to be reckoned in novels at all. Dickens's work is to be reckoned always by characters, sometimes by groups, oftener by episodes, but never by novels. You cannot discuss whether "Nicholas Nickleby" is a good novel, or whether "Our Mutual Friend" is a bad novel.

Strictly, there is no such novel as "Nicholas Nickleby." There is no such novel as "Our Mutual Friend." They are simply lengths cut from the flowing and mixed substance called Dickens—a substance of which any given length will be certain to contain a given proportion of brilliant and of bad stuff. You can say, according to your opinions, "the Crummles part is perfect," or "the Boffins are a mistake," just as a man watching a river go by him could count here a floating flower, and there a streak of scum. But you cannot artistically divide the output into books. The best of his work can be found in the worst of his works. "The Tale of Two Cities" is a good novel; "Little Dorrit" is not a good novel. But the description of "The Circumlocution Office" in "Little Dorrit" is quite as good as the description of "Tellson's Bank" in "The Tale of Two Cities." "The Old Curiosity Shop" is not so good as "David Copperfield," but Swiveller is quite as good as Micawber. Nor is there any reason why these superb creatures, as a general rule, should be in one novel any more than another. There is no reason why Sam Weller, in the course of his wanderings, should not wander into "Nicholas Nickleby." There is no reason why Major Bagstock, in his brisk way, should not walk straight out of " Dombey and Son " and straight into " Martin Chuzzlewit." To this generalization some modification should be added. " Pickwick " stands by itself, and has even a sort of unity in not pretending to unity. " David Copperfield," in a less degree, stands by itself, as being the only book in which Dickens wrote of himself; and " The Tale of Two Cities " stands by itself as being the only book in which Dickens slightly altered himself. But as a whole, this should be firmly grasped, that the units of Dickens, the primary elements, are not the stories, but the characters who affect the stories—or, more often still, the characters who do not affect the stories.

This is a plain matter; but, unless it be stated and felt, Dickens may be greatly misunderstood and greatly underrated. For not only is his whole machinery directed to facilitating the self-display of certain characters, but something more deep and more unmodern still is also true of him. It is also true that all the *moving* machinery exists only to display entirely *static* character. Things in the Dickens story shift and change only in order to give us glimpses of great characters that do not change at all. If we had a sequel of Pickwick ten years afterwards, Pickwick would be exactly the same age. We know he would not have fallen into that strange and beautiful second childhood which soothed and simplified the end of Colonel Newcome. Newcome, throughout the book, is in an atmosphere of time: Pickwick, throughout the book, is not. This will probably be taken by most modern people as praise of Thackeray and dispraise of Dickens. But this only shows how few modern people understand Dickens. It also shows how few understand the faiths and the fables of mankind. The matter can only be roughly stated in one way. Dickens did not strictly make a literature; he made a mythology.

For a few years our corner of Western Europe has had a fancy for this thing we call fiction; that is, for writing down our own lives or similar lives in order to look at them. But though we call it fiction, it differs from older literatures chiefly in being less fictitious. It imitates not only life, but the limitations of life; it not only reproduces life, it reproduces death. But outside us, in every other country, in every other age, there has been going on from the beginning a more fictitious kind of fiction. I mean the kind now called folklore, the literature of the people. Our modern novels, which deal with men as they are, are chiefly produced by a small and educated section of the society. But this other literature deals with men greater than they are—with demi-gods and heroes; and that is far too important a matter to be trusted to the educated classes. The fashioning of these portents is a popular trade, like ploughing or bricklaying; the men who made hedges, the men who made ditches, were the men who made deities. Men could not elect their kings, but they could elect their gods. So we find ourselves faced with a fundamental contrast between what is called fiction and what is called folklore. The one exhibits an abnormal degree of dexterity operating within our daily limitations; the other exhibits quite normal desires extended beyond those limitations. Fiction means the common things as seen by the uncommon people. Fairy tales mean the uncommon things as seen by the common people.

As our world advances through history towards its present epoch, it becomes more specialist, less democratic, and folklore turns gradually into fiction. But it is only slowly that the old elfin fire fades into the light of common realism. For ages after our characters have dressed up in the clothes of mortals they betray the blood of the gods. Even our phraseology is full of relics of this. When a modern novel is devoted to the bewilderments of a weak young clerk who cannot decide which woman he wants to marry, or which new religion he believes in, we still give this knock-kneed cad the name of "the hero"—the name which is the crown of Achilles. The popular preference for a story with "a happy ending" is not, or at least was not, a mere sweet-stuff optimism; it is the remains of the old idea of the triumph of the dragon-slayer, the ultimate apotheosis of the man beloved of heaven.

But there is another and more intangible trace of this fading supernaturalism—a trace very vivid to the reader, but very elusive to the critic. It is a certain air of endlessness in the episodes, even in the shortest episodes—a sense that, although we leave them, they still go on. Our modern attraction to short stories is not an accident of form; it is the sign of a real sense of fleetingness and fragility; it means that existence is only an impression, and, perhaps, only an illusion. A short story of to-day has the air of a dream; it has the irrevocable beauty of a falsehood; we get a glimpse of grey streets of London or red plains of India, as in an opium vision; we see people,—arresting people, with fiery and appealing faces. But when the story is ended, the people are ended. We have no instinct of anything ultimate and enduring behind the episodes. The moderns, in a word, describe life in short stories because they are possessed with the sentiment that life itself is an uncommonly short story, and perhaps not a true one. But in this elder literature, even in the comic literature (indeed, especially in the comic literature), the reverse is true. The characters are felt to be fixed things of which we have fleeting glimpses; that is, they are felt to be divine. Uncle Toby is talking for ever, as the elves are dancing for ever. We feel that whenever we hammer on the house of Falstaff, Falstaff will be at home. We feel it as a Pagan would feel that, if a cry broke the silence after ages of unbelief, Apollo would still be listening in his temple. These writers may tell short stories, but we feel they are only parts of a long story. And herein lies the peculiar significance, the peculiar sacredness even, of penny dreadfuls and the common printed matter made for our errand-boys. Here in dim and desperate forms, under the ban of our base culture, stormed at by silly magistrates, sneered at by silly schoolmasters, —here is the old popular literature still popular; here is the unmistakable voluminousness, the thousand and one tales of Dick Deadshot, like the thousand and one tales of Robin Hood. Here is the splendid and static boy, the boy who remains a boy through a thousand volumes and a thousand years. Here in mean alleys and dim shops, shadowed and shamed by the police, mankind is still driving its dark trade in heroes. And elsewhere, and in all other ages, in braver fashion, under cleaner skies the same eternal tale-telling goes on, and the whole mortal world is a factory of immortals.

Dickens was a mythologist rather than a novelist; he was the last of the mythologists, and perhaps the greatest. He did not always manage to make his characters men, but he always managed, at the least, to make them gods. They are creatures like Punch or Father Christmas. They live statically, in a perpetual summer of being themselves. It was not the aim of Dickens to show the effect of time and circumstance upon a character; it was not even his aim to show the effect of a character on time and circumstance. It is worth remark, in passing, that whenever he tried to describe change in a character, he made a mess of it, as in the repentance of Dombey or the apparent deterioration of Boffin. It was his aim to show character hung in a kind of happy void, in a world apart from time—yes, and essentially apart from circumstance, though the phrase may seem odd in connection with the godlike horse-play of "Pickwick." But all the Pickwickian events, wild as they often are, were only designed to display the greater wildness of souls, or sometimes merely to bring the reader within touch, so to speak, of that wildness. The author would have fired Mr. Pickwick out of a cannon to get him to Wardle's by Christmas; he would have taken the roof off to drop him into Bob Sawyer's party. But once put Pickwick at Wardle's, with his punch and a group of gorgeous personalities, and nothing will move him from his chair. Once he is at Sawyer's party, he forgets how he got there; he forgets Mrs. Bardell and all his story. For the story was but an incantation to call up a god, and the god (Mr. Jack Hopkins) is present in divine power. Once the great characters are face to face, the ladder by which they climbed is forgotten and falls down, the structure of the story drops to pieces, the plot is abandoned, the other characters deserted at every kind of crisis; the whole crowded thoroughfare of the tale is blocked by two or three talkers, who take their immortal ease as if they were already in Paradise. For they do not exist for the story; the story exists for them; and they know it.

To every man alive, one must hope, it has in some manner happened that he has talked with his more fascinating friends round a table on some night when all the numerous personalities unfolded themselves like great tropical flowers. All fell into their parts as in some delightful impromptu play. Every man was more himself than he had ever been in this vale of tears. Every man was a beautiful caricature of himself. The man who has known such nights will understand the exaggerations of "Pickwick." The man who has not known such nights will not enjoy "Pickwick" nor (I imagine) heaven. For, as I have said, Dickens is, in this matter, close to popular religion, which is the ultimate and reliable religion. He conceives an endless joy; he conceives creatures as permanent as Puck or Pan—creatures whose will to live æons upon æons cannot satisfy. He is not come, as a writer, that his creatures may copy life and copy its narrowness; he is come that they may have life, and that they may have it more abundantly. It is absurd indeed that Christians should be called the enemies of life because they wish life to last for ever; it is more absurd still to call the old comic writers dull because they wished their unchanging characters to last for ever. Both popular religion, with its endless joys, and the old comic story, with its endless jokes, have in our time faded together. We are too weak to desire that undying vigour. We believe that you can have too much of a good thing—a blasphemous belief, which at one blow wrecks all the heavens that men have hoped for. The grand old defiers of God were not afraid of an eternity of torment. We have come to be afraid of an eternity of joy. It is not my business here to take sides in this division between those who like life and long novels and those who like death and short stories; my only business is to point out that those who see in Dickens's unchanging characters and recurring catch-words a mere stiffness and lack of living movement miss the point and nature of his work. His tradition is another tradition altogether; his aim is another aim altogether to those of the modern novelists who trace the alchemy of experience and the autumn tints of character. He is there, like the common people of all ages, to make deities; he is there, as I have said, to exaggerate life in the direction of life. The spirit he at bottom celebrates is that of two friends drinking wine together and talking through the night. But for him they are two deathless friends talking through an endless night and pouring wine from an inexhaustible bottle.

This, then, is the first firm fact to grasp about "Pickwick" — about "Pickwick" more than about any of the other stories. It is, first and foremost, a supernatural story. Mr. Pickwick was a fairy. So was old Mr. Weller. This does not imply that they were suited to swing in a trapeze of gossamer; it merely implies that if they had fallen out of it on their heads they would not have died. But, to speak more strictly, Mr. Samuel Pickwick is not the fairy; he is the fairy prince; that is to say, he is the abstract wanderer and wonderer, the Ulysses of Comedy—the half-human and half-elfin creature—human enough to wander, human enough to wonder, but still sustained with that merry fatalism that is natural to immortal beings—sustained by that hint of divinity which tells him in the darkest hour that he is doomed to live happily ever afterwards. He has set out walking to the end of the world, but he knows he will find an inn there.

And this brings us to the best and boldest element of originality in "Pickwick." It has not, I think, been observed, and it may be that Dickens did not observe it. Certainly he did not plan it; it grew gradually, perhaps out of the unconscious part of his soul, and warmed the whole story like a slow fire. Of course it transformed the whole story also; transformed it out of all likeness to itself. About this latter point was waged one of the numberless little wars of Dickens. It was a part of his pugnacious vanity that he refused to admit the truth of the mildest criticism. Moreover, he used his inexhaustible ingenuity to find an apologia that was generally an afterthought. Instead of laughingly admitting, in answer to criticism, the glorious improbability of Pecksniff, he retorted with a sneer, clever and very unjust, that he was not surprised that the Pecksniffs should deny the portrait of Pecksniff. When it was objected that the pride of old Paul Dombey breaks as abruptly as a stick, he tried to make out that there had been an absorbing psychological struggle going on in that gentleman all the time, which the reader was too stupid to perceive. Which is, I am afraid, rubbish. And so, in a similar vein, he answered those who pointed out to him the obvious and not very shocking fact that our sentiments about Pickwick are very different in the second part of the book from our sentiments in the first: that we find ourselves at the beginning setting out in the company of a farcical old fool, if not a farcical old humbug, and that we find ourselves at the end saying farewell to a fine old English merchant, a monument of genial sanity. Dickens answered with the same ingenious self-justification as in the other cases—that surely it often happened that a man met us first arrayed in his more grotesque qualities, and that fuller acquaintance unfolded his more serious merits. This, of course, is quite true;

but I think any honest admirer of "Pickwick" will feel that it is not an answer. For the fault in "Pickwick" (if it be a fault) is a change, not in the hero but in the whole atmosphere. The point is not that Pickwick turns into a different kind of man; it is that "The Pickwick Papers" turns into a different kind of book. And however artistic both parts may be, this combination must, in strict art, be called inartistic. A man is quite artistically justified in writing a tale in which a man as cowardly as Bob Acres becomes a man as brave as Hector. But a man is not artistically justified in writing a tale which begins in the style of "The Rivals" and ends in the style of the "Iliad." In other words, we do not mind the hero changing in the course of a book; but we are not prepared for the author changing in the course of the book. And the author did change in the course of this book. He made, in the midst of this book a great discovery, which was the discovery of his destiny, or, what is more important, of his duty. That discovery turned him from the author of "Sketches by Boz" to the author of "David Copperfield." And that discovery constituted the thing of which I have spoken—the outstanding and arresting original feature in "The Pickwick Papers."

" Pickwick," I have said, is a romance of adventure, and Samuel Pickwick is the romantic adventurer. So much is indeed obvious. But the strange and stirring discovery which Dickens made was this—that having chosen a fat old man of the middle classes as a good thing of which to make a butt, he found that a fat old man of the middle classes is the very best thing of which to make a romantic adventurer. " Pickwick " is supremely original in that it is the adventures of an old man. It is a fairy tale in which the victor is not the youngest of the three brothers, but one of the oldest of their uncles. The result is both noble and new and true. There is nothing which so much needs simplicity as adventure. And there is no one who so much possesses simplicity as an honest and elderly man of business. For romance he is better than a troop of young troubadours; for the swaggering young fellow anticipates his adventures, just as he anticipates his income. Hence, both the adventures and the income, when he comes up to them, are not there. But a man in late middle-age has grown used to the plain necessities, and his first holiday is a second youth. A good man, as Thackeray said with such thorough and searching truth, grows simpler as he grows older. Samuel Pickwick in his youth was probably an insufferable young coxcomb. He knew then, or thought he knew, all about the confidence tricks of swindlers like Jingle. He knew then, or thought he knew, all about the amatory designs of sly ladies like Mrs. Bardell. But years and real life have relieved him of this idle and evil knowledge. He has had the high good luck in losing the follies of youth, to lose the wisdom of youth also. Dickens has caught, in a manner at once wild and convincing, this queer innocence of the afternoon of life. The round, moon-like face, the round, moon-like spectacles of Samuel Pickwick move through the tale as emblems of a certain spherical simplicity. They are fixed in that grave surprise that may be seen in babies; that grave surprise which is the only real happiness that is possible to man. Pickwick's round face is like a round and honourable mirror, in which are reflected all the fantasies of earthly existence; for surprise is, strictly speaking, the only kind of reflection. All this grew gradually on Dickens. It is odd to recall to our minds the original plan, the plan of the Nimrod Club, and the author who was to be wholly occupied in playing practical jokes on his characters. He had chosen (or somebody else had chosen) that corpulent old simpleton as a person peculiarly fitted to fall down trap-doors, to shoot over butter slides, to struggle with apple-pie beds, to be tipped out of carts and dipped into horse-ponds. But Dickens, and Dickens only, discovered as he went on how fitted the fat old man was to rescue ladies, to defy tyrants, to dance, to leap, to experiment with life, to be a *deus ex machinâ,* and even a knight-errant. Dickens made this discovery. Dickens went into the Pickwick Club to scoff, and Dickens remained to pray.

Molière and his marquises are very much amused when M. Jourdain. the fat old middle-class fellow, discovers with delight that he has been talking prose all his life. I have often wondered whether Molière saw how in this fact M. Jourdain towers above them all and touches the stars. He has the freshness to enjoy a fresh fact, the freshness to enjoy an old one. He can feel that the common thing prose is an accomplishment like verse; and it is an accomplishment like verse; it is the miracle of language. He can feel the subtle taste of water, and roll it on his tongue like wine. His simple vanity and voracity, his innocent love of living, his ignorant love of learning, are things far fuller of romance than the weariness and foppishness of the sniggering cavaliers. When he consciously speaks prose, he unconsciously thinks poetry. It would be better for us all if we were as conscious that supper is supper or that life is life, as this true romantic was that prose is actually prose. M. Jourdain is here the type, Mr. Pickwick is elsewhere the type, of this true and neglected thing, the romance of the middle classes. It is the custom in our little epoch to sneer at the middle classes. Cockney artists profess to find the bourgeoisie dull; as if artists had any business to find anything dull. Decadents talk contemptuously of its conventions and its set tasks; it never occurs to them that conventions and set tasks are the very way to keep that greenness in the grass and that redness in the roses—which they had lost for ever. Stevenson, in his incomparable "Lantern Bearers," describes the ecstasy of a schoolboy in the mere fact of buttoning a dark lantern under a dark great-coat. If you wish for that ecstasy of the schoolboy, you must have the boy; but you must also have the school. Strict opportunities and defined hours are the very outline of that enjoyment. A man like Mr. Pickwick has been at school all his life, and when he comes out he astonishes the youngsters. His heart, as that acute psychologist, Mr. Weller, points out, had been born later than his body. It will be remembered that Mr. Pickwick also, when on the escapade of Winkle and Miss Allen, took immoderate pleasure in the performances of a dark lantern which was not dark enough, and was nothing but a nuisance to everybody. His soul also was with Stevenson's boys on the grey sands of Haddington, talking in the dark by the sea. He also was of the league of the "Lantern Bearers." Stevenson, I remember, says that in the shops of that town they could purchase "penny Pickwicks (that remarkable cigar)." Let us hope they smoked them, and that the rotund ghost of Pickwick hovered over the rings of smoke.

Pickwick goes through life with that god-like gullibility which is the key to all adventures. The greenhorn is the ultimate victor in everything; it is he that gets the most out of life. Because Pickwick is led away by Jingle, he will be led to the White Hart Inn, and see the only Weller cleaning boots in the courtyard. Because he is bamboozled by Dodson and Fogg, he will enter the prison house like a paladin, and rescue the man and the woman who have wronged him most. His soul will never starve for exploits or excitements who is wise enough to be made a fool of. He will make himself happy in the traps that have been laid for him; he will roll in their nets and sleep. All doors will fly open to him who has a mildness more defiant than mere courage. The whole is unerringly expressed in one fortunate phrase—he will be always "taken in." To be taken in everywhere is to see the inside of everything. It is the hospitality of circumstance. With torches and trumpets, like a guest, the greenhorn is taken in by Life. And the sceptic is cast out by it.

CHAPTER V

THE GREAT POPULARITY

THERE is one aspect of Charles Dickens which must be of interest even to that subterranean race which does not admire his books. Even if we are not interested in Dickens as a great event in English literature, we must still be interested in him as a great event in English history. If he had not his place with Fielding and Thackeray, he would still have his place with Wat Tyler and Wilkes; for the man led a mob. He did what no English statesman, perhaps, has really done; he called out the people. He was popular in a sense of which we moderns have not even a notion. In that sense there is no popularity now. There are no popular authors to-day. We call such authors as Mr. Guy Boothby or Mr. William Le Queux popular authors. But this is popularity altogether in a weaker sense; not only in quantity, but in quality. The old popularity was positive; the new is negative. There is a great deal of difference between the eager man who wants to read a book, and the tired man who wants a book to read. A man reading a Le Queux mystery wants to get to the end of it. A man reading the Dickens novel wished that it might never end. Men read a Dickens story six times because they knew it so well. If a man can read a Le Queux story six times it is only because he can forget it six times. In short, the Dickens novel was popular, not because it was an unreal world, but because it was a real world; a world in which the soul could live. The modern " shocker " at its very best is an interlude in life. But in the days when Dickens's work was coming out in serial, people talked as if real life were itself the interlude between one issue of " Pickwick " and another.

In reaching the period of the publication of " Pickwick," we reach this sudden apotheosis of Dickens. Henceforward he filled the literary world in a way hard to imagine. Fragments of that huge fashion remain in our daily language; in the talk of every trade or public question are embedded the wrecks of that enormous religion. Men give out the airs of Dickens without even opening his books; just as Catholics can live in a tradition of Christianity without having looked at the New Testament. The man in the street has more memories of Dickens, whom he has not read, than of Marie Corelli, whom he has. There is nothing in any way parallel to this omnipresence and vitality in the great comic characters of Boz. There are no modern Bumbles and Pecksniffs, no modern Gamps and Micawbers. Mr. Rudyard Kipling (to take an author of a higher type than those before mentioned) is called, and called justly, a popular author; that is to say, he is widely read, greatly enjoyed, and highly remunerated; he has achieved the paradox of at once making poetry and making money. But let any one who wishes to see the difference try the experiment of assuming the Kipling characters to be common property like the Dickens characters. Let any one go into an average parlour and allude to Strickland as he would allude to Mr. Bumble, the Beadle. Let any one say that somebody is "a perfect Learoyd," as he would say "a perfect Pecksniff." Let any one write a comic paragraph for a halfpenny paper, and allude to Mrs. Hawksbee instead of to Mrs. Gamp. He will soon discover that the modern world has forgotten its own fiercest booms more completely than it has forgotten this formless tradition from its fathers. The mere dregs of it come to more than any contemporary excitement; the gleaning of the grapes of "Pickwick" is more than the whole vintage of "Soldiers Three." There is one instance, and I think only one, of an exception to this generalization; there is one figure in our popular literature which would really be recognized by the populace. Ordinary men would understand you if you referred currently to Sherlock Holmes. Sir Arthur Conan Doyle would no doubt be justified in rearing his head to the stars, remembering that Sherlock Holmes is the only really familiar figure in modern fiction. But let him droop that head again with a gentle sadness, remembering that if Sherlock Holmes is the only familiar figure in modern fiction, Sherlock Holmes is also the only familiar figure in the Sherlock Holmes tales. Not many people could say offhand what was the name of the owner of Silver Blaze, or whether Mrs. Watson was dark or fair. But if Dickens had written the Sherlock Holmes stories, every character in them would have been equally arresting and memorable. A Sherlock Holmes would have cooked the dinner for Sherlock Holmes; a Sherlock Holmes would have driven his cab. If Dickens brought in a man merely to carry a letter, he had time for a touch or two, and made him a giant. Dickens not only conquered the world, he conquered it with minor characters. Mr. John Smauker, the servant of Mr. Cyrus Bantam, though he merely passes across the stage, is almost as vivid to us as Mr.

Samuel Weller, the servant of Mr. Samuel Pickwick. The young man with the lumpy forehead, who only says " Esker " to Mr. Podsnap's foreign gentleman, is as good as Mr. Podsnap himself. They appear only for a fragment of time, but they belong to eternity. We have them only for an instant, but they have us for ever.

In dealing with Dickens, then, we are dealing with a man whose public success was a marvel and almost a monstrosity. And here I perceive that my friend, the purely artistic critic, primed with Flaubert and Turgenev, can contain himself no longer. He leaps to his feet, upsetting his cup of cocoa, and asks contemptuously what all this has to do with criticism. " Why begin your study of an author," he says, " with trash about popularity? Boothby is popular, and Le Queux is popular, and Mother Siegel is popular. If Dickens was even more popular, it may only mean that Dickens was even worse. The people like bad literature. If your object is to show that Dickens was good literature, you should rather apologize for his popularity, and try to explain it away. You should seek to show that Dickens's work was good literature, although it was popular. Yes, that is your task, to prove that Dickens was admirable, although he was admired! "

I ask the artistic critic to be patient for a little and to believe that I have a serious reason for registering this historic popularity. To that we shall come presently. But as a manner of approach I may perhaps ask leave to examine this actual and fashionable statement, to which I have supposed him to have recourse—the statement that the people like bad literature, and even like literature because it is bad. This way of stating the thing is an error, and in that error lies matter of much import to Dickens and his destiny in letters. The public does not like bad literature. The public likes a certain kind of literature and likes that kind of literature even when it is bad better than another kind of literature even when it is good. Nor is this unreasonable; for the line between different types of literature is as real as the line between tears and laughter; and to tell people who can only get bad comedy that you have some first-class tragedy is as irrational as to offer a man who is shivering over weak warm coffee a really superior sort of ice.

Ordinary people dislike the delicate modern work, not because it is good or because it is bad, but because it is not the thing that they asked for. If, for instance, you find them pent in sterile streets and hungering for adventure and a violent secrecy, and if you then give them their choice between "A Study in Scarlet," a good detective story, and "The Autobiography of Mark Rutherford," a good psychological monologue, no doubt they will prefer "A Study in Scarlet." But they will not do so because "The Autobiography of Mark Rutherford" is a very good monologue, but because it is evidently a very poor detective story. They will be indifferent to "Les Aveugles," not because it is good drama, but because it is bad melodrama. They do not like good introspective sonnets; but neither do they like bad introspective sonnets, of which there are many. When they walk behind the brass of the Salvation Army band instead of listening to harmonies at Queen's Hall, it is always assumed that they prefer bad music. But it may be merely that they prefer military music, music marching down the open street, and that if Dan Godfrey's band could be smitten with salvation and lead them, they would like that even better. And while they might easily get more satisfaction out of a screaming article in *The War Cry* than out of a page of Emerson about the Over-soul, this would not be because the page of Emerson is another and superior kind of literature. It would be because the page of Emerson is another (and inferior) kind of religion.

Dickens stands first as a defiant monument of what happens when a great literary genius has a literary taste akin to that of the community. For this kinship was deep and spiritual. Dickens was not like our ordinary demagogues and journalists. Dickens did not write what the people wanted. Dickens wanted what the people wanted. And with this was connected that other fact which must never be forgotten, and which I have more than once insisted on, that Dickens and his school had a hilarious faith in democracy and thought of the service of it as a sacred priesthood. Hence there was this vital point in his popularism, that there was no condescension in it. The belief that the rabble will only read rubbish can be read between the lines of all our contemporary writers, even of those writers whose rubbish the rabble reads. Mr. Fergus Hume has no more respect for the populace than Mr. George Moore. The only difference lies between those writers who will consent to talk down to the people, and those writers who will not consent to talk down to the people. But Dickens never talked down to the people. He talked up to the people. He approached the people like a deity and poured out his riches and his blood. This is what makes the immortal bond between him and the masses of men. He had not merely produced something they could understand, but he took it seriously, and toiled and agonized to produce it. They were not only enjoying one of the best writers, they were enjoying the best he could do. His raging and sleepless nights, his wild walks in the darkness, his note-books crowded, his nerves in rags, all this extraordinary output was but a fit sacrifice to the ordinary man. He climbed towards the lower classes. He panted upwards on weary wings to reach the heaven of the poor.

His power, then, lay in the fact that he expressed with an energy and brilliancy quite uncommon the things close to the common mind. But with this mere phrase, the common mind, we collide with a current error. Commonness and the common mind are now generally spoken of as meaning in some manner inferiority and the inferior mind; the mind of the mere mob. But the common mind means the mind of all the artists and heroes; or else it would not be common. Plato had the common mind; Dante had the common mind; or that mind was not common. Commonness means the quality common to the saint and the sinner, to the philosopher and the fool; and it was this that Dickens grasped and developed. In everybody there is a certain thing

that loves babies, that fears death, that likes sunlight: that thing enjoys Dickens. And everybody does not mean uneducated crowds; everybody means everybody: everybody means Mrs. Meynell. This lady, a cloistered and fastidious writer, has written one of the best eulogies of Dickens that exist, an essay in praise of his pungent perfection of epithet. And when I say that everybody understands Dickens I do not mean that he is suited to the untaught intelligence. I mean that he is so plain that even scholars can understand him.

The best expression of the fact, however, is to be found in noting the two things in which he is most triumphant. In order of artistic value, next after his humour, comes his horror. And both his humour and his horror are of a kind strictly to be called human; that is, they belong to the basic part of us, below the lowest roots of our variety. His horror for instance is a healthy churchyard horror, a fear of the grotesque defamation called death; and this every man has, even if he also has the more delicate and depraved fears that come of an evil spiritual outlook. We may be afraid of a fine shade with Henry James; that is, we may be afraid of the world. We may be afraid of a taut silence with Maeterlinck; that is, we may be afraid of our own souls. But every one will certainly be afraid of a Cock Lane Ghost, including Henry James and Maeterlinck. This latter is literally a mortal fear, a fear of death; it is not the immortal fear, or fear of damnation, which belongs to all the more refined intellects of our day. In a word, Dickens does, in the exact sense, make the flesh creep; he does not, like the decadents, make the soul crawl. And the creeping of the flesh on being reminded of its fleshly failure is a strictly universal thing which we can all feel, while some of us are as yet uninstructed in the art of spiritual crawling. In the same way the Dickens mirth is a part of man and universal. All men can laugh at broad humour, even the subtle humourists. Even the modern *flâneur,* who can smile at a particular combination of green and yellow, would laugh at Mr. Lammle's request for Mr. Fledgeby's nose. In a word—the common things are common—even to the uncommon people.

These two primary dispositions of Dickens, to make the flesh creep and to make the sides ache, were a sort of twins of his spirit; they were never far apart and the fact of their affinity is interestingly exhibited in the first two novels.

Generally he mixed the two up in a book and mixed a great many other things with them. As a rule he cared little if he kept six stories of quite different colours running in the same book. The effect was sometimes similar to that of playing six tunes at once. He does not mind the coarse tragic figure of Jonas Chuzzlewit crossing the mental stage which is full of the allegorical pantomime of Eden, Mr. Chollop and *The Watertoast Gazette,* a scene which is as much of a satire as "Gulliver," and nearly as much of a fairy tale. He does not mind binding up a rather pompous sketch of prostitution in the same book with an adorable impossibility like Bunsby. But "Pickwick" is so far a coherent thing that it is coherently comic and consistently rambling. And as a consequence his next book was, upon the whole, coherently and consistently horrible. As his natural turn for terrors was kept down in "Pickwick," so his natural turn for joy and laughter is kept down in "Oliver Twist." In "Oliver Twist" the smoke of the thieves' kitchen hangs over the whole tale, and the shadow of Fagin falls everywhere. The little lamp-lit rooms of Mr. Brownlow and Rose Maylie are to all appearance purposely kept subordinate, a mere foil to the foul darkness without. It was a strange and appropriate accident that Cruikshank and not "Phiz" should have illustrated this book. There was about Cruikshank's art a kind of cramped energy which is almost the definition of the criminal mind. His drawings have a dark strength: yet he does not only draw morbidly, he draws meanly. In the doubled-up figure and frightful eyes of Fagin in the condemned cell there is not only a baseness of subject; there is a kind of baseness in the very technique of it. It is not drawn with the free lines of a free man; it has the half-witted secrecies of a hunted thief. It does not look merely like a picture of Fagin; it looks like a picture by Fagin. Among these dark and detestable plates there is one which has with a kind of black directness, the dreadful poetry that does inhere in the story, stumbling as it often is. It represents Oliver asleep at an open window in the house of one of his humaner patrons. And outside the window, but as big and close as if they were in the room stand Fagin and the foul-faced Monk, staring at him with dark monstrous visages and great, white wicked eyes, in the style of the simple deviltry of the draughtsman. The very *naïveté* of the horror is horrifying: the very woodenness of the two wicked men seems to make them worse than mere men who are wicked. But this picture of big devils at the window-sill does express, as has been suggested above, the thread of poetry in the whole thing; the sense, that is, of the thieves as a kind of army of devils compassing earth and sky, crying for Oliver's soul and besieging the house in which he is barred for safety. In this matter there is, I think, a difference between the author and the illustrator. In Cruikshank there was surely something morbid; but, sensitive and sentimental as Dickens was, there was nothing morbid in him. He had, as Stevenson had, more of the mere boy's love of suffocating stories of blood and darkness; of skulls, of gibbets, of all the things, in a word, that are sombre without being sad. There is a ghastly joy in remembering our boyish reading about Sikes and his flight; especially about the voice of that unbearable pedlar which went on in a monotonous and maddening sing-song, "will wash out grease-stains, mud-stains, blood-stains," until Sikes fled almost screaming. For this boyish mixture of appetite and repugnance there is a good popular phrase, "supping on horrors." Dickens supped on horrors as he supped on Christmas pudding. He supped on horrors because he was an optimist and could sup on anything. There was no saner or simpler schoolboy than Traddles, who covered all his books with skeletons.

"Oliver Twist" had begun in Bentley's *Miscellany,* which Dickens edited in 1837. It was interrupted by a blow that for the moment broke the author's spirit and seemed to have broken his heart. His wife's sister, Mary Hogarth, died suddenly. To Dickens his wife's family seems to have been like his own; his affections were heavily committed to the sisters, and of this one he was peculiarly fond. All his life, through much conceit and sometimes something bordering on selfishness, we can feel the redeeming note of an almost tragic tenderness; he was a man who could really have died of love or sorrow. He took up the work of "Oliver Twist" again later in the year, and finished it at the end of 1838. His work was incessant and almost bewildering. In 1838 he had already brought out the first number of "Nicholas Nickleby." But the great popularity went booming on; the whole world was roaring for books by Dickens, and more books by Dickens, and Dickens was labouring night and day like a factory. Among other things he edited the "Memoirs of Grimaldi." The incident is only worth mentioning for the sake of one more example of the silly ease with which Dickens was drawn by criticism and the clever ease with which he managed, in these small squabbles, to defend himself. Somebody mildly suggested that, after all, Dickens had never known Grimaldi. Dickens was down on him like a thunderbolt, sardonically asking how close an intimacy Lord Braybrooke had with Mr. Samuel Pepys.

"Nicholas Nickleby" is the most typical perhaps of the tone of his earlier works. It is in form a very rambling, old-fashioned romance, the kind of romance in which the hero is only a convenience for the frustration of the villain. Nicholas is what is called in theatricals a stick. But any stick is good enough to beat a Squeers with. That strong thwack, that simplified energy is the whole object of such a story; and the whole of this tale is full of a kind of highly picturesque platitude. The wicked aristocrats, Sir Mulberry Hawk, Lord Frederick Verisopht and the rest are inadequate versions of the fashionable profligate. But this is not (as some suppose) because Dickens in his vulgarity could not comprehend the refinement of patrician vice. There is no idea more vulgar or more ignorant than the notion that a gentleman is generally what is called refined. The error of the Hawk conception is that, if anything, he is too refined. Real aristocratic blackguards do not swagger and rant so well. A real fast baronet would not have defied Nicholas in the tavern with so much oratorical dignity. A real fast baronet would probably have been choked with apoplectic embarrassment and said nothing at all. But Dickens read into this aristocracy a grandiloquence and a natural poetry which, like all melodrama, is really the precious jewel of the poor.

But the book contains something which is much more Dickensian. It is exquisitely characteristic of Dickens that the truly great achievement of the story is the person who delays the story. Mrs. Nickleby with her beautiful mazes of memory does her best to prevent the story of Nicholas Nickleby from being told. And she does well. There is no particular necessity that we should know what happens to Madeline Bray. There is a desperate and crying necessity that we should know that Mrs. Nickleby once had a foot-boy who had a wart on his nose and a driver who had a green shade over his left eye. If Mrs. Nickleby is a fool, she is one of those fools who are wiser than the world. She stands for a great truth which we must not forget; the truth that experience is not in real life a saddening thing at all. The people who have had misfortunes are generally the people who love to talk about them. Experience is really one of the gaieties of old age, one of its dissipations. Mere memory becomes a kind of debauch. Experience may be disheartening to those who are foolish enough to try to co-ordinate it and to draw deductions from it. But to those happy souls, like Mrs. Nickleby, to whom relevancy is nothing, the whole of their past life is like an inexhaustible fairyland. Just as we take a rambling walk because we know that a whole district is beautiful, so they indulge a rambling mind because they know that a whole existence is interesting. A boy does not plunge into his future more romantically and at random, than they plunge into their past.

Another gleam in the book is Mr. Mantalini. Of him, as of all the really great comic characters of Dickens, it is impossible to speak with any critical adequacy. Perfect absurdity is a direct thing, like physical pain, or a strong smell. A joke is a fact. However indefensible it is it cannot be attacked. However defensible it is it cannot be defended. That Mr. Mantalini should say in praising the "outline" of his wife, "The two Countesses had no outlines, and the Dowager's was a demd outline," this can only be called an unanswerable absurdity. You may try to analyse it, as Charles Lamb did the indefensible joke about the hare; you may dwell for a moment on the dark distinctions between the negative disqualification of the Countesses and the positive disqualification of the Dowager, but you will not capture the violent beauty of it in any way. "She will be a lovely widow; I shall be a body. Some handsome women will cry; she will laugh demnedly." This vision of demoniac heartlessness has the same defiant finality. I mention the matter here, but it has to be remembered in connection with all the comic masterpieces of Dickens. Dickens has greatly suffered with the critics precisely through this stunning simplicity in his best work. The critic is called upon to describe his sensations while enjoying Mantalini and Micawber, and he can no more describe them than he can describe a blow in the face. Thus Dickens, in this self-conscious, analytical and descriptive age, loses both ways. He is doubly unfitted for the best modern criticism. His bad work is below that criticism. His good work is above it.

But gigantic as were Dickens's labours, gigantic as were the exactions from him, his own plans were more gigantic still. He had the type of mind that wishes to do every kind of work at once; to do everybody's work as well as its own. There floated before him a vision of a monstrous magazine, entirely written by himself. It is true that when this scheme came to be discussed, he suggested that other pens might be occasionally employed; but, reading between the lines, it is sufficiently evident that he thought of the thing as a kind of vast multiplication of himself, with Dickens as editor, opening letters, Dickens as leader-writer writing leaders, Dickens as reporter reporting meetings, Dickens as reviewer reviewing books, Dickens, for all I know, as office-boy, opening and shutting doors. This serial, of which he spoke to Messrs. Chapman and Hall, began and broke off and remains as a colossal fragment bound together under the title of "Master Humphrey's Clock." One characteristic thing he wished to have in the periodical. He suggested an Arabian Nights of London, in which Gog and Magog, the giants of the city, should give forth chronicles as enormous as themselves. He had a taste for these schemes or frameworks for many tales. He made and abandoned many; many he half-fulfilled. I strongly suspect that he meant Major Jackman, in "Mrs. Lirriper's Lodgings" and "Mrs. Lirriper's Legacy," to start a series of studies of that lady's lodgers, a kind of history of No. 81 Norfolk Street, Strand. "The Seven Poor Travellers" was planned for seven stories; we will not say seven poor stories. Dickens had meant, probably, to write a tale for each article of "Somebody's Luggage": he only got as far as the hat and the boots. This gigantesque scale of literary architecture, huge and yet curiously cosy, is characteristic of his spirit, fond of size and yet fond of comfort. He liked to have story within story, like room within room of some labyrinthine but comfortable castle. In this spirit he wished "Master Humphrey's Clock" to begin, and to be a big frame or bookcase for numberless novels. The clock started; but the clock stopped.

In the prologue by Master Humphrey reappears Mr. Pickwick and Sam Weller, and of that resurrection many things have been said, chiefly expressions of a reasonable regret. Doubtless they do not add much to their author's reputation, but they add a great deal to their author's pleasure. It was ingrained in him to wish to meet old friends. All his characters are, so to speak, designed to be old friends; in a sense every Dickens character is an old friend, even when he first appears. He comes to us mellow out of many implied interviews, and carries the firelight on his face. Dickens was simply pleased to meet Pickwick again, and being pleased, he made the old man too comfortable to be amusing.

But "Master Humphrey's Clock" is now scarcely known except as the shell of one of the well-known novels. "The Old Curiosity Shop" was published in accordance with the original "Clock" scheme. Perhaps the most typical thing about it is the title. There seems no reason in particular, at the first and most literal glance, why the story should be called after the Old Curiosity Shop. Only two of the characters have anything to do with such a shop, and they leave us for ever in the first few pages. It is as if Thackeray had called the whole novel of "Vanity Fair" "Miss Pinkerton's Academy." It is as if Scott had given the whole story of "The Antiquary" the title of "The Hawes Inn." But when we feel the situation with more fidelity we realize that this title is something in the nature of a key to the whole Dickens romance. His tales always started from some splendid hint in the streets. And shops, perhaps the most poetical of all things, often set off his fancy galloping. Every shop, in fact, was to him the door of romance. Among all the huge serial schemes of which we have spoken, it is a matter of wonder that he never started an endless periodical called "The Street," and divided it into shops. He could have written an exquisite romance called "The Baker's Shop"; another called "The Chemist's Shop"; another called "The Oil Shop," to keep company with "The Old Curiosity Shop." Some incomparable baker he invented and forgot. Some gorgeous chemist might have been. Some more than mortal oilman is lost to us for ever. This Old Curiosity Shop he did happen to linger by: its tale he did happen to tell.

Around " Little Nell," of course, a controversy raged and rages; some implored Dickens not to kill her at the end of the story: some regret that he did not kill her at the beginning. To me the chief interest in this young person lies in the fact that she is an example, and the most celebrated example of what must have been, I think, a personal peculiarity, perhaps a personal experience of Dickens. There is, of course, no paradox at all in saying that if we find in a good book a wildly impossible character it is very probable indeed that it was copied from a real person. This is one of the commonplaces of good art criticism. For although people talk of the restraints of fact and the freedom of fiction, the case for most artistic purposes is quite the other way. Nature is as free as air: art is forced to look probable. There may be a million things that do happen, and yet only one thing that convinces us as likely to happen. Out of a million possible things there may be only one appropriate thing. I fancy, therefore, that many stiff, unconvincing characters are copied from the wild freak-show of real life. And in many parts of Dickens's work there is evidence of some peculiar affection on his part for a strange sort of little girl; a little girl with a premature sense of responsibility and duty; a sort of saintly precocity. Did he know some little girl of this kind? Did she die, perhaps, and remain in his memory in colours too ethereal and pale? In any case there are a great number of them in his works. Little Dorrit was one of them, and Florence Dombey with her brother, and even Agnes in infancy; and, of course, Little Nell. And, in any case, one thing is evident; whatever charm these children may have they have not the charm of childhood. They are not little children: they are "little mothers." The beauty and divinity in a child lie in his not being worried, not being conscientious, not being like Little Nell. Little Nell has never any of the sacred bewilderment of a baby. She never wears that face, beautiful but almost half-witted, with which a real child half understands that there is evil in the universe.

As usual, however, little as the story has to do with the title, the splendid and satisfying pages have even less to do with the story. Dick Swiveller is perhaps the noblest of all the noble creations of Dickens. He has all the overwhelming absurdity of Mantalini, with the addition of being human and credible, for he knows he is absurd.

His high-falutin is not done because he seriously thinks it right and proper, like that of Mr. Snodgrass, nor is it done because he thinks it will serve his turn, like that of Mr. Pecksniff, for both these beliefs are improbable; it is done because he really loves high-falutin, because he has a lonely literary pleasure in exaggerative language. Great draughts of words are to him like great draughts of wine—pungent and yet refreshing, light and yet leaving him in a glow. In unerring instinct for the perfect folly of a phrase he has no equal, even among the giants of Dickens. "I am sure," says Miss Wackles, when she had been flirting with Cheggs, the market-gardener, and reduced Mr. Swiveller to Byronic renunciation, "I am sure I'm very sorry if—" "Sorry," said Mr. Swiveller, "sorry in the possession of a Cheggs!" The abyss of bitterness is unfathomable. Scarcely less precious is the pose of Mr. Swiveller when he imitates the stage brigand. After crying, "Some wine here! Ho!" he hands the flagon to himself with profound humility, and receives it haughtily. Perhaps the very best scene in the book is that between Mr. Swiveller and the single gentleman with whom he endeavours to remonstrate for having remained in bed all day: "We cannot have single gentlemen coming into the place and sleeping like double gentlemen without paying extra. . . . An equal amount of slumber was never got out of one bed, and if you want to sleep like that you must pay for a double-bedded room." His relations with the Marchioness are at once purely romantic and purely genuine; there is nothing even of Dickens's legitimate exaggerations about them. A shabby, larky, good-natured clerk would, as a matter of fact, spend hours in the society of a little servant girl if he found her about the house. It would arise partly from a dim kindliness, and partly from that mysterious instinct which is sometimes called, mistakenly, a love of low company—that mysterious instinct which makes so many men of pleasure find something soothing in the society of uneducated people, particularly uneducated women. It is the instinct which accounts for the otherwise unaccountable popularity of barmaids.

And still the pot of that huge popularity boiled. In 1841 another novel was demanded, and " Barnaby Rudge " supplied. It is chiefly of interest as an embodiment of that other element in Dickens, the picturesque or even the pictorial. Barnaby Rudge, the idiot with his rags and his feathers and his raven, the bestial hangman, the blind mob—all make a picture, though they hardly make a novel. One touch there is in it of the richer and more humorous Dickens, the boy-conspirator, Mr. Sim Tappertit. But he might have been treated with more sympathy—with as much sympathy, for instance, as Mr. Dick Swiveller; for he is only the romantic guttersnipe, the bright boy at the particular age when it is most fascinating to found a secret society and most difficult to keep a secret. And if ever there was a romantic guttersnipe on earth it was Charles Dickens. "Barnaby Rudge" is no more an historical novel than Sim's secret league was a political movement; but they are both beautiful creations. When all is said, however, the main reason for mentioning the work here is that it is the next bubble in the pot, the next thing that burst out of that whirling, seething head. The tide of it rose and smoked and sang till it boiled over the pot of Britain and poured over all America. In the January of 1842 he set out for the United States.

CHAPTER VI

DICKENS AND AMERICA

THE essential of Dickens's character was the conjunction of common sense with uncommon sensibility. The two things are not, indeed, in such an antithesis as is commonly imagined. Great English literary authorities, such as Jane Austen and Mr. Chamberlain, have put the word " sense " and the word " sensibility " in a kind of opposition to each other. But not only are they not opposite words: they are actually the same word. They both mean receptiveness or approachability by the facts outside us. To have a sense of colour is the same as to have a sensibility to colour. A person who realizes that beef-steaks are appetizing shows his sensibility. A person who realizes that moonrise is romantic shows his sense. But it is not difficult to see the meaning and need of the popular distinction between sensibility and sense, particularly in the form called common sense. Common sense is a sensibility duly distributed in all normal directions; sensibility has come to mean a specialized sensibility in one. This is unfortunate, for it is not the sensibility that is bad, but the specializing; that is, the lack of sensibility to everything else. A young lady who stays out all night to look at the stars should not be blamed for her sensibility to starlight, but for her insensibility to other people. A poet who recites his own verses from ten to five with the tears rolling down his face should decidedly be rebuked for his lack of sensibility—his lack of sensibility to those grand rhythms of the social harmony, crudely called manners. For all politeness is a long poem, since it is full of recurrences. This balance of all the sensibilities we call sense; and it is in this capacity that it becomes of great importance as an attribute of the character of Dickens.

Dickens, I repeat, had common sense and uncommon sensibility. That is to say, the proportion of interests in him was about the same as that of an ordinary man, but he felt all of them more excitedly. This is a distinction not easy for us to keep in mind, because we hear to-day chiefly of two types, the dull man who likes ordinary things mildly, and the extraordinary man who likes extraordinary things wildly. But Dickens liked quite ordinary things; he merely made an extraordinary fuss about them. His excitement was sometimes like an epileptic fit; but it must not be confused with the fury of the man of one idea or one line of ideas. He had the excess of the eccentric, but not the defects, the narrowness. Even when he raved like a maniac he did not rave like a monomaniac. He had no particular spot of sensibility or spot of insensibility: he was merely a normal man minus a normal self-command. He had no special point of mental pain or repugnance, like Ruskin's horror of steam and iron, or Mr. Bernard Shaw's permanent irritation against romantic love. He was annoyed at the ordinary annoyances: only he was more annoyed than was necessary. He did not desire strange delights, blue wine or black women with Baudelaire, or cruel sights east of Suez with Mr. Kipling. He wanted what a healthy man wants, only he was ill with wanting it. To understand him, in a word, we must keep well in mind the medical distinction between delicacy and disease. Perhaps we shall comprehend it and him more clearly if we think of a woman rather than a man. There was much that was feminine about Dickens, and nothing more so than this abnormal normality. A woman is often, in comparison with a man, at once more sensitive and more sane.

This distinction must be especially remembered in all his quarrels. And it must be most especially remembered in what may be called his great quarrel with America, which we have now to approach. The whole matter is so typical of Dickens's attitude to everything and anything, and especially of Dickens's attitude to anything political, that I may ask permission to approach the matter by another, a somewhat long and curving avenue.

Common sense is a fairy thread, thin and faint, and as easily lost as gossamer. Dickens (in large matters) never lost it. Take, as an example, his political tone or drift throughout his life. His views, of course, may have been right or wrong; the reforms he supported may have been successful or otherwise: that is not a matter for this book. But if we compare him with the other men that wanted the same things (or the other men that wanted the other things) we feel a startling absence of cant, a startling sense of humanity as it is, and of the eternal weakness. He was a fierce democrat, but in his best vein he laughed at the cocksure Radical of common life, the red-faced man who said, "Prove it!" when anybody said anything. He fought for the right to elect; but he would not whitewash elections. He believed in parliamentary government; but he did not, like our contemporary newspapers, pretend that parliament is something much more heroic and imposing than it is. He fought for the rights of the grossly oppressed Nonconformists; but he spat out of his mouth the unction of that too easy seriousness with which they oiled everything, and held up to them like a horrible mirror the foul fat face of Chadband. He saw that Mr. Podsnap thought too little of places outside England. But he saw that Mrs. Jellaby thought too much of them. In the last book he wrote he gives us, in Mr. Honeythunder, a hateful and wholesome picture of all the Liberal catchwords pouring out of one illiberal man. But perhaps the best evidence of this steadiness and sanity is the fact that, dogmatic as he was, he never tied himself to any passing dogma: he never got into any *cul de sac* of civic or economic fanaticism: he went down the broad road of the Revolution. He never admitted that economically, we must make hells of workhouses, any more than Rousseau would have admitted it. He never said the State had no right to teach children or save their bones, any more than Danton would have said it. He was a fierce Radical; but he was never a Manchester Radical. He used the test of Utility, but he was never a Utilitarian. While economists were writing soft words he wrote "Hard Times," which Macaulay called "sullen Socialism," because it was not complacent

Whiggism. But Dickens was never a Socialist any more than he was an Individualist; and, whatever else he was, he certainly was not sullen. He was not even a politician of any kind. He was simply a man of very clear, airy judgment on things that did not inflame his private temper, and he perceived that any theory that tried to run the living State entirely on one force and motive was probably nonsense. Whenever the Liberal philosophy had embedded in it something hard and heavy and lifeless, by an instinct he dropped it out. He was too romantic, perhaps, but he would have to do only with real things. He may have cared too much about Liberty. But he cared nothing about " Laissez faire."

Now, among many interests of his contact with America this interest emerges as infinitely the largest and most striking, that it gave a final example of this queer, unexpected coolness and candour of his, this abrupt and sensational rationality. Apart altogether from any question of the accuracy of his picture of America, the American indignation was particularly natural and inevitable. For the large circumstances of the age must be taken into account. At the end of the previous epoch the whole of our Christian civilization had been startled from its sleep by trumpets to take sides in a bewildering Armageddon, often with eyes still misty. Germany and Austria found themselves on the side of the old order, France and America on the side of the new. England, as at the Reformation, took up eventually a dark middle position, maddeningly difficult to define. She created a democracy, but she kept an aristocracy: she reformed the House of Commons, but left the magistracy (as it is still) a mere league of gentlemen against the world. But underneath all this doubt and compromise there was in England a great and perhaps growing mass of dogmatic democracy; certainly thousands, probably millions expected a Republic in fifty years. And for these the first instinct was obvious. The first instinct was to look across the Atlantic to where lay a part of ourselves already Republican, the van of the advancing English on the road to liberty. Nearly all the great Liberals of the nineteenth century enormously idealized America. On the other hand to the Americans, fresh from their first epic of arms, the defeated mother country, with its coronets and county magistrates, was only a broken feudal keep.

So much is self-evident. But nearly halfway through the nineteenth century there came out of England the voice of a violent satirist. In its political quality it seemed like the half-choked cry of the frustrated republic. It had no patience with the pretence that England was already free, that we had gained all that was valuable from the Revolution. It poured a cataract of contempt on the so-called working compromises of England, on the oligarchic cabinets, on the two artificial parties, on the government offices, on the J.P.'s, on the vestries, on the voluntary charities. This satirist was Dickens, and it must be remembered that he was not only fierce, but uproariously readable. He really damaged the things he struck at, a very rare thing. He stepped up to the grave official of the vestry, really trusted by the rulers, really feared like a god by the poor, and he tied round his neck a name that choked him; never again now can he be anything but Bumble. He confronted the fine old English gentleman who gives his patriotic services for nothing as a local magistrate, and he nailed him up as Nupkins, an owl in open day. For to this satire there is literally no answer; it cannot be denied that a man like Nupkins can be and is a magistrate, so long as we adopt the amazing method of letting the rich man of a district actually be the judge in it. We can only avoid the vision of the fact by shutting our eyes, and imagining the nicest rich man we can think of; and that, of course, is what we do. But Dickens, in this matter, was merely realistic; he merely asked us to look on Nupkins, on the wild, strange thing that we had made. Thus Dickens seemed to see England not at all as the country where freedom slowly broadened down from precedent to precedent, but as a rubbish heap of seventeenth century bad habits abandoned by everybody else. That is, he looked at England almost with the eyes of an American democrat.

And so, when the voice, swelling in volume, reached America and the Americans, the Americans said, " Here is a man who will hurry the old country along, and tip her kings and beadles into the sea. Let him come here, and we will show him a race of free men such as he dreams of, alive upon the ancient earth. Let him come here and tell the English of the divine democracy towards which he drives them. There he has a monarchy and an oligarchy to make game of. Here is a republic for him to praise." It seemed, indeed, a very natural sequel, that having denounced undemocratic England as the wilderness, he should announce democratic America as the promised land. Any ordinary person would have prophesied that as he had pushed his rage at the old order almost to the edge of rant, he would push his encomium of the new order almost to the edge of cant. Amid a roar of republican idealism, compliments, hope, and anticipatory gratitude, the great democrat entered the great democracy. He looked about him; he saw a complete America, unquestionably progressive, unquestionably self-governing. Then, with a more than American coolness, and a more than American impudence, he sat down and wrote "Martin Chuzzlewit." That tricky and perverse sanity of his had mutinied again. Common sense is a wild thing, savage, and beyond rules; and it had turned on them and rent them.

The main course of action was as follows; and it is right to record it before we speak of the justice of it. When I speak of his sitting down and writing "Martin Chuzzlewit," I use, of course, an elliptical expression. He wrote the notes of the American part of "Martin Chuzzlewit" while he was still in America; but it was a later decision presumably that such impressions should go into a book, and it was little better than an afterthought that they should go into "Martin Chuzzlewit." Dickens had an uncommonly bad habit (artistically speaking) of altering a story in the middle as he did in the case of "Our Mutual Friend." And it is on record that he only sent young Martin to America because he did not know what else to do with him, and because (to say truth) the sales were falling off. But the first action, which Americans regarded as an equally hostile one, was the publication of "American Notes," the history of which should first be given. His notion of visiting America had come to him as a very vague notion, even before the appearance of "The Old Curiosity Shop." But it had grown in him through the whole ensuing period in the plaguing and persistent way that ideas did grow in him and live with him. He contended against the idea in a certain manner. He had much to induce him to contend against it. Dickens was by this time not only a husband, but a father, the father of several children, and their existence made a difficulty in itself. His wife, he said, cried whenever the project was mentioned. But it was a point in him that he could never, with any satisfaction, part with a project. He had that restless optimism, that kind of nervous optimism, which would always tend to say "Yes"; which is stricken with an immortal repentance, if ever it says "No." The idea of seeing America might be doubtful, but the idea of not seeing America was dreadful. "To miss this opportunity would be a sad thing," he says. ". . . God willing, I think it *must* be managed somehow!" It was managed somehow.

First of all he wanted to take his children as well as his wife. Final obstacles to this fell upon him, but they did not frustrate him. A serious illness fell on him; but that did not frustrate him. He sailed for America in 1842.

He landed in America, and he liked it. As John Forster very truly says, it is due to him, as well as to the great country that welcomed him, that his first good impression should be recorded, and that it should be "considered independently of any modification it afterwards underwent." But the modification it afterwards underwent was, as I have said above, simply a sudden kicking against cant, that is, against repetition. He was quite ready to believe that all Americans were free men. He would have believed it if they had not all told him so. He was quite prepared to be pleased with America. He would have been pleased with it if it had not been so much pleased with itself. The "modification" his view underwent did not arise from any "modification" of America as he first saw it. His admiration did not change because America changed. It changed because America did not change. The Yankees enraged him at last, not by saying different things, but by saying the same things. They were a republic; they were a new and vigorous nation; it seemed natural that they should say so to a famous foreigner first stepping on to their shore. But it seemed maddening that they should say so to each other in every car and drinking saloon from morning till night. It was not that the Americans in any way ceased from praising him. It was rather that they went on praising him. It was not merely that their praises of him sounded beautiful when he first heard them. Their praises of themselves sounded beautiful when he first heard them. That democracy was grand, and that Charles Dickens was a remarkable person, were two truths that he certainly never doubted to his dying day. But, as I say, it was a soulless repetition that stung his sense of humour out of sleep; it woke like a wild beast for hunting, the lion of his laughter. He had heard the truth once too often. He had heard the truth for the nine hundred and ninety-ninth time, and he suddenly saw that it was falsehood.

It is true that a particular circumstance sharpened and defined his disappointment. He felt very hotly, as he felt everything, whether selfish or unselfish, the injustice of the American piracies of English literature, resulting from the American copyright laws. He did not go to America with any idea of discussing this; when, some time afterwards, somebody said that he did, he violently rejected the view as only describable "in one of the shortest words in the English language." But his entry into America was almost triumphal; the rostrum or pulpit was ready for him; he felt strong enough to say anything. He had been most warmly entertained by many American men of letters, especially by Washington Irving, and in his consequent glow of confidence he stepped up to the dangerous question of American copyright. He made many speeches attacking the American law and theory of the matter as unjust to English writers and to American readers. The effect appears to have astounded him. "I believe there is no country," he writes, "on the face of the earth where there is less freedom of opinion on any subject in reference to which there is a broad difference of opinion than in this. There! I write the words with reluctance, disappointment, and sorrow; but I believe it from the bottom of my soul. . . . The notion that I, a man alone by myself in America, should venture to suggest to the Americans that there was one point on which they were neither just to their own countrymen nor to us, actually struck the boldest dumb! Washington Irving, Prescott, Hoffman, Bryant, Halleck, Dana, Washington Allston—every man who writes in this country is devoted to the question, and not one of them *dares* to raise his voice and complain of the atrocious state of the law. . . . The wonder is that a breathing man can be found with temerity enough to suggest to the Americans the possibility of their having done wrong. I wish you could have seen the faces that I saw down both sides of the table at Hartford when I began to talk about Scott. I wish you could have heard how I gave it out. My blood so boiled when I thought of the monstrous injustice that I felt as if I were twelve feet high when I thrust it down their throats."

That is almost a portrait of Dickens. We can almost see the erect little figure, its face and hair like a flame.

For such reasons, among others, Dickens was angry with America. But if America was angry with Dickens, there were also reasons for it. I do not think that the rage against his copyright speeches was, as he supposed, merely national insolence and self-satisfaction. America is a mystery to any good Englishman; but I think Dickens managed somehow to touch it on a queer nerve. There is one thing, at any rate, that must strike all Englishmen who have the good fortune to have American friends; that is, that while there is no materialism so crude or so material as American materialism, there is also no idealism so crude or so ideal as American idealism. America will always affect an Englishman as being soft in the wrong place and hard in the wrong place; coarse exactly where all civilized men are delicate, delicate exactly where all grown-up men are coarse. Some beautiful ideal runs through this people, but it runs aslant. The only existing picture in which the thing I mean has been embodied is in Stevenson's "Wrecker," in the blundering delicacy of Jim Pinkerton. America has a new delicacy, a coarse, rank refinement. But there is another way of embodying the idea, and that is to say this—that nothing is more likely than that the Americans thought it very shocking in Dickens, the divine author, to talk about being done out of money. Nothing would be more American than to expect a genius to be too high-toned for trade. It is certain that they deplored his selfishness in the matter, it is probable that they deplored his indelicacy. A beautiful young dreamer, with flowing brown hair, ought not to be even conscious of his copyrights. For it is quite unjust to say that the Americans worship the dollar. They really do worship intellect—another of the passing superstitions of our time.

If America had then this Pinkertonian propriety, this new, raw sensibility, Dickens was the man to rasp it. He was its precise opposite in every way. The decencies he did respect were old-fashioned and fundamental. On top of these he had that lounging liberty and comfort which can only be had on the basis of very old conventions, like the carelessness of gentlemen and the deliberation of rustics. He had no fancy for being strung up to that taut and quivering ideality demanded by American patriots and public speakers. And there was something else also, connected especially with the question of copyright and his own pecuniary claims. Dickens was not in the least desirous of being thought too "high-souled" to want his wages, nor was he in the least ashamed of asking for them. Deep in him (whether the modern reader likes the quality or no) was a sense very strong in the old Radicals—very strong especially in the old English Radicals—a sense of personal *rights,* one's own rights included, as something not merely useful but sacred. He did not think a claim any less just and solemn because it happened to be selfish; he did not divide claims into selfish and unselfish, but into right and wrong. It is significant that when he asked for his money, he never asked for it with that shamefaced cynicism, that sort of embarrassed brutality, with which the modern man of the world mutters something about business being business or looking after number one. He asked for his money in a valiant and ringing voice, like a man asking for his honour. While his American critics were moaning and sneering at his interested motives as a disqualification, he brandished his interested motives like a banner. "It is nothing to them," he cries in astonishment, "that, of all men living, I am the greatest loser by it" (the Copyright Law). "It is nothing that I have a claim to speak and be heard." The thing they set up as a barrier he actually presents as a passport. They think that he, of all men, ought not to speak because he is interested. He thinks that he, of all men, ought to speak because he is wronged.

But this particular disappointment with America in the matter of the tyranny of its public opinion was not merely the expression of the fact that Dickens was a typical Englishman; that is, a man with a very sharp insistence upon individual freedom. It also worked back ultimately to that larger and vaguer disgust of which I have spoken—the disgust at the perpetual posturing of the people before a mirror. The tyranny was irritating, not so much because of the suffering it inflicted on the minority, but because of the awful glimpses that it gave of the huge and imbecile happiness of the majority. The very vastness of the vain race enraged him, its immensity, its unity, its peace. He was annoyed more with its contentment than with any of its discontents. The thought of that unthinkable mass of millions, every one of them saying that Washington was the greatest man on earth, and that the Queen lived in the Tower of London, rode his riotous fancy like a nightmare. But to the end he retained the outlines of his original republican ideal and lamented over America not as being too Liberal, but as not being Liberal enough. Among others, he used these somewhat remarkable words: "I tremble for a Radical coming here, unless he is a Radical on principle, by reason and reflection, and from the sense of right. I fear that if he were anything else he would return home a Tory. . . . I say no more on that head for two months from this time, save that I do fear that the heaviest blow ever dealt at liberty will be dealt by this country, in the failure of its example on the earth."

We are still waiting to see if that prediction has been fulfilled; but nobody can say that it has been falsified.

He went west on the great canals; he went south

and touched the region of slavery; he saw America superficially indeed, but as a whole. And the great mass of his experience was certainly pleasant, though he vibrated with anticipatory passion against slave-holders, though he swore he would accept no public tribute in the slave country (a resolve which he broke under the pressure of the politeness of the south), yet his actual collisions with slavery and its upholders were few and brief. In these he bore himself with his accustomed vivacity and fire, but it would be a great mistake to convey the impression that his mental reaction against America was chiefly, or even largely, due to his horror at the negro problem. Over and above the cant of which we have spoken, the weary rush of words, the chief complaint he made was a complaint against bad manners; and on a large view his anti-Americanism would seem to be more founded on spitting than on slavery. When, however, it did happen that the primary morality of man-owning came up for discussion, Dickens displayed an honourable impatience. One man, full of anti-abolitionist ardour, buttonholed him and bombarded him with the well-known argument in defence of slavery, that it was not to the financial interest of a slave-owner to damage or weaken his own slaves. Dickens, in telling the story of this interview, writes as follows: " I told him quietly that it was not a man's interest to get drunk, or to steal, or to game, or to indulge in any other vice; but he *did* indulge in it for all that. That cruelty and the abuse of irresponsible power were two of the bad passions of human nature, with the gratification of which considerations of interest or of ruin had nothing whatever to do. . . ." It is hardly possible to doubt that Dickens, in telling the man this, told him something sane and logical and unanswerable. But it is perhaps permissible to doubt whether he told it to him quietly.

He returned home in the spring of 1842, and in the later part of the year his " American Notes " appeared, and the cry against him that had begun over copyright swelled into a roar in his rear. Yet when we read the " Notes " we can find little offence in them, and, to say truth, less interest than usual. They are no true picture of America, or even of his vision of America, and this for two reasons. First, that he deliberately excluded from them all mention of that copyright question which had really given him his glimpse of how tyrannical a democracy can be. Second, that here he chiefly criticizes America for faults which are not, after all, especially American. For example, he is indignant with the inadequate character of the prisons, and compares them unfavourably with those in England, controlled by Lieutenant Tracey, and by Chesterton at Coldbath Fields, two reformers of prison discipline for whom he had a high regard. But it was a mere accident that American gaols were inferior to English. There was and is nothing in the American spirit to prevent their effecting all the reforms of Tracey and Chesterton, nothing to prevent their doing anything that money and energy and organization can do. America might have (for all I know, does have) a prison system cleaner and more humane and more efficient than any other in the world. And the evil genius of America might still remain—everything might remain that makes Pogram or Chollop irritating or absurd. And against the evil genius of America Dickens was now to strike a second and a very different blow.

In January, 1843, appeared the first number of the novel called "Martin Chuzzlewit." The earlier part of the book and the end, which have no connection with America or the American problem, in any case require a passing word. But except for the two gigantic grotesques on each side of the gateway of the tale, Pecksniff and Mrs. Gamp, "Martin Chuzzlewit" will be chiefly admired for its American excursion. It is a good satire embedded in an indifferent novel. Mrs. Gamp is, indeed, a sumptuous study, laid on in those rich, oily, almost greasy colours that go to make the English comic characters, that make the very diction of Falstaff fat, and quaking with jolly degradation. Pecksniff also is almost perfect, and much too good to be true. The only other thing to be noticed about him is that here, as almost everywhere else in the novels, the best figures are at their best when they have least to do. Dickens's characters are perfect as long as he can keep them out of his stories. Bumble is divine until a dark and practical secret is entrusted to him—as if anybody but a lunatic would entrust a secret to Bumble. Micawber is noble when he is doing nothing; but he is quite unconvincing when he is spying on Uriah Heep, for obviously neither Micawber nor any one else would employ Micawber as a private detective. Similarly, while Pecksniff is the best thing in the story, the story is the worst thing in Pecksniff. His plot against old Martin can only be described by saying that it is as silly as old Martin's plot against him. His fall at the end is one of the rare falls of Dickens. Surely it was not necessary to take Pecksniff so seriously. Pecksniff is a merely laughable character; he is so laughable that he is lovable. Why take such trouble to unmask a man whose mask you have made transparent? Why collect all the characters to witness the exposure of a man in whom none of the characters believe? Why toil and triumph to have the laugh of a man who was only made to be laughed at?

But it is the American part of "Martin Chuzzlewit" which is our concern, and which is memorable. It has the air of a great satire; but if it is only a great slander, it is still great. His serious book on America was merely a squib, perhaps a damp squib. In any case, we all know that America will survive such serious books. But his fantastic book may survive America. It may survive America as "The Knights" has survived Athens. "Martin Chuzzlewit" has this quality of great satire that the critic forgets to ask whether the portrait is true to the original, because the portrait is so much more important than the original. Who cares whether Aristophanes correctly describes Kleon, who is dead, when he so perfectly describes the demagogue, who cannot die? Just as little, it may be, will some future age care whether the ancient civilization of the west, the lost cities of New York and St. Louis, were fairly depicted in the colossal monument of Elijah Pogram. For there is much more in the American episodes than their intoxicating absurdity; there is more than humour in the young man who made the speech about the British Lion, and said, " I taunt that lion. Alone I dare him; " or in the other man who told Martin that when he said that Queen Victoria did not live in the Tower of London he " fell into an error not uncommon among his countrymen." He has his finger on the nerve of an evil which was not only in his enemies, but in himself. The great democrat has hold of one of the dangers of democracy. The great optimist confronts a horrible nightmare of optimism. Above all, the genuine Englishman attacks a sin that is not merely American, but English also. The eternal, complacent iteration of patriotic half-truths; the perpetual buttering of one's self all over with the same stale butter; above all, the big defiances of small enemies, or the very urgent challenges to very distant enemies; the cowardice so habitual and unconscious that it wears the plumes of courage—all this is an English temptation as well as an American one. " Martin Chuzzlewit " may be a caricature of America. America may be a caricature of England. But in the gravest college, in the quietest country house of England, there is the seed of the same essential madness that fills Dickens's book, like an asylum, with brawling

Chollops and raving Jefferson Bricks. That essential madness is the idea that the good patriot is the man who feels at ease about his country. This notion of patriotism was unknown in the little pagan republics where our European patriotism began. It was unknown in the Middle Ages. In the eighteenth century, in the making of modern politics, a "patriot" meant a discontented man. It was opposed to the word "courtier," which meant an upholder of the *status quo*. In all other modern countries, especially in countries like France and Ireland, where real difficulties have been faced, the word "patriot" means something like a political pessimist. This view and these countries have exaggerations and dangers of their own; but the exaggeration and danger of England is the same as the exaggeration and danger of *The Watertoast Gazette*. The thing which is rather foolishly called the Anglo-Saxon civilization is at present soaked through with a weak pride. It uses great masses of men not to procure discussion but to procure the pleasure of unanimity; it uses masses like bolsters. It uses its organs of public opinion not to warn the public, but to soothe it. It really succeeds not only in ignoring the rest of the world, but actually in forgetting it. And when a civilization really forgets the rest of the world—lets it fall as something obviously dim and barbaric—then there is only one adjective for the ultimate fate of that civilization, and that adjective is " Chinese."

Martin Chuzzlewit's America is a mad-house: but it is a mad-house we are all on the road to. For completeness and even comfort are almost the definitions of insanity. The lunatic is the man who lives in a small world but thinks it is a large one: he is the man who lives in a tenth of the truth, and thinks it is the whole. The madman cannot conceive any cosmos outside a certain tale or conspiracy or vision. Hence the more clearly we see the world divided into Saxons and non-Saxons, into our splendid selves and the rest, the more certain we may be that we are slowly and quietly going mad. The more plain and satisfying our state appears, the more we may know that we are living in an unreal world. For the real world is not satisfying. The more clear become the colours and facts of Anglo-Saxon superiority, the more surely we may know we are in a dream. For the real world is not clear or plain. The real world is full of bracing bewilderments and brutal surprises. Comfort is the blessing and the curse of the English, and of Americans of the Pogram type also. With them it is a loud comfort, a wild comfort, a screaming and capering comfort; but comfort at bottom still. For there is but an inch of difference between the cushioned chamber and the padded cell.

CHAPTER VII

DICKENS AND CHRISTMAS

In the July of 1844 Dickens went on an Italian tour, which he afterwards summarized in the book called "Pictures from Italy." They are, of course, very vivacious, but there is no great need to insist on them, considered as Italian sketches; there is no need whatever to worry about them as a phase of the mind of Dickens when he travelled out of England. He never travelled out of England. There is no trace in all these amusing pages that he really felt the great foreign things which lie in wait for us in the south of Europe, the Latin civilization, the Catholic Church, the art of the centre, the endless end of Rome. His travels are not travels in Italy, but travels in Dickensland. He sees amusing things; he describes them amusingly. But he would have seen things just as good in a street in Pimlico, and described them just as well. Few things were racier even in his raciest novel, than his description of the marionette play of the death of Napoleon. Nothing could be more perfect than the figure of the doctor, which had something wrong with its wires, and hence " hovered about the couch and delivered medical opinions in the air." Nothing could be better as a catching of the spirit of all popular drama than the colossal depravity of the wooden image of " Sir Udson Low." But there is nothing Italian about it. Dickens would have made just as good fun, indeed just the same fun, of a Punch and Judy show performing in Long Acre or Lincoln's Inn Fields.

Dickens uttered just and sincere satire on Plornish and Podsnap; but Dickens was as English as any Podsnap or any Plornish. He had a hearty humanitarianism, and a hearty sense of justice to all nations, so far as he understood it. But that very kind of humanitarianism, that very kind of justice, were English. He was the Englishman of the type that made Free Trade, the most English of all things, since it was at once calculating and optimistic. He respected catacombs and gondolas, but that very respect was English. He wondered at brigands and volcanoes, but that very wonder was English. The very conception that Italy consists of these things was an English conception. The root things he never understood, the Roman legend, the ancient life of the Mediterranean, the world-old civilization of the vine and olive, the mystery of the immutable Church. He never understood these things, and I am glad he never understood them: he could only have understood them by ceasing to be the inspired cockney that he was, the rousing English Radical of the great Radical age in England. That spirit of his was one of the things that we have had which were truly national. All other forces we have borrowed, especially those which flatter us most. Imperialism is foreign, socialism is foreign, militarism is foreign, education is foreign, strictly even Liberalism is foreign. But Radicalism was our own; as English as the hedge-rows.

Dickens abroad, then, was for all serious purposes simply the Englishman abroad; the Englishman abroad is for all serious purposes, simply the Englishman at home. Of this generalization one modification must be made. Dickens did feel a direct pleasure in the bright and busy exterior of the French life, the clean caps, the coloured uniforms, the skies like blue enamel, the little green trees, the little white houses, the scene picked out in primary colours, like a child's picture-book. This he felt, and this he put (by a stroke of genius) into the mouth of Mrs. Lirriper, a London landlady on a holiday: for Dickens always knew that it is the simple and not the subtle who feel differences; and he saw all his colours through the clear eyes of the poor. And in thus taking to his heart the streets as it were, rather than the spires of the Continent, he showed beyond question that combination of which we have spoken—of common sense with uncommon sensibility. For it is for the sake of the streets and shops and the coats and hats, that we should go abroad; they are far better worth going to see than the castles and cathedrals and Roman camps. For the wonders of the world are the same all over the world, at least all over the European world. Castles that throw valleys in shadow, minsters that strike the sky, roads so old that they seem to have been made by the gods, these are in all Christian countries. The marvels of man are at all our doors. A labourer hoeing turnips in Sussex has no need to be ignorant that the bones of Europe are the Roman roads. A clerk living in Lambeth has no need not to know that there was a Christian art exuberant in the thirteenth century; for only across the river he can see the live stones of the Middle Ages surging together towards the stars. But exactly the things that do strike the traveller as extraordinary are the ordinary things, the food, the clothes, the vehicles; the strange things are cosmopolitan, the common things are national and peculiar. Cologne spire is lifted on the same arches as Canterbury; but the thing you cannot see out of Germany is a German beer-garden. There is no need for a Frenchman to go to look at Westminster Abbey as a piece of English architecture; it is not, in the special sense, a piece of English architecture. But a hansom cab is a piece of English architecture; a thing produced by the peculiar poetry of our cities, a symbol of a certain reckless comfort which is really English; a thing to draw a pilgrimage of the nations. The imaginative Englishman will be found all day in a *café;* the imaginative Frenchman in a hansom cab.

This sort of pleasure Dickens took in the Latin life; but no deeper kind. And the strongest of all possible indications of his fundamental detachment from it can be found in one fact. A great part of the time that he was in Italy he was engaged in writing "The Chimes," and such Christmas tales, tales of Christmas in the English towns, tales full of fog and snow and hail and happiness.

Dickens could find in any street divergences between man and man deeper than the divisions of nations. His fault was to exaggerate differences. He could find types almost as distinct as separate tribes of animals in his own brain and his own city, those two homes of a magnificent chaos. The only two southerners introduced prominently into his novels, the two in "Little Dorrit," are popular English foreigners, I had almost said stage foreigners. Villainy is, in English eyes, a southern trait, therefore one of the foreigners is villainous. Vivacity is, in English eyes, another southern trait, therefore the other foreigner is vivacious. But we can see from the outlines of both that Dickens did not have to go to Italy to get them. While poor panting millionaires, poor tired earls and poor God-forsaken American men of culture are plodding about Italy for literary inspiration, Charles Dickens made up the whole of that Italian romance (as I strongly suspect) from the faces of two London organ-grinders.

In the sunlight of the southern world, he was still dreaming of the firelight of the north. Among the palaces and the white campanile, he shut his eyes to see Marylebone and dreamed a lovely dream of chimney-pots. He was not happy he said, without streets. The very foulness and smoke of London were lovable in his eyes and fill his Christmas tales with a vivid vapour. In the clear skies of the south he saw afar off the fog of London like a sunset cloud and longed to be in the core of it.

This Christmas tone of Dickens, in connection

with his travels is a matter that can only be expressed by a parallel with one of his other works. Much the same that has here been said of his "Pictures from Italy" may be said about his "Child's History of England;" with the difference that while the "Pictures from Italy," do in a sense add to his fame, the "History of England" in almost every sense detracts from it. But the nature of the limitation is the same. What Dickens was travelling in distant lands, that he was travelling in distant ages; a sturdy, sentimental English Radical with a large heart and a narrow mind. He could not help falling into that besetting sin or weakness of the modern progressive, the habit of regarding the contemporary questions as the eternal questions and the latest word as the last. He could not get out of his head the instinctive conception that the real problem before St. Dunstan was whether he should support Lord John Russell or Sir Robert Peel. He could not help seeing the remotest peaks lit up by the raging bonfire of his own passionate political crisis. He lived for the instant and its urgency; that is, he did what St. Dunstan did. He lived in an eternal present like all simple men. It is indeed "A Child's History of England;" but the child is the writer and not the reader.

But Dickens in his cheapest cockney utilitarianism, was not only English, but unconsciously historic. Upon him descended the real tradition of "Merry England," and not upon the pallid mediævalists who thought they were reviving it. The Pre-Raphaelites, the Gothicists, the admirers of the Middle Ages, had in their subtlety and sadness the spirit of the present day. Dickens had in his buffoonery and bravery the spirit of the Middle Ages. He was much more mediæval in his attacks on mediævalism than they were in their defences of it. It was he who had the things of Chaucer, the love of large jokes and long stories and brown ale and all the white roads of England. Like Chaucer he loved story within story, every man telling a tale. Like Chaucer he saw something openly comic in men's motley trades. Sam Weller would have been a great gain to the Canterbury Pilgrimage and told an admirable story. Rossetti's Damozel would have been a great bore, regarded as too fast by the Prioress and too priggish by the Wife of Bath. It is said that in the somewhat sickly Victorian revival of feudalism which was called "Young England," a nobleman hired a hermit to live in his grounds. It is also said that the hermit struck for more beer. Whether this anecdote be true or not, it is always told as showing a collapse from the ideal of the Middle Ages to the level of the present day. But in the mere act of striking for beer the holy man was very much more "mediæval" than the fool who employed him.

It would be hard to find a better example of this than Dickens's great defence of Christmas. In fighting for Christmas he was fighting for the old European festival, Pagan and Christian, for that trinity of eating, drinking and praying which to moderns appears irreverent, for the holy day which is really a holiday. He had himself the most babyish ideas about the past. He supposed the Middle Ages to have consisted of tournaments and torture-chambers, he supposed himself to be a brisk man of the manufacturing age, almost a Utilitarian. But for all that he defended the mediæval feast which was going out against the Utilitarianism which was coming in. He could only see all that was bad in mediævalism. But he fought for all that was good in it. And he was all the more really in sympathy with the old strength and simplicity because he only knew that it was good and did not know that it was old. He cared as little for mediævalism as the mediævals did. He cared as much as they did for lustiness and virile laughter and sad tales of good lovers and pleasant tales of good livers. He would have been very much bored by Ruskin and Walter Pater if they had explained to him the strange sunset tints of Lippi and Botticelli. He had no pleasure in looking on the dying Middle Ages. But he looked on the living Middle Ages, on a piece of the old uproarious superstition still unbroken; and he hailed it like a new religion. The Dickens character ate pudding to an extent at which the modern mediævalists turned pale. They would do every kind of honour to an old observance, except observing it. They would pay to a Church feast every sort of compliment except feasting.

And (as I have said) as were his unconscious relations to our European past, so were his unconscious relations to England. He imagined himself to be, if anything, a sort of cosmopolitan; at any rate to be a champion of the charms and merits of continental lands against the arrogance of our island. But he was in truth very much more a champion of the old and genuine England against that comparatively cosmopolitan England which we have all lived to see. And here again the supreme example is Christmas. Christmas is, as I have said, one of numberless old European feasts of which the essence is the combination of religion with merry-making. But among those feasts it is also especially and distinctively English in the style of its merry-making and even in the style of its religion. For the character of Christmas (as distinct, for instance, from the continental Easter) lies chiefly in two things: first on the terrestrial side the note of comfort rather than the note of brightness; and on the spiritual side, Christian charity rather than Christian ecstasy. And comfort is, like charity, a very English instinct. Nay, comfort is, like charity, an English merit; though our comfort may and does degenerate into materialism, just as our charity may (and does) degenerate into laxity and make-believe.

This ideal of comfort belongs peculiarly to England; it belongs peculiarly to Christmas; above all it belongs pre-eminently to Dickens. And it is astonishingly misunderstood. It is misunderstood by the continent of Europe, it is, if possible, still more misunderstood by the English of to-day. On the Continent the restaurateurs provide us with raw beef, as if we were savages; yet old English cooking takes as much care as French. And in England has arisen a parvenu patriotism which represents the English as everything but English; as a blend of Chinese stoicism, Latin militarism, Prussian rigidity, and American bad taste. And so England, whose fault is gentility and whose virtue is geniality, England with her tradition of the great gay gentlemen of Elizabeth, is represented to the four quarters of the world (as in Mr. Kipling's religious poems) in the enormous image of a solemn cad. And because it is very difficult to be comfortable in the suburbs, the suburbs have voted that comfort is a gross and material thing. Comfort, especially this vision of Christmas comfort, is the reverse of a gross or material thing. It is far more poetical, properly speaking, than the Garden of Epicurus. It is far more artistic than the Palace of Art. It is more artistic because it is based upon a contrast, a contrast between the fire and wine within the house and the winter and the roaring rains without. It is far more poetical, because there is in it a note of defence, almost of war; a note of being besieged by the snow and hail; of making merry in the belly of a fort. The man who said that an Englishman's house is his castle said much more than he meant. The Englishman thinks of his house as something fortified, and provisioned, and his very surliness is at root romantic. And this sense would naturally be strongest in wild winter nights, when the lowered portcullis and the lifted drawbridge do not merely bar people out, but bar people in. The Englishman's house is most sacred, not merely when the King cannot enter it, but when the Englishman cannot get out of it.

This comfort, then, is an abstract thing, a principle. The English poor shut all their doors and windows till their rooms reek like the Black Hole. They are suffering for an idea. Mere animal hedonism would not dream, as we English do, of winter feasts and little rooms, but of eating fruit in large and idle gardens. Mere sensuality would desire to please all its senses. But to our good dreams this dark and dangerous background is essential; the highest pleasure we can imagine is a defiant pleasure, a happiness that stands at bay. The word "comfort" is not indeed the right word, it conveys too much of the slander of mere sense; the true word is "cosiness," a word not translatable. One, at least, of the essentials of it is smallness, smallness in preference to largeness, smallness for smallness's sake. The merry-maker wants a pleasant parlour, he would not give twopence for a pleasant continent. In our difficult time, of course, a fight for mere space has become necessary. Instead of being greedy for ale and Christmas pudding we are greedy for mere air, an equally sensual appetite. In abnormal conditions this is wise; and the illimitable veldt is an excellent thing for nervous people. But our fathers were large and healthy enough to make a thing humane, and not worry about whether it was hygienic. They were big enough to get into small rooms.

Of this quite deliberate and artistic quality in the close Christmas chamber, the standing evidence is Dickens in Italy. He created these dim firelit tales like little dim red jewels, as an artistic necessity, in the centre of an endless summer. Amid the white cities of Tuscany he hungered for something romantic, and wrote about a rainy Christmas. Amid the pictures of the Uffizi he starved for something beautiful, and fed his memory on London fog. His feeling for the fog was especially poignant and typical. In the first of his Christmas tales, the popular " Christmas Carol," he suggested the very soul of it in one simile, when he spoke of the dense air, suggesting that " Nature was brewing on a large scale." This sense of the thick atmosphere as something to eat or drink, something not only solid but satisfactory, may seem almost insane, but it is no exaggeration of Dickens's emotion. We speak of a fog " that you could cut with a knife." Dickens would have liked the phrase as suggesting that the fog was a colossal cake. He liked even more his own phrase of the Titanic brewery, and no dream would have given him a wilder pleasure than to grope his way to some such tremendous vats and drink the ale of the giants.

There is a current prejudice against fogs, and Dickens, perhaps, is their only poet. Considered hygienically no doubt this may be more or less excusable. But, considered poetically, fog is not undeserving, it has a real significance. We have in our great cities abolished the clean and sane darkness of the country. We have outlawed night and sent her wandering in wild meadows; we have lit eternal watch-fires against her return. We have made a new cosmos, and as a consequence our own sun and stars. And, as a consequence also, and most justly, we have made our own darkness. Just as every lamp is a warm human moon, so every fog is a rich human nightfall. If it were not for this mystic accident we should never see darkness, and he who has never seen darkness has never seen the sun. Fog for us is the chief form of that outward pressure which compresses mere luxury into real comfort. It makes the world small, in the same spirit as in that common and happy cry that the world is small, meaning that it is full of friends. The first man that emerges out of the mist with a light, is for us Prometheus, a saviour bringing fire to men. He is that greatest and best of all men, greater than the heroes, better than the saints, Man Friday. Every rumble of a cart, every cry in the distance, marks the heart of humanity beating undaunted in the darkness. It is wholly human; man toiling in his own cloud. If real darkness is like the embrace of God, this is the dark embrace of man.

In such a sacred cloud the tale called "The Christmas Carol" begins, the first and most typical of all his Christmas tales. It is not irrelevant to dilate upon the geniality of this darkness, because it is characteristic of Dickens that his atmospheres are more important than his stories. The Christmas atmosphere is more important than Scrooge, or the ghosts either; in a sense, the background is more important than the figures. The same thing may be noticed in his dealings with that other atmosphere (besides that of good humour) which he excelled in creating, an atmosphere of mystery and wrong, such as that which gathers round Mrs. Clennam, rigid in her chair, or old Miss Havisham, ironically robed as a bride. Here again the atmosphere altogether eclipses the story, which often seems disappointing in comparison. The secrecy is sensational; the secret is tame. The surface of the thing seems more awful than the core of it. It seems almost as if these grisly figures, Mrs. Chadband and Mrs. Clennam, Miss Havisham and Miss Flite, Nemo and Sally Brass, were keeping something back from the author as well as from the reader. When the book closes we do not know their real secret. They soothed the optimistic Dickens with something less terrible than the truth. The dark house of Arthur Clennam's childhood really depresses us; it is a true glimpse into that quiet street in hell, where live the children of that unique dispensation which theologians call Calvinism and Christians devil-worship. But some stranger crime had really been done there, some more monstrous blasphemy or human sacrifice than the suppression of some silly document advantageous to the silly Dorrits. Something worse than a common tale of jilting lay behind the masquerade and madness of the awful Miss Havisham. Something worse was whispered by the misshapen Quilp to the sinister Sally in that wild, wet summer-house by the river, something worse than the clumsy plot against the clumsy Kit. These dark pictures seem almost as if they were literally visions; things, that is, that Dickens saw but did not understand.

And as with his backgrounds of gloom, so with his backgrounds of good-will, in such tales as "The Christmas Carol." The tone of the tale is kept throughout in a happy monotony, though the tale is everywhere irregular and in some places weak. It has the same kind of artistic unity that belongs to a dream. A dream may begin with the end of the world and end with a tea-party; but either the end of the world will seem as trivial as a tea-party or that tea-party will be as terrible as the day of doom. The incidents change wildly; the story scarcely changes at all. "The Christmas Carol" is a kind of philanthropic dream, an enjoyable nightmare, in which the scenes shift bewilderingly and seem as miscellaneous as the pictures in a scrap-book, but in which there is one constant state of the soul, a state of rowdy benediction and a hunger for human faces. The beginning is about a winter day and a miser; yet the beginning is in no way bleak. The author starts with a kind of happy howl; he bangs on our door like a drunken carol singer; his style is festive and popular; he compares the snow and hail to philanthropists who "come down handsomely"; he compares the fog to unlimited beer. Scrooge is not really inhuman at the beginning any more than he is at the end. There is a heartiness in his inhospitable sentiments that is akin to humour and therefore to humanity; he is only a crusty old bachelor, and had (I strongly suspect) given away turkeys secretly all his life. The beauty and the real blessing of the story do not lie in the mechanical plot of it, the repentance of Scrooge, probable or improbable; they lie in the great furnace of real happiness that glows through Scrooge and everything round him; that great furnace, the heart of Dickens. Whether the Christmas visions would or would not convert Scrooge, they convert us. Whether or no the visions were evoked by real Spirits of the Past, Present, and Future, they were evoked by that truly exalted order of angels who are correctly called High Spirits. They are impelled and sustained by a quality which our contemporary artists ignore or almost deny, but which in a life decently lived is as normal and attainable as sleep, positive, passionate, conscious joy. The story sings from end to end like a happy man going home; and, like a happy and good man, when it cannot sing it yells. It is lyric and exclamatory, from the first exclamatory words of it. It is strictly a Christmas Carol.

Dickens, as has been said, went to Italy with this kindly cloud still about him, still meditating on Yule mysteries. Among the olives and the orange-trees he wrote his second great Christmas tale, "The Chimes" (at Genoa in 1844), a Christmas tale only differing from "The Christmas Carol" in being fuller of the grey rains of winter and the north. "The Chimes" is, like the "Carol," an appeal for charity and mirth, but it is a stern and fighting appeal: if the other is a Christmas carol, this is a Christmas war-song. In it Dickens hurled himself with even more than his usual militant joy and scorn into an attack upon a cant, which he said made his blood boil. This cant was nothing more nor less than the whole tone taken by three-quarters of the political and economic world towards the poor. It was a vague and vulgar Benthamism with a rollicking Tory touch in it. It explained to the poor their duties with a cold and coarse philanthropy unendurable by any free man. It had also at its command a kind of brutal banter, a loud good-humour which Dickens sketches savagely in Alderman Cute. He fell furiously on all their ideas: the cheap advice to live cheaply, the base advice to live basely, above all, the preposterous primary assumption that the rich are to advise the poor and not the poor the rich. There were and are hundreds of these benevolent bullies. Some say that the poor should give up having children, which means that they should give up their great virtue of sexual sanity. Some say that they should give up "treating" each other, which means that they should give up all that remains to them of the virtue of hospitality. Against all of this Dickens thundered very thoroughly in "The Chimes." It may be remarked in passing that this affords another instance of a confusion already referred to, the confusion whereby Dickens supposed himself to be exalting the present over the past, whereas he was really dealing deadly blows at things strictly peculiar to the present. Embedded in this very book is a somewhat useless interview between Trotty Veck and the church bells, in which the latter lectures the former for having supposed (why I don't know) that they were expressing regret for the disappearance of the Middle Ages. There is no reason why Trotty Veck or any one else should idealize the Middle Ages, but certainly he was the last man in the world to be asked to idealize the nineteenth century, seeing that the smug and stingy philosophy, which poisons his life through the book, was an exclusive creation of that century. But, as I have said before, the fieriest mediævalist may forgive Dickens for disliking the good things the Middle Ages took away, considering how he loved whatever good things the Middle Ages left behind. It matters very little that he hated old feudal castles when they were already old. It matters very much that he hated the New Poor Law while it was still new.

The moral of this matter in "The Chimes" is essential. Dickens had sympathy with the poor in the Greek and literal sense; he suffered with them mentally; for the things that irritated them were the things that irritated him. He did not pity the people, or even champion the people, or even merely love the people; in this matter he was the people. He alone in our literature is the voice not merely of the social substratum, but even of the subconsciousness of the substratum. He utters the secret anger of the humble. He says what the uneducated only think, or even only feel, about the educated. And in nothing is he so genuinely such a voice as in this fact of his fiercest mood being reserved for methods that are counted scientific and progressive. Pure and exalted atheists talk themselves into believing that the working-classes are turning with indignant scorn from the churches. The working-classes are not indignant against the churches in the least. The things the working-classes really are indignant against are the hospitals. The people has no definite disbelief in the temples of theology. The people has a very fiery and practical disbelief in the temples of physical science. The things the poor hate are the modern things, the rationalistic things—doctors, inspectors, poor law guardians, professional philanthropy. They never showed any reluctance to be helped by the old and corrupt monasteries. They will often die rather than be helped by the modern and efficient workhouse. Of all this anger, good or bad, Dickens is the voice of an accusing energy. When, in "The Christmas Carol," Scrooge refers to the surplus population, the Spirit tells him, very justly, not to speak till he knows what the surplus is and where it is. The implication is severe but sound. When a group of superciliously benevolent economists look down into the abyss for the surplus population, assuredly there is only one answer that should be given to them; and that is to say, "If there is a surplus, you are a surplus." And if any one were ever cut off, they would be. If the barricades went up in our streets and the poor became masters, I think the priests would escape, I fear the gentlemen would; but I believe the gutters would be simply running with the blood of philanthropists.

Lastly, he was at one with the poor in this chief matter of Christmas, in the matter, that is, of special festivity. There is nothing on which the poor are more criticized than on the point of spending large sums on small feasts; and though there are material difficulties, there is nothing in which they are more right. It is said that a Boston paradox-monger said, " Give us the luxuries of life and we will dispense with the necessities." But it is the whole human race that says it, from the first savage wearing feathers instead of clothes to the last costermonger having a treat instead of three meals.

The third of his Christmas stories, "The Cricket on the Hearth," calls for no extensive comment, though it is very characteristic. It has all the qualities which we have called dominant qualities in his Christmas sentiment. It has cosiness, that is the comfort that depends upon a discomfort surrounding it. It has a sympathy with the poor, and especially with the extravagance of the poor; with what may be called the temporary wealth of the poor. It has the sentiment of the hearth, that is, the sentiment of the open fire being the red heart of the room. That open fire is the veritable flame of England, still kept burning in the midst of a mean civilization of stoves. But everything that is valuable in " The Cricket on the Hearth " is perhaps as well expressed in the title as it is in the story. The tale itself, in spite of some of those inimitable things that Dickens never failed to say, is a little too comfortable to be quite convincing. " The Christmas Carol " is the conversion of an anti-Christmas character. " The Chimes " is a slaughter of anti-Christmas characters. "The Cricket," perhaps, fails for lack of this crusading note. For everything has its weak side, and when full justice has been done to this neglected note of poetic comfort, we must remember that it has its very real weak side. The defect of it in the work of Dickens was that he tended sometimes to pile up the cushions until none of the characters could move. He is so much interested in effecting his state of static happiness that he forgets to make a story at all. His princes at the start of the story begin to live happily ever afterwards. We feel this strongly in "Master Humphrey's Clock," and we feel it sometimes in these Christmas stories. He makes his characters so comfortable that his characters begin to dream and drivel. And he makes his reader so comfortable that his reader goes to sleep.

The actual tale of the carrier and his wife sounds somewhat sleepily in our ears; we cannot keep our attention fixed on it, though we are conscious of a kind of warmth from it as from a great wood fire. We know so well that everything will soon be all right that we do not suspect when the carrier suspects, and are not frightened when the gruff Tackleton growls. The sound of the Christmas festivities at the end comes fainter on our ears than did the shout of the Cratchits or the bells of Trotty Veck. All the good figures that followed Scrooge when he came growling out of the fog fade into the fog again.

CHAPTER VIII

THE TIME OF TRANSITION

DICKENS was back in London by the June of 1845. About this time he became the first editor of *The Daily News*, a paper which he had largely planned and suggested, and which, I trust, remembers its semi-divine origin. That his thoughts had been running, as suggested in the last chapter, somewhat monotonously on his Christmas domesticities, is again suggested by the rather singular fact that he originally wished *The Daily News* to be called *The Cricket*. Probably he was haunted again with his old vision of a homely, tale-telling periodical such as had broken off in "Master Humphrey's Clock." About this time, however, he was peculiarly unsettled. Almost as soon as he had taken the editorship he threw it up; and having only recently come back to England, he soon made up his mind to go back to the Continent. In the May of 1846 he ran over to Switzerland and tried to write "Dombey and Son" at Lausanne. Tried to, I say, because his letters are full of an angry impotence. He could not get on. He attributed this especially to his love of London and his loss of it, " the absence of streets and numbers of figures. . . . *My* figures seem disposed to stagnate without crowds about them." But he also, with shrewdness, attributed it more generally to the laxer and more wandering life he had led for the last two years, the American tour, the Italian tour, diversified, generally speaking, only with slight literary productions. His ways were never punctual or healthy, but they were also never unconscientious as far as work was concerned. If he walked all night he could write all day. But in this strange exile or interregnum he did not seem able to fall into any habits, even bad habits. A restlessness beyond all his experience had fallen for a season upon the most restless of the children of men.

It may be a mere coincidence: but this break in his life very nearly coincided with the important break in his art. " Dombey and Son," planned in all probability some time before, was destined to be the last of a quite definite series, the early novels of Dickens. The difference between the books from the beginning up to " Dombey," and the books from " David Copperfield " to the end may be hard to state dogmatically, but is evident to every one with any literary sense. Very coarsely, the case may be put by saying that he diminished, in the story as a whole, the practice of pure caricature. Still more coarsely it may be put in the phrase that he began to practise realism. If we take Mr. Stiggins, say, as a clergyman depicted at the beginning of his literary career, and Mr. Crisparkle, say, as a clergyman depicted at the end of it, it is evident that the difference does not merely consist in the fact that the first is a less desirable clergyman than the second. It consists in the nature of our desire for either of them. The glory of Mr. Crisparkle partly consists in the fact that he might really exist anywhere, in any country town into which we may happen to stray. The glory of Mr. Stiggins wholly consists in the fact that he could not possibly exist anywhere except in the head of Dickens. Dickens has the secret recipe of that divine dish. In some sense, therefore, when we say that he became less of a caricaturist we mean that he became less of a creator. That original violent vision of all things which he had seen from his boyhood began to be mixed with other men's milder visions and with the light of common day. He began to understand and practise other than his own mad merits; began to have some movement towards the merits of other writers, towards the mixed emotion of

Thackeray, or the solidity of George Eliot. And this must be said for the process; that the fierce wine of Dickens could endure some dilution. On the whole, perhaps, his primal personalism was all the better when surging against some saner restraints. Perhaps a flavour of strong Stiggins goes a long way. Perhaps the colossal Crummles might be cut down into six or seven quite credible characters. For my own part, for reasons which I shall afterwards mention, I am in real doubt about the advantage of this realistic education of Dickens. I am not sure that it made his books better; but I am sure it made them less bad. He made fewer mistakes undoubtedly; he succeeded in eliminating much of the mere rant or cant of his first books; he threw away much of the old padding, all the more annoying, perhaps, in a literary sense, because he did not mean it for padding, but for essential eloquence. But he did not produce anything actually better than Mr. Chuckster. But then there is nothing better than Mr. Chuckster. Certain works of art, such as the Venus of Milo, exhaust our aspiration. Upon the whole this may, perhaps, be safely said of the transition. Those who have any doubt about Dickens can have no doubt of the superiority of the later books. Beyond question they have less of what annoys us in Dickens. But do not, if you are in the company of any ardent adorers of Dickens (as I hope for your sake you are) do not insist too urgently and exclusively on the splendour of Dickens's last works, or they will discover that you do not like him.

" Dombey and Son " is the last novel in the first manner: " David Copperfield " is the first novel in the last. The increase in care and realism in the second of the two is almost startling. Yet even in " Dombey and Son " we can see the coming of a change, however faint, if we compare it with his first fantasies, such as " Nicholas Nickleby " or " The Old Curiosity Shop." The central story is still melodrama, but it is much more tactful and effective melodrama. Melodrama is a form of art, legitimate like any other, as noble as farce, almost as noble as pantomime. The essence of melodrama is that it appeals to the moral sense in a highly simplified state, just as farce appeals to the sense of humour in a highly simplified state. Farce creates people who are so intellectually simple as to hide in packing-cases or pretend to be their own aunts. Melodrama creates people so morally simple as to kill their enemies in Oxford Street, and repent on seeing their mother's photograph. The object of the simplification in farce and melodrama is the same, and quite artistically legitimate, the object of gaining a resounding rapidity of action which subtleties would obstruct. And this can be done well or ill. The simplified villain can be a spirited charcoal sketch or a mere black smudge. Carker is a spirited charcoal sketch: Ralph Nickleby is a mere black smudge. The tragedy of Edith Dombey teems with unlikelihood, but it teems with life. That Dombey should give his own wife censure through his own business manager is impossible, I will not say in a gentleman, but in a person of ordinary sane self-conceit. But once having got the inconceivable trio before the footlights, Dickens gives us good ringing dialogue, very different from the mere rants in which Ralph Nickleby figures in the unimaginable character of a rhetorical money-lender. And there is another point of technical improvement in this book over such books as "Nicholas Nickleby." It has not only a basic idea, but a good basic idea. There is a real artistic opportunity in the conception of a solemn and selfish man of affairs, feeling for his male heir his first and last emotion, mingled of a thin flame of tenderness and a strong flame of pride. But with all these possibilities, the serious episode of the Dombeys serves ultimately only to show how unfitted

Dickens was for such things, how fitted he was for something opposite.

The incurable poetic character, the hopelessly non-realistic character of Dickens's essential genius could not have a better example than the story of the Dombeys. For the story itself is probable; it is the treatment that makes it unreal. In attempting to paint the dark pagan devotion of the father (as distinct from the ecstatic and Christian devotion of the mother), Dickens was painting something that was really there. This is no wild theme, like the wanderings of Nell's grandfather, or the marriage of Gride. A man of Dombey's type would love his son as he loves Paul. He would neglect his daughter as he neglects Florence. And yet we feel the utter unreality of it all, while we feel the utter reality of monsters like Stiggins or Mantalini. Dickens could only work in his own way, and that way was the wild way. We may almost say this: that he could only make his characters probable if he was allowed to make them impossible. Give him license to say and do anything, and he could create beings as vivid as our own aunts and uncles. Keep him to likelihood and he could not tell the plainest tale so as to make it seem likely. The story of "Pickwick" is credible, although it is not possible. The story of Florence Dombey is incredible although it is true.

An excellent example can be found in the same story. Major Bagstock is a grotesque, and yet he contains touch after touch of Dickens's quiet and sane observation of things as they are. He was always most accurate when he was most fantastic. Dombey and Florence are perfectly reasonable, but we simply know that they do not exist. The Major is mountainously exaggerated, but we all feel that we have met him at Brighton. Nor is the rationale of the paradox difficult to see; Dickens exaggerated when he had found a real truth to exaggerate. It is a deadly error (an error at the back of much of the false placidity of our politics) to suppose that lies are told with excess and luxuriance, and truths told with modesty and restraint. Some of the most frantic lies on the face of life are told with modesty and restraint; for the simple reason that only modesty and restraint will save them. Many official declarations are just as dignified as Mr. Dombey, because they are just as fictitious. On the other hand, the man who has found a truth dances about like a boy who has found a shilling; he breaks into extravagances, as the Christian churches broke into gargoyles. In one sense truth alone can be exaggerated; nothing else can stand the strain. The outrageous Bagstock is a glowing and glaring exaggeration of a thing we have all seen in life—the worst and most dangerous of all its hypocrisies. For the worst and most dangerous hypocrite is not he who affects unpopular virtue, but he who affects popular vice. The jolly fellow of the saloon bar and the racecourse is the real deceiver of mankind; he has misled more than any false prophet, and his victims cry to him out of hell. The excellence of the Bagstock conception can best be seen if we compare it with the much weaker and more improbable knavery of Pecksniff. It would not be worth a man's while, with any worldly object, to pretend to be a holy and high-minded architect. The world does not admire holy and high-minded architects. The world does admire rough and tough old army men who swear at waiters and wink at women. Major Bagstock is simply the perfect prophecy of that decadent jingoism which corrupted England of late years. England has been duped, not by the cant of goodness, but by the cant of badness. It has been fascinated by a quite fictitious cynicism, and reached that last and strangest of all impostures in which the mask is as repulsive as the face.

"Dombey and Son" provides us with yet another instance of this general fact in Dickens. He could only get to the most solemn emotions adequately if he got to them through the grotesque. He could only, so to speak, really get into the inner chamber by coming down the chimney, like his own most lovable lunatic in "Nicholas Nickleby." A good example is such a character as Toots. Toots is what none of Dickens's dignified characters are, in the most serious sense, a true lover. He is the twin of Romeo. He has passion, humility, self-knowledge, a mind lifted into all magnanimous thoughts, everything that goes with the best kind of romantic love. His excellence in the art of love can only be expressed by the somewhat violent expression that he is as good a lover as Walter Gay is a bad one. Florence surely deserved her father's scorn if she could prefer Gay to Toots. It is neither a joke nor any kind of exaggeration to say that in the vacillations of Toots, Dickens not only came nearer to the psychology of true love than he ever came elsewhere, but nearer than any one else ever came. To ask for the loved one, and then not to dare to cross the threshold, to be invited by her, to long to accept, and then to lie in order to decline, these are the funny things that Mr. Toots did, and that every honest man who yells with laughter at him has done also. For the moment, however, I only mention this matter as a pendent case to the case of Major Bagstock, an example of the way in which Dickens had to be ridiculous in order to begin to be true. His characters that begin solemn end futile; his characters that begin frivolous end solemn in the best sense. His foolish figures are not only more entertaining than his serious figures, they are also much more serious. The Marchioness is not only much more laughable than Little Nell; she is also much more of all that Little Nell was meant to be; much more really devoted, pathetic, and brave. Dick Swiveller is not only a much funnier fellow than Kit, he is also a much more genuine fellow, being free from that slight stain of "meekness," or the snobbishness of the respectable poor, which the wise and perfect Chuckster wisely and perfectly perceived in Kit. Susan Nipper is not only more of a comic character than Florence; she is more of a heroine than Florence any day of the week. In "Our Mutual Friend" we do not, for some reason or other, feel really very much excited about the fall or rescue of Lizzie Hexam. She seems too romantic to be really pathetic. But we do feel excited about the rescue of Miss Lammle, because she is, like Toots, a holy fool; because her pink nose and pink elbows, and candid outcry and open indecent affections do convey to us a sense of innocence helpless among human dragons, of Andromeda tied naked to a rock. Dickens had to make a character humorous before he could make it human; it was the only way he knew, and he ought to have always adhered to it. Whether he knew it or not, the only two really touching figures in " Martin Chuzzlewit " are the Misses Pecksniff. Of the things he tried to treat unsmilingly and grandly we can all make game to our heart's content. But when once he has laughed at a thing it is sacred for ever.

" Dombey," however, means first and foremost the finale of the early Dickens. It is difficult to say exactly in what it is that we perceive that the old crudity ends there, and does not reappear in " David Copperfield " or in any of the novels after it. But so certainly it is. In detached scenes and characters, indeed, Dickens kept up his farcical note almost or quite to the end. But this is the last farce; this is the last work in which a farcical license is tacitly claimed, a farcical note struck to start with. And in a sense his next novel may be called his first novel. But the growth of this great novel, " David Copperfield," is a thing very interesting, but at the same time very dark, for it is a growth in the soul. We have seen that Dickens's mind was in a stir of change; that he was dreaming of art, and even of realism. Hugely delighted as he invariably was with his own books, he was humble enough to be ambitious. He was even humble enough to be envious. In the matter of art, for instance, in the narrower sense, of arrangement and proportion in fictitious things, he began to be conscious of his deficiency, and even, in a stormy sort of way, ashamed of it; he tried to gain completeness even while raging at any one who called him incomplete. And in this matter of artistic construction, his ambition (and his success too) grew steadily up to the instant of his death. The end finds him attempting things that are at the opposite pole to the frank formlessness of "Pickwick." His last book, "The Mystery of Edwin Drood," depends entirely upon construction, even upon a centralized strategy. He staked everything upon a plot; he who had been the weakest of plotters, weaker than Sim Tappertit. He essayed a detective story, he who could never keep a secret; and he has kept it to this day. A new Dickens was really being born when Dickens died.

And as with art, so with reality. He wished to show that he could construct as well as anybody. He also wished to show that he could be as accurate as anybody. And in this connection (as in many others) we must recur constantly to the facts mentioned in connection with America and with his money-matters. We must recur, I mean, to the central fact that his desires were extravagant in quantity, but not in quality; that his wishes were excessive, but not eccentric. It must never be forgotten that sanity was his ideal, even when he seemed almost insane. It was thus with his literary aspirations. He was brilliant; but he wished sincerely to be solid. Nobody out of an asylum could deny that he was a genius and an unique writer; but he did not wish to be an unique writer, but an universal writer. Much of the manufactured pathos or rhetoric against which his enemies quite rightly rail, is really due to his desire to give all sides of life at once, to make his book a cosmos instead of a tale. He was sometimes really vulgar in his wish to be a literary Whiteley, an universal provider. Thus it was that he felt about realism and truth to life. Nothing is easier than to defend Dickens as Dickens, but Dickens wished to be everybody else. Nothing is easier than to defend Dickens's world as a fairyland, of which he alone has the key; to defend him as one defends Maeterlinck, or any other original writer. But Dickens was not content with being original, he had a wild wish to be true. He loved truth so much in the abstract that he sacrificed to the shadow of it his own glory. He denied his own divine originality, and pretended that he had plagiarized from life. He disowned his own soul's children, and said he had picked them up in the street.

And in this mixed and heated mood of anger and ambition, vanity and doubt, a new and great design was born. He loved to be romantic, yet he desired to be real. How if he wrote of a thing that was real and showed that it was romantic? He loved real life; but he also loved his own way. How if he wrote his own real life, but wrote it in his own way? How if he showed the carping critics who doubted the existence of his strange characters, his own yet stranger existence? How if he forced these pedants and unbelievers to admit that Weller and Pecksniff, Crummles and Swiveller, whom they thought so improbably wild and wonderful, were less wild and wonderful than Charles Dickens? What if he ended the quarrels about whether his romances could occur, by confessing that his romance had occurred?

For some time past, probably during the greater part of his life, he had made notes for an autobiography. I have already quoted an admirable passage from these notes, a passage reproduced in "David Copperfield," with little more alteration than a change of proper names—the passage which describes Captain Porter and the debtor's petition in the Marshalsea. But he probably perceived at last what a less keen intelligence must ultimately have perceived, that if an autobiography is really to be honest it must be turned into a work of fiction. If it is really to tell the truth, it must at all costs profess not to. No man dare say of himself, over his own name, how badly he has behaved. No man dare say of himself, over his own name, how well he has behaved. Moreover, of course a touch of fiction is almost always essential to the real conveying of fact, because fact, as experienced, has a fragmentariness which is bewildering at first hand and quite blinding at second hand. Facts have at least to be sorted into compartments and the proper head and tail given to each. The perfection and pointedness of art are a sort of substitute for the pungency of actuality. Without this selection and completion our life seems a tangle of unfinished tales, a heap of novels, all volume one. Dickens determined to make one complete novel of it.

For though there are many other aspects of "David Copperfield," this autobiographical aspect is, after all, the greatest. The point of the book is, that unlike all the other books of Dickens, it is concerned with quite common actualities, but it is concerned with them warmly and with the war-like sympathies. It is not only both realistic and romantic; it is realistic because it is romantic. It is human nature described with the human exaggeration. We all know the actual types in the book; they are not like the turgid and preternatural types elsewhere in Dickens. They are not purely poetic creations like Mr. Kenwiggs or Mr. Bunsby. We all know that they exist. We all know the stiff-necked and humorous old-fashioned nurse, so conventional and yet so original, so dependent and yet so independent. We all know the intrusive stepfather, the abstract strange male, coarse, handsome, sulky, successful; a breaker-up of homes. We all know the erect and sardonic spinster, the spinster who is so mad in small things and so sane in great ones. We all know the cock of the school; we all know Steerforth, the creature whom the gods love and even the servants respect. We know his poor and aristocratic mother, so proud, so gratified, so desolate. We know the Rosa Dartle type, the lonely woman in whom affection itself has stagnated into a sort of poison.

But while these are real characters they are

real characters lit up with the colours of youth and passion. They are real people romantically felt; that is to say, they are real people felt as real people feel them. They are exaggerated, like all Dickens's figures: but they are not exaggerated as personalities are exaggerated by an artist; they are exaggerated as personalities are exaggerated by their own friends and enemies. The strong souls are seen through the glorious haze of the emotions that strong souls really create. We have Murdstone as he would be to a boy who hated him; and rightly, for a boy would hate him. We have Steerforth as he would be to a boy who adored him; and rightly, for a boy would adore him. It may be that if these persons had a mere terrestrial existence, they appeared to other eyes more insignificant. It may be that Murdstone in common life was only a heavy business man with a human side that David was too sulky to find. It may be that Steerforth was only an inch or two taller than David, and only a shade or two above him in the lower middle classes; but this does not make the book less true. In cataloguing the facts of life the author must not omit that massive fact, illusion.

When we say the book is true to life we must stipulate that it is especially true to youth; even to boyhood. All the characters seem a little larger than they really were, for David is looking up at them. And the early pages of the book are in particular astonishingly vivid. Parts of it seem like fragments of our forgotten infancy. The dark house of childhood, the loneliness, the things half understood, the nurse with her inscrutable sulks and her more inscrutable tenderness, the sudden deportations to distant places, the seaside and its childish friendships, all this stirs in us when we read it, like something out of a previous existence. Above all, Dickens has excellently depicted the child enthroned in that humble circle which only in after years he perceives to have been humble. Modern and cultured persons, I believe, object to their children seeing kitchen company or being taught by a woman like Peggoty. But surely it is more important to be educated in a sense of human dignity and equality than in anything else in the world. And a child who has once had to respect a kind and capable woman of the lower classes will respect the lower classes for ever. The true way to overcome the evil in class distinctions is not to denounce them as revolutionists denounce them, but to ignore them as children ignore them.

The early youth of David Copperfield is psychologically almost as good as his childhood. In one touch especially Dickens pierced the very core of the sensibility of boyhood; it was when he made David more afraid of a manservant than of anybody or anything else. The lowering Murdstone, the awful Mrs. Steerforth are not so alarming to him as Mr. Littimer, the unimpeachable gentleman's gentleman. This is exquisitely true to the masculine emotions, especially in their undeveloped state. A youth of common courage does not fear anything violent, but he is in mortal fear of anything correct. This may or may not be the reason that so few female writers understand their male characters, but this fact remains: that the more sincere and passionate and even headlong a lad is the more certain he is to be conventional. The bolder and freer he seems the more the traditions of the college or the rules of the club will hold him with their gyves of gossamer; and the less afraid he is of his enemies the more cravenly he will be afraid of his friends. Herein lies indeed the darkest peril of our ethical doubt and chaos. The fear is that as morals become less urgent, manners will become more so; and men who have forgotten the fear of God will retain the fear of Littimer. We shall merely sink into a much meaner bondage. For when you break the great laws, you do not get liberty; you do not even get anarchy. You get the small laws.

The sting and strength of this piece of fiction, then, do (by a rare accident) lie in the circumstance that it was so largely founded on fact. "David Copperfield" is the great answer of a great romancer to the realists. David says in effect: "What! you say that the Dickens tales are too purple really to have happened! Why, this is what happened to me, and it seemed the most purple of all. You say that the Dickens heroes are too handsome and triumphant! Why, no prince or paladin in Ariosto was ever so handsome and triumphant as the Head Boy seemed to me walking before me in the sun. You say the Dickens villains are too black! Why, there was no ink in the devil's ink-stand black enough for my own stepfather when I had to live in the same house with him. The facts are quite the other way to what you suppose. This life of grey studies and half tones, the absence of which you regret in Dickens, is only life as it is looked at. This life of heroes and villains is life as it is lived. The life a man knows best is exactly the life he finds most full of fierce certainties and battles between good and ill—his own. Oh, yes, the life we do not care about may easily be a psychological comedy. Other people's lives may easily be human documents. But a man's own life is always a melodrama."

There are other effective things in "David Copperfield;" they are not all autobiographical, but they nearly all have this new note of quietude and reality. Micawber is gigantic; an immense assertion of the truth that the way to live is to exaggerate everything. But of him I shall have to speak more fully in another connection. Mrs. Micawber, artistically speaking, is even better. She is very nearly the best thing in Dickens. Nothing could be more absurd, and at the same time more true, than her clear, argumentative manner of speech as she sits smiling and expounding in the midst of ruin. What could be more lucid and logical and unanswerable than her statement of the prolegomena of the Medway problem, of which the first step must be to "see the Medway," or of the coal-trade, which required talent and capital. "Talent Mr. Micawber has. Capital Mr. Micawber has not." It seems as if something should have come at last out of so clear and scientific an arrangement of ideas. Indeed if (as has been suggested) we regard "David Copperfield" as an unconscious defence of the poetic view of life, we might regard Mrs. Micawber as an unconscious satire on the logical view of life. She sits as a monument of the hopelessness and helplessness of reason in the face of this romantic and unreasonable world.

As I have taken " Dombey and Son " as the book before the transition, and " David Copperfield " as typical of the transition itself, I may perhaps take " Bleak House " as the book after the transition. " Bleak House " has every characteristic of his new realistic culture. Dickens never, as in his early books, revels now in the parts he likes and scamps the parts he does not, after the manner of Scott. He does not, as in previous tales, leave his heroes and heroines mere walking gentlemen and ladies with nothing at all to do but walk: he expends upon them at least ingenuity. By the expedients (successful or not) of the self-revelation of Esther or the humorous inconsistencies of Rick, he makes his younger figures if not lovable at least readable. Everywhere we see this tighter and more careful grip. He does not, for instance, when he wishes to denounce a dark institution, sandwich it in as a mere episode in a rambling story of adventure, as the debtor's prison is embedded in the body of Pickwick or the low Yorkshire school in the body of Nicholas Nickleby. He puts the Court of Chancery in the centre of the stage, a sombre and sinister temple, and groups round it in artistic relation decaying and fantastic figures, its offspring and its satirists. An old dipsomaniac keeps a rag and bone shop, type of futility and antiquity, and calls himself the Lord Chancellor. A little mad old maid hangs about the courts on a forgotten or imaginary law-suit, and says with perfect and pungent irony, "I am expecting a judgment shortly, on the Day of Judgment." Rick and Ada and Esther are not mere strollers who have strayed into the court of law, they are its children, its symbols, and its victims. The righteous indignation of the book is not at the red heat of anarchy, but at the white heat of art. Its anger is patient and plodding, like some historic revenge. Moreover, it slowly and carefully creates the real psychology of oppression. The endless formality, the endless unemotional urbanity, the endless hope deferred, these things make one feel the fact of injustice more than the madness of Nero. For it is not the activeness of tyranny that maddens, but its passiveness. We hate the deafness of the god more than his strength. Silence is the unbearable repartee.

Again we can see in this book strong traces of an increase in social experience. Dickens, as his fame carried him into more fashionable circles, began really to understand something of what is strong and what is weak in the English upper class. Sir Leicester Deadlock is a far more effective condemnation of oligarchy than the ugly swagger of Sir Mulberry Hawke, because pride stands out more plainly in all its impotence and insolence as the one weakness of a good man, than as one of the million weaknesses of a bad one. Dickens, like all young Radicals, had imagined in his youth that aristocracy rested upon the hardness of somebody; he found, as we all do, that it rests upon the softness of everybody. It is very hard not to like Sir Leicester Deadlock, not to applaud his silly old speeches, so foolish, so manly, so genuinely English, so disastrous to England. It is true that the English people love a lord, but it is not true that they fear him; rather, if anything, they pity him; there creeps into their love something of the feeling they have towards a baby or a black man. In their hearts they think it admirable that Sir Leicester Deadlock should be able to speak at all. And so a system, which no iron laws and no bloody battles could possibly force upon a people, is preserved from generation to generation by pure, weak good-nature.

In " Bleak House " occurs the character of Harold Skimpole, the character whose alleged likeness to Leigh Hunt has laid Dickens open to so much disapproval. Unjust disapproval, I think, as far as fundamental morals are concerned. In method he was a little clamorous and clumsy, as, indeed, he was apt to be. But when he said that it was possible to combine a certain tone of conversation taken from a particular man with other characteristics which were not meant to be his, he surely said what all men who write stories know. A work of fiction often consists in combining a pair of whiskers seen in one street with a crime seen in another. He may quite possibly have really meant only to make Leigh Hunt's light philosophy the mask for a new kind of scamp, as a variant on the pious mask of Pecksniff or the candid mask of Bagstock. He may never once have had the unfriendly thought, "Suppose Hunt behaved like a rascal!" he may have only had the fanciful thought, "Suppose a rascal behaved like Hunt!"

But there is a good reason for mentioning Skimpole especially. In the character of Skimpole, Dickens displayed again a quality that was very admirable in him—I mean a disposition to see things sanely and to satirize even his own faults. He was commonly occupied in satirizing the Gradgrinds, the economists, the men of Smiles and Self-

Help. For him there was nothing poorer than their wealth, nothing more selfish than their self-denial. And against them he was in the habit of pitting the people of a more expansive habit—the happy Swivellers and Micawbers, who, if they were poor, were at least as rich as their last penny could make them. He loved that great Christian carelessness that seeks its meat from God. It was merely a kind of uncontrollable honesty that forced him into urging the other side. He could not disguise from himself or from the world that the man who began by seeking his meat from God might end by seeking his meat from his neighbour, without apprising his neighbour of the fact. He had shown how good irresponsibility could be; he could not stoop to hide how bad it could be. He created Skimpole; and Skimpole is the dark underside of Micawber.

In attempting Skimpole he attempted something with a great and urgent meaning. He attempted it, I say; I do not assert that he carried it through. As has been remarked, he was never successful in describing psychological change; his characters are the same yesterday, to-day, and for ever. And critics have complained very justly of the crude villainy of Skimpole's action in the matter of Joe and Mr. Bucket. Certainly Skimpole had no need to commit a clumsy treachery to win a clumsy bribe; he had only to call on Mr. Jarndyce. He had lost his honour too long to need to sell it.

The effect is bad; but I repeat that the aim was great. Dickens wished, under the symbol of Skimpole, to point out a truth which is perhaps the most terrible in moral psychology. I mean the fact that it is by no means easy to draw the line between light and heavy offence. He desired to show that there are no faults, however kindly, that we can afford to flatter or to let alone; he meant that perhaps Skimpole had once been as good a man as Swiveller. If flattered or let alone, our kindliest fault can destroy our kindliest virtue. A thing may begin as a very human weakness, and end as a very inhuman weakness. Skimpole means that the extremes of evil are much nearer than we think. A man may begin by being too generous to pay his debts, and end by being too mean to pay his debts. For the vices are very strangely in league, and encourage each other. A sober man may become a drunkard through being a coward. A brave man may become a coward through being a drunkard. That is the thing Dickens was darkly trying to convey in Skimpole—that a man might become a mountain of selfishness if he attended only to the Dickens virtues. There is nothing that can be neglected; there is no such thing (he meant) as a peccadillo.

I have dwelt on this consciousness of his because, alas, it had a very sharp edge for himself. Even while he was permitting a fault, originally small, to make a comedy of Skimpole, a fault, originally small, was making a tragedy of Charles Dickens. For Dickens also had a bad quality, not intrinsically very terrible, which he allowed to wreck his life. He also had a small weakness that could sometimes become stronger than all his strengths. His selfishness was not, it need hardly be said, the selfishness of Gradgrind; he was particularly compassionate and liberal. Nor was it in the least the selfishness of Skimpole. He was entirely self-dependent, industrious, and dignified. His selfishness was wholly a selfishness of the nerves. Whatever his whim or the temperature of the instant told him to do, must be done. He was the type of man who would break a window if it would not open and give him air. And this weakness of his had, by the time of which we speak, led to a breach between himself and his wife which he was too exasperated and excited to heal in time. Everything must be put right, and put right at once, with him. If London bored him, he must go to the Continent at once; if the Continent bored him, he must come back to London at once. If the day was too noisy, the whole household must be quiet; if night was too quiet, the whole household must wake up. Above all, he had this supreme character of the domestic despot—that his good temper was, if possible, more despotic than his bad temper. When he was miserable (as he often was, poor fellow), they only had to listen to his railings. When he was happy they had to listen to his novels. All this, which was mainly mere excitability, did not seem to amount to much; it did not in the least mean that he had ceased to be a clean-living and kind-hearted and quite honest man. But there was this evil about it—that he did not resist his little weakness at all; he pampered it as Skimpole pampered his. And it separated him and his wife. A mere silly trick of temperament did everything that the blackest misconduct could have done. A random sensibility, started about the shuffling of papers or the shutting of a window, ended by tearing two clean, Christian people from each other, like a blast of bigamy or adultery.

CHAPTER IX

LATER LIFE AND WORKS

I HAVE deliberately in this book mentioned only such facts in the life of Dickens as were, I will not say significant (for all facts must be significant, including the million facts that can never be mentioned by anybody), but such facts as illustrated my own immediate meaning. I have observed this method consistently and without shame because I think that we can hardly make too evident a chasm between books which profess to be statements of all ascertainable facts, and books which (like this one) profess only to contain a particular opinion or a summary deducible from the facts. Books like Forster's exhaustive work and others exist, and are as accessible as St. Paul's Cathedral; we have them in common as we have the facts of the physical universe; and it seems highly desirable that the function of making an exhaustive catalogue and that of making an individual generalization should not be confused. No catalogue, of course, can contain all the facts even of five minutes; every catalogue, however long and learned, must be not only a bold, but, one may say, an audacious selection. But if a great many facts are given, the reader gains a blurred belief that all the facts are being given. In a professedly personal judgment it is therefore clearer and more honest to give only a few illustrative facts, leaving the other obtainable facts to balance them. For thus it is made quite clear that the thing is a sketch, an affair of a few lines.

It is as well, however, to make at this point a pause sufficient to indicate the main course of the later life of the novelist. And it is best to begin with the man himself, as he appeared in those last days of popularity and public distinction. Many are still alive who remember him in his after-dinner speeches, his lectures, and his many public activities; as I am not one of these, I cannot correct my notions with that flash of the living features without which a description may be subtly and entirely wrong. Once a man is dead, if it be only yesterday, the newcomer must piece him together from descriptions really as much at random as if he were describing Cæsar or Henry II. Allowing, however, for this inevitable falsity, a figure vivid and a little fantastic, does walk across the stage of Forster's "Life."

Dickens was of a middle size and his vivacity

and relative physical insignificance probably gave rather the impression of small size; certainly of the absence of bulk. In early life he wore, even for that epoch, extravagant clusters of brown hair, and in later years, a brown moustache and a fringe of brown beard (cut like a sort of broad and bushy imperial) sufficiently individual in shape to give him a faint air as of a foreigner. His face had a peculiar tint or quality which is hard to describe even after one has contrived to imagine it. It was the quality which Mrs. Carlyle felt to be, as it were, metallic, and compared to clear steel. It was, I think, a sort of pale glitter and animation, very much alive and yet with something deathly about it, like a corpse galvanized by a god. His face (if this was so) was curiously a counterpart of his character. For the essence of Dickens's character was that it was at once tremulous and yet hard and sharp, just as the bright blade of a sword is tremulous and yet hard and sharp. He vibrated at every touch and yet he was indestructible; you could bend him, but you could not break him. Brown of hair and beard, somewhat pale of visage (especially in his later days of excitement and ill-health) he had quite exceptionally bright and active eyes; eyes that were always darting about like brilliant birds to pick up all the tiny things of which he made more, perhaps, than any novelist has done; for he was a sort of poetical Sherlock Holmes. The mouth behind the brown beard was large and mobile, like the mouth of an actor; indeed he was an actor, in many things too much of an actor. In his lectures, in later years, he could turn his strange face into any of the innumerable mad masks that were the faces of his grotesque characters. He could make his face fall suddenly into the blank inanity of Mrs. Raddle's servant, or swell, as if to twice its size, into the apoplectic energy of Mr. Sergeant Buzfuz. But the outline of his face itself, from his youth upwards, was cut quite delicate and decisive, and in repose and its own keen way, may even have looked effeminate.

The dress of the comfortable classes during the later years of Dickens was, compared with ours, somewhat slipshod and somewhat gaudy. It was the time of loose pegtop trousers of an almost Turkish oddity, of large ties, of loose short jackets and of loose long whiskers. Yet even this expansive period, it must be confessed, considered Dickens a little too flashy or, as some put it, too Frenchified in his dress. He wore velvet coats; he wore wild waistcoats that were like incredible sunsets; he wore large hats of an unnecessary and startling whiteness. He did not mind being seen in sensational dressing-gowns; nay, he had his portrait painted in one of them. All this is not meritorious; neither is it particularly discreditable; it is a characteristic only, but an important one. He was an absolutely independent and entirely self-respecting man. But he had none of that old dusty, half-dignified English feeling upon which Thackeray was so sensitive; I mean the desire to be regarded as a private gentleman, which means at bottom the desire to be left alone. This again is not a merit; it is only one of the milder aspects of aristocracy. But meritorious or not, Dickens did not possess it. He had no objection to being stared at, if he were also admired. He did not exactly pose in the oriental manner of Disraeli; his instincts were too clean for that; but he did pose somewhat in the French manner, of some leaders like Mirabeau and Gambetta. Nor had he the dull desire to "get on" which makes men die contented as inarticulate Under Secretaries of State. He did not desire success so much as fame, the old human glory, the applause and wonder of the people. Such he was as he walked down the street in his white hat, probably with a slight swagger.

His private life consisted of one tragedy and ten thousand comedies. By one tragedy I mean one real and rending moral tragedy—the failure of his marriage. He loved his children dearly, and more than one of them died; but in sorrows like these there is no violence and above all no shame. The end of life is not tragic like the end of love. And by the ten thousand comedies I mean the whole texture of his life, his letters, his conversation, which were one incessant carnival of insane and inspired improvisation. So far as he could prevent it, he never permitted a day of his life to be ordinary. There was always some prank, some impetuous proposal, some practical joke, some sudden hospitality, some sudden disappearance. It is related of him (I give one anecdote out of a hundred) that in his last visit to America, when he was already reeling as it were under the blow that was to be mortal, he remarked quite casually to his companions that a row of painted cottages looked exactly like the painted shops in a pantomime. No sooner had the suggestion passed his lips than he leapt at the nearest doorway and in exact imitation of the clown in the harlequinade, beat conscientiously with his fist, not on the door (for that would have burst the canvas scenery of course), but on the side of the doorpost. Having done this he lay down ceremoniously across the doorstep for the owner to fall over him if he should come rushing out. He then got up gravely and went on his way. His whole life was full of such unexpected energies, precisely like those of the pantomime clown. Dickens had indeed a great and fundamental affinity with the landscape, or rather house-scape, of the harlequinade. He liked high houses, and sloping roofs, and deep areas. But he would have been really happy if some good fairy of the eternal pantomime had given him the power of flying off the roofs and pitching harmlessly down the height of the houses and bounding out of the areas like an indiarubber ball. The divine lunatic in " Nicholas Nickleby " comes nearest to his dream. I really think Dickens would rather have been that one of his characters than any of the others. With what excitement he would have struggled down the chimney. With what ecstatic energy he would have hurled the cucumbers over the garden wall.

His letters exhibit even more the same incessant creative force. His letters are as creative as any of his literary creations. His shortest postcard is often as good as his ablest novel; each one of them is spontaneous; each one of them is different. He varies even the form and shape of the letter as far as possible; now it is in absurd French! now it is from one of his characters; now it is an advertisement for himself as a stray dog. All of them are very funny; they are not only very funny, but they are quite as funny as his finished and published work. This is the ultimately amazing thing about Dickens; the amount there is of him. He wrote, at the very least, sixteen thick important books packed full of original creation. And if you had burnt them all he could have written sixteen more, as a man writes idle letters to his friend.

In connection with this exuberant part of his nature there is another thing to be noted, if we are to make a personal picture of him. Many modern people, chiefly women, have been heard to object to the Bacchic element in the books of Dickens, that celebration of social drinking as a supreme symbol of social living, which those books share with almost all the great literature of mankind, including the New Testament. Undoubtedly there is an abnormal amount of drinking in a page of Dickens, as there is an abnormal amount of fighting, say, in a page of Dumas. If you reckon up the beers and brandies of Mr. Bob Sawyer, with the care of an arithmetician and the deductions of a pathologist, they rise alarmingly, like a rising tide at sea. Dickens did defend drink clamorously, praised it with passion, and described whole orgies of it with enormous gusto. Yet it is wonderfully typical of his prompt and impatient nature that he himself drank comparatively little. He was the type of man who could be so eager in praising the cup that he left the cup untasted. It was a part of his active and feverish temperament that he did not drink wine very much. But it was a part of his humane philosophy, of his religion, that he did drink wine. To healthy European philosophy, wine is a symbol; to European religion it is a sacrament. Dickens approved it because it was a great human institution, one of the rites of civilization, and this it certainly is. The teetotaller who stands outside it may have perfectly clear ethical reasons of his own, as a man may have who stands outside education or nationality, who refuses to go to an University or to serve in an Army. But he is neglecting one of the great social things that man has added to nature. The teetotaller has chosen a most unfortunate phrase for the drunkard when he says that the drunkard is making a beast of himself. The man who drinks ordinarily makes nothing but an ordinary man of himself. The man who drinks excessively makes a devil of himself. But nothing connected with a human and artistic thing like wine can bring one nearer to the brute life of nature. The only man who is, in the exact and literal sense of the words, making a beast of himself is the teetotaller.

The tone of Dickens towards religion, though like that of most of his contemporaries, philosophically disturbed and rather historically ignorant, had an element that was very characteristic of himself. He had all the prejudices of his time. He had, for instance, that dislike of defined dogmas, which really means a preference for unexamined dogmas. He had the usual vague notion that the whole of our human past was packed with nothing but insane Tories. He had, in a word, all the old Radical ignorances which went along with the old Radical acuteness and courage and public spirit. But this spirit tended, in almost all the others who held it, to a specific dislike of the Church of England; and a disposition to set the other sects against it, as truer types of inquiry, or of individualism. Dickens had a definite tenderness for the Church of England. He might have even called it a weakness for the Church of England, but he had it. Something in those placid services, something in that reticent and humane liturgy pleased him against all the tendencies of his time; pleased him in the best part of himself, his virile love of charity and peace. Once, in a puff of anger at the Church's political stupidity (which is indeed profound), he left it for a week or two and went to an Unitarian Chapel; in a week or two he came back. This curious and sentimental hold of the English Church upon him increased with years. In the book he was at work on when he died he describes the Minor Canon, humble, chivalrous, tender-hearted, answering with indignant simplicity the froth and platform righteousness of the sectarian philanthropist. He upholds Canon Crisparkle and satirizes Mr. Honeythunder. Almost every one of the other Radicals, his friends, would have upheld Mr. Honeythunder and satirized Canon Crisparkle.

I have mentioned this matter for a special reason. It brings us back to that apparent contradiction or dualism in Dickens to which, in one connection or another, I have often adverted, and which, in one shape or another, constitutes the whole crux of his character. I mean the union of a general wildness approaching lunacy, with a sort of secret moderation almost amounting to mediocrity. Dickens was, more or less, the man I have described—sensitive, theatrical, amazing, a bit of a dandy, a bit of a buffoon. Nor are such characteristics, whether weak or wild, entirely accidents or externals. He had some false theatrical tendencies integral in his nature. For instance, he had one most unfortunate habit, a habit that often put him in the wrong, even when he happened to be in the right. He had an incurable habit of explaining himself. This reduced his admirers to the mental condition of the authentic but hitherto uncelebrated little girl who said to her mother, "I think I should understand if only you wouldn't explain." Dickens always would explain. It was a part of that instinctive publicity of his which made him at once a splendid democrat and a little too much of an actor. He carried it to the craziest lengths. He actually wanted to have printed in *Punch,* it is said, an apology for his own action in the matter of his marriage. That incident alone is enough to suggest that his external offers and proposals were sometimes like screams heard from Bedlam. Yet it remains true that he had in him a central part that was pleased only by the most decent and the most reposeful rites, by things of which the Anglican prayer-book is very typical. It is certainly true that he was often extravagant. It is most certainly equally true that he detested and despised extravagance.

The best explanation can be found in his literary genius. His literary genius consisted in a contradictory capacity at once to entertain and to deride—very ridiculous ideas. If he is a buffoon, he is laughing at buffoonery. His books were in some ways the wildest on the face of the world. Rabelais did not introduce into Paphlagonia or the Kingdom of the Coqcigrues satiric figures more frantic and misshapen than Dickens made to walk about the Strand and Lincoln's Inn. But for all that, you come, in the core of him, on a sudden quietude and good sense. Such, I think, was the core of Rabelais, such were all the far-stretching and violent satirists. This is a point essential to Dickens, though very little comprehended in our current tone of thought. Dickens was an immoderate jester, but a moderate thinker. He was an immoderate jester because he was a moderate thinker. What we moderns call the wildness of his imagination was actually created by what we moderns call the tameness of his thought. I mean that he felt the full insanity of all extreme tendencies, because he was himself so sane; he felt eccentricities, because he was in the centre. We are always, in these days, asking our violent prophets to write violent satires; but violent prophets can never possibly write violent satires. In order to write satire like that of Rabelais—satire that juggles with the stars and kicks the world about like a football—it is necessary to be one's self temperate, and even mild. A modern man like Nietzsche, a modern man like Gorky, a modern man like d'Annunzio, could not possibly write real and riotous satire. They are themselves too much on the borderlands. They could not be a success as caricaturists, for they are already a great success as caricatures.

I have mentioned his religious preference merely as an instance of this interior moderation. To say, as some have done, that he attacked Nonconformity is quite a false way of putting it. It is clean across the whole trend of the man and his time to suppose that he could have felt bitterness against any theological body as a theological body; but anything like religious extravagance, whether Protestant or Catholic, moved him to an extravagance of satire. And he flung himself into the drunken energy of Stiggins, he piled up to the stars the " verbose flights of stairs " of Mr. Chadband, exactly because his own conception of religion was the quiet and impersonal Morning Prayer. It is typical of him that he had a peculiar hatred for speeches at the graveside.

An even clearer case of what I mean can be found in his political attitude. He seemed to some an almost anarchic satirist. He made equal fun of the systems which reformers made war on, and of the instruments on which reformers relied. He made no secret of his feeling that the average English premier was an accidental ass. In two superb sentences he summed up and swept away the whole British constitution: "England, for the last week, has been in an awful state. Lord Coodle would go out, Sir Thomas Doodle wouldn't come in, and there being no people in England to speak of except Coodle and Doodle, the country has been without a government." He lumped all cabinets and all government offices together, and made the same game of them all. He created his most staggering humbugs, his most adorable and incredible idiots, and set them on the highest thrones of our national system. To many moderate and progressive people, such a satirist seemed to be insulting heaven and earth, ready to wreck society for some mad alternative, prepared to pull down St. Paul's, and on its ruins erect a gory guillotine. Yet, as a matter of fact, this apparent wildness of his came from his being, if anything, a very moderate politician. It came, not at all from fanaticism, but from a rather rational detachment. He had the sense to see that the British constitution was not democracy, but the British constitution. It was an artificial system—like any other, good in some ways, bad in others. His satire of it sounded wild to those that worshipped it; but his satire of it arose not from his having any wild enthusiasm against it, but simply from his not having, like every one else, a wild enthusiasm for it. Alone, as far as I know, among all the great Englishmen of that age, he realized the thing that Frenchmen and Irishmen understand. I mean the fact that popular government is one thing, and representative government another. He realized that representative government has many minor disadvantages, one of them being that it is never representative. He speaks of his " hope to have made every man in England feel something of the contempt for the House of Commons that I have." He says also these two things, both of which are wonderfully penetrating as coming from a good Radical in 1855, for they contain a perfect statement of the peril in which we now stand, and which may, if it please God, sting us into avoiding the long vista at the end of which one sees so clearly the dignity and the decay of Venice—

" I am hourly strengthened," he says, " in my old belief, that our political aristocracy and our tuft-hunting are the death of England. In all this business I don't see a gleam of hope. As to the popular spirit, it has come to be so entirely separated from the Parliament and the Government, and so perfectly apathetic about them both, that I seriously think it a most portentous sign." And he says also this: "I really am serious in thinking—and I have given as painful consideration to the subject as a man with children to live and suffer after him can possibly give it—that representative government is become altogether a failure with us, that the English gentilities and subserviences render the people unfit for it, and the whole thing has broken down since the great seventeenth century time, and has no hope in it."

These are the words of a wise and perhaps melancholy man, but certainly not of an unduly excited one. It is worth noting, for instance, how much more directly Dickens goes to the point than Carlyle did, who noted many of the same evils. But Carlyle fancied that our modern English government was wordy and long-winded because it was democratic government. Dickens saw, what is certainly the fact, that it is wordy and long-winded because it is aristocratic government, the two most pleasant aristocratic qualities being a love of literature and an unconsciousness of time. But all this amounts to the same conclusion of the matter. Frantic figures like Stiggins and Chadband were created out of the quietude of his religious preference. Wild creations like the Barnacles and the Bounderbys were produced in a kind of ecstasy of the ordinary, of the obvious in political justice. His monsters were made out of his level and his moderation, as the old monsters were made out of the level sea.

Such was the man of genius we must try to imagine; violently emotional, yet with a good judgment; pugnacious, but only when he thought himself oppressed; prone to think himself oppressed, yet not cynical about human motives. He was a man remarkably hard to understand or to reanimate. He almost always had reasons for his action; his error was that he always expounded them. Sometimes his nerve snapped; and then he was mad. Unless it did so he was quite unusually sane.

Such a rough sketch at least must suffice us in order to summarize his later years. Those years were occupied, of course, in two main additions to his previous activities. The first was the series of public readings and lectures which he now began to give systematically. The second was his successive editorship of *Household Words* and of *All the Year Round*. He was of a type that enjoys every new function and opportunity. He had been so many things in his life, a reporter, an actor, a conjurer, a poet. As he had enjoyed them all, so he enjoyed being a lecturer, and enjoyed being an editor. It is certain that his audiences (who sometimes stacked themselves so thick that they lay flat on the platform all round him) enjoyed his being a lecturer. It is not so certain that the subeditors enjoyed his being an editor. But in both connections the main matter of importance is the effect on the permanent work of Dickens himself. The readings were important for this reason, that they fixed, as if by some public and pontifical pronouncement, what was Dickens's interpretation of Dickens's work. Such a knowledge is mere tradition, but it is very forcible. My own family has handed on to me, and I shall probably hand on to the next generation, a definite memory of how Dickens made his face suddenly like the face of an idiot in impersonating Mrs. Raddle's servant, Betsy. This does serve one of the permanent purposes of tradition; it does make it a little more difficult for any ingenious person to prove that Betsy was meant to be a brilliant satire on the over-cultivation of the intellect.

As for his relation to his two magazines, it is chiefly important, first for the admirable things that he wrote in the magazines himself (one cannot forbear to mention the inimitable monologue of the waiter in "Somebody's Luggage"), and secondly for the fact that in his capacity of editor he made one valuable discovery. He discovered Wilkie Collins. Wilkie Collins was the one man of unmistakable genius who has a certain affinity with Dickens; an affinity in this respect, that they both combine in a curious way a modern and cockney and even commonplace opinion about things with a huge elemental sympathy with strange oracles and spirits and old night. There were no two men in Mid-Victorian England, with their top-hats and umbrellas, more typical of its rationality and dull reform; and there were no two men who could touch them at a ghost story. No two men would have more contempt for superstitions; and no two men could so create the superstitious thrill. Indeed, our modern mystics make a mistake when they wear long hair or loose ties to attract the spirits. The elves and the old gods when they revisit the earth really go straight for a dull top-hat. For it means simplicity, which the gods love.

Meanwhile his books, which, as brilliant as ever, were appearing from time to time, bore witness to that increasing tendency to a more careful and responsible treatment which we have marked in the transition which culminated in "Bleak House." His next important book, "Hard Times," strikes an almost unexpected note of severity. The characters are indeed exaggerated, but they are bitterly and deliberately exaggerated; they are not exaggerated with the old unconscious high spirits of Nicholas Nickleby or Martin Chuzzlewit. Dickens exaggerates Bounderby because he really hates him. He exaggerated Pecksniff because he really loved him. "Hard Times" is not one of the greatest books of Dickens; but it is perhaps in a sense one of his greatest monuments. It stamps and records the reality of Dickens's emotion on a great many things that were then considered unphilosophical grumblings, but which since have swelled into the immense phenomenon of the socialist philosophy. To call Dickens a Socialist is a wild exaggeration; but the truth and peculiarity of his position might be expressed thus: that even when everybody thought that Liberalism meant individualism he was emphatically a Liberal and emphatically not an individualist. Or the truth might be better still stated in this manner: that he saw that there was a secret thing, called humanity, to which both extreme socialism and extreme individualism were profoundly and inexpressibly indifferent, and that this permanent and presiding humanity was the thing he happened to understand; he knew that individualism is nothing and non-individualism is nothing but the keeping of the commandment of man. He felt, as a novelist should, that the question is too much discussed as to whether a man is in favour of this or that scientific philosophy; that there is another question, whether the scientific philosophy is in favour of the man. That is why such books as "Hard Times" will remain always a part of the power and tradition of Dickens. He saw that economic systems are not things like the stars, but things like the lamp-posts, manifestations of the human mind, and things to be judged by the human heart.

Thenceforward until the end his books grow consistently graver and, as it were, more responsible; he improves as an artist if not always as a creator. "Little Dorrit" (published in 1857) is at once in some ways so much more subtle and in every way so much more sad than the rest of his work that it bores Dickensians and especially pleases George Gissing. It is the only one of the Dickens tales which could please Gissing, not only by its genius, but also by its atmosphere. There is something a little modern and a little sad, something also out of tune with the main trend of Dickens's moral feeling, about the description of the character of Dorrit as actually and finally weakened by his wasting experiences, as not lifting any cry above the conquered years. It is but a faint fleck of shadow. But the illimitable white light of human hopefulness, of which I spoke at the beginning, is ebbing away, the work of the revolution is growing weaker everywhere; and the night of necessitarianism cometh when no man can work. For the first time in a book by Dickens perhaps we really do feel that the hero is forty-five. Clennam is certainly very much older than Mr. Pickwick.

This was indeed only a fugitive grey cloud; he went on to breezier operations. But whatever they were, they still had the note of the later days. They have a more cautious craftsmanship; they have a more mellow and a more mixed human sentiment. Shadows fell upon his page from the other and sadder figures out of the Victorian decline. A good instance of this is his next book, "The Tale of Two Cities" (1859). In dignity and eloquence it almost stands alone among the books by Dickens, but it also stands alone among his books in this respect, that it is not entirely by Dickens. It owes its inspiration avowedly to the passionate and cloudy pages of Carlyle's "French Revolution." And there is something quite essentially inconsistent between Carlyle's disturbed and half-sceptical transcendentalism and the original school and spirit to which Dickens belonged, the lucid and laughing decisiveness of the old convinced and contented Radicalism. Hence the genius of Dickens cannot save him, just as the great genius of Carlyle could not save him from making a picture of the French Revolution, which was delicately and yet deeply erroneous. Both tend too much to represent it as a mere elemental outbreak of hunger or vengeance; they do not see enough that it was a war for intellectual principles, even for intellectual platitudes. We, the modern English, cannot easily understand the French Revolution, because we cannot easily understand the idea of bloody battle for pure common sense; we cannot understand common sense in arms and conquering. In modern England common sense appears to mean putting up with existing conditions. For us a practical politician really means a man who can be thoroughly trusted to do nothing at all; that is where his practicality comes in. The French feeling—the feeling at the back of the Revolution—was that the more sensible a man was, the more you must look out for slaughter.

In all the imitators of Carlyle, including Dickens, there is an obscure sentiment that the thing for which the Frenchmen died must have been something new and queer, a paradox, a strange idolatry. But when such blood ran in the streets, it was for the sake of a truism; when those cities were shaken to their foundations, they were shaken to their foundations by a truism.

I have mentioned this historical matter because it illustrates these later and more mingled influences which at once improve and as it were perplex the later work of Dickens. For Dickens had in his original mental composition capacities for understanding this cheery and sensible element in the French Revolution far better than Carlyle. The French Revolution was, among other things, French, and, so far as that goes, could never have a precise counterpart in so jolly and autochthonous an Englishman as Charles Dickens. But there was a great deal of the actual and unbroken tradition of the Revolution itself in his early radical indictments; in his denunciations of the Fleet Prison there was a great deal of the capture of the Bastille. There was, above all, a certain reasonable impatience which was the essence of the old Republican, and which is quite unknown to the Revolutionist in modern Europe. The old Radical did not feel exactly that he was "in revolt;" he felt if anything that a number of idiotic institutions had revolted against reason and against him. Dickens, I say, had the revolutionary idea, though an English form of it, by clear and conscious inheritance; Carlyle had to rediscover the Revolution by a violence of genius and vision. If Dickens, then, took from Carlyle (as he said he did) his image of the Revolution, it does certainly mean that he had forgotten something of his own youth and come under the more complex influences of the end of the nineteenth century. His old hilarious and sentimental view of human nature seems for a moment dimmed in "Little Dorrit." His old political simplicity has been slightly disturbed by Carlyle.

I repeat that this graver note is varied, but it remains a graver note. We see it struck, I think, with particular and remarkable success in "Great Expectations" (1860-61). This fine story is told with a consistency and quietude of individuality which is rare in Dickens. But so far had he travelled along the road of a heavier reality, that he even intended to give the tale an unhappy ending, making Pip lose Estella for ever; and he was only dissuaded from it by the robust romanticism of Bulwer-Lytton. But the best part of the tale—the account of the vacillations of the hero between the humble life to which he owes everything, and the gorgeous life from which he expects something, touch a very true and somewhat tragic part of morals; for the great paradox of morality (the paradox to which only the religions have given an adequate expression) is that the very vilest kind of fault is exactly the most easy kind. We read in books and ballads about the wild fellow who might kill a man or smoke opium, but who would never stoop to lying or cowardice or to "anything mean." But for actual human beings opium and slaughter have only occasional charm; the permanent human temptation is the temptation to be mean. The one standing probability is the probability of becoming a cowardly hypocrite. The circle of the traitors is the lowest of the abyss, and it is also the easiest to fall into. That is one of the ringing realities of the Bible, that it does not make its great men commit grand sins; it makes its great men (such as David and St. Peter) commit small sins and behave like sneaks.

Dickens has dealt with this easy descent of desertion, this silent treason, with remarkable accuracy in the account of the indecisions of Pip. It contains a good suggestion of that weak romance which is the root of all snobbishness: that the mystery which belongs to patrician life excites us more than the open, even the indecent virtues of the humble. Pip is keener about Miss Havisham, who may mean well by him, than about Joe Gargery, who evidently does. All this is very strong and wholesome; but it is still a little stern. "Our Mutual Friend" (1864) brings us back a little into his merrier and more normal manner; some of the satire, such as that upon Veneering's election, is in the best of his old style, so airy and fanciful, yet hitting so suddenly and so hard. But even here we find the fuller and more serious treatment of psychology; notably in the two facts that he creates a really human villain, Bradley Headstone, and also one whom we might call a really human hero, Eugene, if it were not that he is much too human to be called a hero at all. It has been said (invariably by cads) that Dickens never described a gentleman; it is like saying that he never described a zebra. A gentleman is a very rare animal among human creatures, and to people like Dickens, interested in all humanity, not a supremely important one. But in Eugene Wrayburne he does, whether consciously or not, turn that accusation with a vengeance. For he not only describes a gentleman but describes the inner weakness and peril that belong to a gentleman, the devil that is always rending the entrails of an idle and agreeable man. In Eugene's purposeless pursuit of Lizzie Hexam, in his yet more purposeless torturing of Bradley Headstone, the author has marvellously realized that singular empty obstinacy that drives the whims and pleasures of a leisured class. He sees that there is nothing that such a man more stubbornly adheres to, than the thing that he does not particularly want to do. We are still in serious psychology.

His last book represents yet another new departure, dividing him from the chaotic Dickens of days long before. His last book is not merely an attempt to improve his power of construction in a story: it is an attempt to rely entirely on that power of construction. It not only has a plot, it is a plot. "The Mystery of Edwin Drood" (1870) was in such a sense, perhaps, the most ambitious book that Dickens ever attempted. It is, as every one knows, a detective story, and certainly a very successful one, as is attested by the tumult of discussion as to its proper solution. In this, quite apart from its unfinished state, it stands, I think, alone among the author's works. Elsewhere, if he introduced a mystery, he seldom took the trouble to make it very mysterious. "Our Mutual Friend" was finished, but if only half of it were readable, I think any one could see that John Rokesmith was John Harman. "Bleak House" is finished, but if it were only half finished I think any one would guess that Lady Deadlock and Nemo had sinned in the past. "Edwin

Drood" is not finished; for in the very middle of it Dickens died.

He had altogether overstrained himself in a last lecturing tour in America. He was a man in whom any serious malady would naturally make very rapid strides; for he had the temper of an irrational invalid. I have said before that there was in his curious character something that was feminine. Certainly there was nothing more entirely feminine than this, that he worked because he was tired. Fatigue bred in him a false and feverish industry, and his case increased, like the case of a man who drinks to cure the effects of drink. He died in 1870; and the whole nation mourned him as no public man has ever been mourned; for prime ministers and princes were private persons compared with Dickens. He had been a great popular king, like a king of some more primal age whom his people could come and see, giving judgment under an oak tree. He had in essence held great audiences of millions, and made proclamations to more than one of the nations of the earth. His obvious omnipresence in every part of public life was like the omnipresence of the sovereign. His secret omnipresence in every house and hut of private life was more like the omnipresence of a deity. Compared with that popular leadership all the fusses of the last forty years are diversions in idleness. Compared with such a case as his it may be said that we play with our politicians, and manage to endure our authors. We shall never have again such a popularity until we have again a people.

He left behind him this almost sombre fragment, "The Mystery of Edwin Drood." As one turns it over the tragic element of its truncation mingles somewhat with an element of tragedy in the thing itself: the passionate and predestined Landless, or the half maniacal Jasper carving devils out of his own heart. The workmanship of it is very fine; the right hand has not only not lost, but is still gaining its cunning. But as we turn the now enigmatic pages the thought creeps into us again which I have suggested earlier, and which is never far off the mind of a true lover of Dickens. Had he lost or gained by the growth of technique and probability in his later work? His later characters were more like men; but were not his earlier characters more like immortals? He has become able to perform a social scene so that it is possible at any rate; but where is that Dickens who once performed the impossible? Where is that young poet who created such majors and architects as nature will never dare to create?

Dickens learnt to describe daily life as Thackeray and Jane Austen could describe it; but Thackeray could not have thought such a thought as Crummles; and it is painful to think of Miss Austen attempting to imagine Mantalini. After all, we feel there are many able novelists; but there is only one Dickens, and whither has he fled?

He was alive to the end. And in this last dark and secretive story of Edwin Drood he makes one splendid and staggering appearance, like a magician saying farewell to mankind. In the centre of this otherwise reasonable and rather melancholy book, this grey story of a good clergyman and the quiet Cloisterham Towers, Dickens has calmly inserted one entirely delightful and entirely insane passage. I mean the frantic and inconceivable epitaph of Mrs. Sapsea, that which describes her as "the reverential wife" of Thomas Sapsea, speaks of her consistency in "Looking up to him," and ends with the words, spaced out so admirably on the tombstone, "Stranger pause. And ask thyself this question, Canst thou do likewise? If not, with a blush retire." Not the wildest tale in Pickwick contains such an impossibility as that; Dickens dare scarcely have introduced it, even as one of Jingle's lies. In no human churchyard will you find that invaluable tombstone; indeed, you could scarcely find it in any world where there are churchyards. You could scarcely have such immortal folly as that in a world where there is also death. Mr. Sapsea is one of the golden things stored up for us in a better world.

Yes, there were many other Dickenses: a clever Dickens, an industrious Dickens, a public-spirited Dickens; but this was the great one. This last outbreak of insane humour reminds us wherein lay his power and his supremacy. The praise of such beatific buffoonery should be the final praise, the ultimate word in his honour. The wild epitaph of Mrs. Sapsea should be the serious epitaph of Dickens.

CHAPTER X

THE GREAT DICKENS CHARACTERS

ALL criticism tends too much to become criticism of criticism; and the reason is very evident. It is that criticism of creation is so very staggering a thing. We see this in the difficulty of criticizing any artistic creation. We see it again in the difficulty of criticizing that creation which is spelt with a capital C. The pessimists who attack the Universe are always under this disadvantage. They have an exhilarating consciousness that they could make the sun and moon better; but they also have the depressing consciousness that they could not make the sun and moon at all. A man looking at a hippopotamus may sometimes be tempted to regard a hippopotamus as an enormous mistake; but he is also bound to confess that a fortunate inferiority prevents him personally from making such mistakes. It is neither a blasphemy nor an exaggeration to say that we feel something of the same difficulty in judging of the very creative element in human literature. And this is the first and last dignity of Dickens; that he was a creator. He did not point out things, he made them. We may disapprove of Mr. Guppy, but we recognize him as a creation flung down like a miracle out of an upper sphere; we can pull him to pieces, but we could not have put him together. We can destroy Mrs. Gamp in our wrath, but we could not have made her in our joy. Under this disadvantage any book about Dickens must definitely labour. Real primary creation (such as the sun or the birth of a child) calls forth not criticism, not appreciation, but a kind of incoherent gratitude. This is why most hymns about God are bad; and this is why most eulogies on Dickens are bad. The eulogists of the divine and of the human creator are alike inclined to appear sentimentalists because they are talking about something so very real. In the same way love-letters always sound florid and artificial because they are about something real.

Any chapter such as this chapter must therefore in a sense be inadequate. There is no way of dealing properly with the ultimate greatness of Dickens, except by offering sacrifice to him as a god; and this is opposed to the etiquette of our time. But something can perhaps be done in the way of suggesting what was the quality of this creation. But even in considering its quality we ought to remember that quality is not the whole question. One of the godlike things about Dickens is his quantity, his quantity as such, the enormous output, the incredible fecundity of his invention. I have said a moment ago that not one of us could have invented Mr. Guppy. But even if we could have stolen Mr. Guppy from Dickens we have still to confront the fact that Dickens would have been able to invent another quite inconceivable character to take his place. Perhaps we could have created Mr. Guppy; but the effort would certainly have exhausted us; we should be ever afterwards wheeled about in a bath-chair at Bournemouth.

Nevertheless there is something that is worth saying about the quality of Dickens. At the very beginning of this review I remarked that the reader must be in a mood, at least, of democracy. To some it may have sounded irrelevant; but the Revolution was as much behind all the books of the nineteenth century as the Catholic religion (let us say) was behind all the colours and carving of the Middle Ages. Another great name of the nineteenth century will afford an evidence of this; and will also bring us most sharply to the problem of the literary quality of Dickens.

Of all these nineteenth century writers there is none, in the noblest sense, more democratic than Walter Scott. As this may be disputed, and as it is relevant, I will expand the remark. There are two rooted spiritual realities out of which grow all kinds of democratic conception or sentiment of human equality. There are two things in which all men are manifestly unmistakably equal. They are not equally clever or equally muscular or equally fat, as the sages of the modern reaction (with piercing insight) perceive. But this is a spiritual certainty, that all men are tragic. And this again, is an equally sublime spiritual certainty, that all men are comic. No special and private sorrow can be so dreadful as the fact of having to die. And no freak or deformity can be so funny as the mere fact of having two legs. Every man is important if he loses his life; and every man is funny if he loses his hat, and has to run after it. And the universal test everywhere of whether a thing is popular, of the people, is whether it employs vigorously these extremes of the tragic and the comic. Shelley, for instance, was an aristocrat, if ever there was one in this world. He was a Republican, but he was not a democrat: in his poetry there is every perfect quality except this pungent and popular stab. For the tragic and the comic you must go, say, to Burns, a poor man. And all over the world, the folk literature, the popular literature, is the same. It consists of very dignified sorrow and very undignified fun. Its sad tales are of broken hearts; its happy tales are of broken heads.

These, I say, are two roots of democratic reality. But they have in more civilized literature, a more civilized embodiment or form. In literature such as that of the nineteenth century the two elements appear somewhat thus. Tragedy becomes a profound sense of human dignity. The other and jollier element becomes a delighted sense of human variety. The first supports equality by saying that all men are equally sublime. The second supports equality by observing that all men are equally interesting.

In this democratic aspect the interest and variety of all men, there is, of course, no democrat so great as Dickens. But in the other matter, in the idea of the dignity of all men, I repeat that there is no democrat so great as Scott. This fact, which is the moral and enduring magnificence of Scott, has been astonishingly overlooked. His rich and dramatic effects are gained in almost every case by some grotesque or beggarly figure rising into a human pride and rhetoric. The common man, in the sense of the paltry man, becomes the common man in the sense of the universal man. He declares his humanity. For the meanest of all the modernites has been the notion that the heroic is an oddity or variation, and that the things that unite us are merely flat or foul. The common things are terrible and startling, death, for instance, and first love: the things that are common are the things that are not commonplace. Into such high and central passions the comic Scott character will suddenly rise. Remember the firm and almost stately answer of the preposterous Nicol Jarvie when Helen Macgregor seeks to browbeat him into condoning lawlessness and breaking his bourgeois decency. That speech is a great monument of the middle class. Molière made M. Jourdain talk prose; but Scott made him talk poetry. Think of the rising and rousing voice of the dull and gluttonous Athelstane when he answers and overwhelms De Bracy. Think of the proud appeal of the old beggar in the " Antiquary " when he rebukes the duellists. Scott was fond of describing kings in disguise. But all his characters are kings in disguise. He was, with all his errors, profoundly possessed with the old religious conception (the only possible democratic basis), the idea that man himself is a king in disguise.

In all this Scott, though a Royalist and a Tory, had in the strangest way the heart of the Revolution. For instance, he regarded rhetoric, the art of the orator, as the immediate weapon of the oppressed. All his poor men make grand speeches, as they did in the Jacobin Club, which Scott would have so much detested. And it is odd to reflect that he was, as an author, giving free speech to fictitious rebels while he was, as a stupid politician, denying it to real ones. But the point for us here is this: that all this popular sympathy of his rests on the graver basis, on the dark dignity of man. "Can you find no way?" asks Sir Arthur Wardour of the beggar when they are cut off by the tide. "I'll give you a farm . . . I'll make you rich." . . . "Our riches will soon be equal," says the beggar, and looks out across the advancing sea.

Now, I have dwelt on this strong point of Scott because it is the best illustration of the one weak point of Dickens. Dickens had little or none of this sense of the concealed sublimity of every separate man. Dickens's sense of democracy was entirely of the other kind: it rested on the other of the two supports of which I have spoken. It rested on the sense that all men were wildly interesting and wildly varied. When a Dickens character becomes excited he becomes more and more himself. He does not, like the Scott beggar, turn more and more into man. As he rises he grows more and more into a gargoyle or grotesque. He does not, like the fine speaker in Scott, grow more classical as he grows more passionate, more universal as he grows more intense. The thing can only be illustrated by a special case. Dickens did more than once, of course, make one of his quaint or humble characters assert himself in a serious crisis or defy the powerful. There is, for instance, the quite admirable scene in which Susan Nipper (one of the greatest of Dickens's achievements) faces and rebukes Mr. Dombey. But it is still true (and quite appropriate in its own place and manner) that Susan Nipper remains a purely comic character throughout her speech, and even grows more comic as she goes on. She is more serious than usual in her meaning, but not more serious in her style. Dickens keeps the natural diction of Nipper, but makes her grow more Nipperish as she grows more warm. But Scott keeps the natural diction of Bailie Jarvie, but insensibly sobers and uplifts that style until it reaches a plain and appropriate eloquence. This plain and appropriate eloquence was (except in a few places at the end of "Pickwick") almost unknown to Dickens. Whenever he made comic characters talk sentiment comically, as in the instance of

Susan, it was a success, but an avowedly extravagant success. Whenever he made comic characters talk sentiment seriously it was an extravagant failure. Humour was his medium; his only way of approaching emotion. Wherever you do not get humour, you get unconscious humour.

As I have said elsewhere in this book Dickens was deeply and radically English; the most English of our great writers. And there is something very English in this contentment with a grotesque democracy; and in this absence of the eloquence and elevation of Scott. The English democracy is the most humorous democracy in the world. The Scotch democracy is the most dignified, while the whole abandon and satiric genius of the English populace come from its being quite undignified in every way. A comparison of the two types might be found, for instance, by putting a Scotch Labour leader like Mr. Keir Hardie alongside an English Labour leader like Mr. Will Crooks. Both are good men, honest and responsible and compassionate; but we can feel that the Scotchman carries himself seriously and universally, the Englishman personally and with an obstinate humour. Mr. Hardie wishes to hold up his head as Man, Mr. Crooks wishes to follow his nose as Crooks. Mr. Keir Hardie is very like a poor man in Walter Scott. Mr. Crooks is very like a poor man in Dickens.

Dickens then had this English feeling of a grotesque democracy. By that is more properly meant a vastly varying democracy. The intoxicating variety of men—that was his vision and conception of human brotherhood. And certainly it is a great part of human brotherhood. In one sense things can only be equal if they are entirely different. Thus, for instance, people talk with a quite astonishing gravity about the inequality or equality of the sexes; as if there could possibly be any inequality between a lock and a key. Wherever there is no element of variety, wherever all the items literally have an identical aim, there is at once and of necessity inequality. A woman is only inferior to man in the matter of being not so manly; she is inferior in nothing else. Man is inferior to woman in so far as he is not a woman; there is no other reason. And the same applies in some degree to all genuine differences. It is a great mistake to suppose that love unites and unifies men. Love diversifies them, because love is directed towards individuality. The thing that really unites men and makes them like to each other is hatred. Thus, for instance, the more we love Germany the more pleased we shall be that

Germany should be something different from ourselves, should keep her own ritual and conviviality and we ours. But the more we hate Germany the more we shall copy German guns and German fortifications in order to be armed against Germany. The more modern nations detest each other the more meekly they follow each other; for all competition is in its nature only a furious plagiarism. As competition means always similarity, it is equally true that similarity always means inequality. If everything is trying to be green, some things will be greener than others; but there is an immortal and indestructible equality between green and red. Something of the same kind of irrefutable equality exists between the violent and varying creations of such a writer as Dickens. They are all equally ecstatic fulfilments of a separate line of development. It would be hard to say that there could be any comparison or inequality, let us say between Mr. Sapsea and Mr. Elijah Pogram. They are both in the same difficulty; they can neither of them contrive to exist in this world; they are both too big for the gate of birth.

Of the high virtue of this variation I shall speak more adequately in a moment; but certainly this love of mere variation (which I have contrasted with the classicism of Scott) is the only intelligent statement of the common case against the exaggeration of Dickens. This is the meaning, the only sane or endurable meaning, which people have in their minds when they say that Dickens is a mere caricaturist. They do not mean merely that Uncle Pumblechook does not exist. A fictitious character ought not to be a person who exists; he ought to be an entirely new combination, an addition to the creatures already existing on the earth. They do not mean that Uncle Pumblechook could not exist; for on that obviously they can have no knowledge whatever. They do not mean that Uncle Pumblechook's utterances are selected and arranged so as to bring out his essential Pumblechookery; to say that is simply to say that he occurs in a work of art. But what they do really mean is this, and there is an element of truth in it. They mean that Dickens nowhere makes the reader feel that Pumblechook has any kind of fundamental human dignity at all. It is nowhere suggested that Pumblechook will some day die. He is felt rather as one of the idle and evil fairies, who are innocuous and yet malignant, and who live for ever because they never really live at all. This dehumanized vitality, this fantasy, this irresponsibility of creation, does in some sense truly belong to Dickens. It is the lower side of his hilarious human variety. But now we come to the higher side of his human variety, and it is far more difficult to state.

Mr. George Gissing, from the point of view of the passing intellectualism of our day, has made (among his many wise tributes to Dickens) a characteristic complaint about him. He has said that Dickens, with all his undoubted sympathy for the lower classes, never made a working man, a poor man, specifically and highly intellectual. An exception does exist, which he must at least have realized—a wit, a diplomatist, a great philosopher. I mean, of course, Mr. Weller. Broadly, however, the accusation has a truth, though it is a truth that Mr. Gissing did not grasp in its entirety. It is not only true that Dickens seldom made a poor character what we call intellectual; it is also true that he seldom made any character what we call intellectual. Intellectualism was not at all present to his imagination. What was present to his imagination was character—a thing which is not only more important than intellect, but is also much more entertaining. When some English moralists write about the importance of having character, they appear to mean only the importance of having a dull character. But character is brighter than wit, and much more complex than sophistry. The whole superiority of the democracy of Dickens over the democracy of such a man as Gissing lies exactly in the fact that Gissing would have liked to prove that poor men could instruct themselves and could instruct others. It was of final importance to Dickens that poor men could amuse themselves and could amuse him. He troubled little about the mere education of that life; he declared two essential things about it—that it was laughable, and that it was livable. The humble characters of Dickens do not amuse each other with epigrams; they amuse each other with themselves. The present that each man brings in hand is his own incredible personality. In the most sacred sense, and in the most literal sense of the phrase, he "gives himself away." Now, the man who gives himself away does the last act of generosity; he is like a martyr, a lover, or a monk. But he is also almost certainly what we commonly call a fool.

The key of the great characters of Dickens is that they are all great fools. There is the same difference between a great fool and a small fool as there is between a great poet and a small poet. The great fool is a being who is above wisdom rather than below it. That element of greatness of which I spoke at the beginning of this book is nowhere more clearly indicated than in such characters. A man can be entirely great while he is entirely foolish. We see this in the epic heroes, such as Achilles. Nay, a man can be entirely great because he is entirely foolish. We see this in all the great comic characters of all the great comic writers of whom Dickens was the last. Bottom the Weaver is great because he is foolish; Mr. Toots is great because he is foolish. The thing I mean can be observed, for instance, in innumerable actual characters. Which of us has not known, for instance, a great rustic?—a character so incurably characteristic that he seemed to break through all canons about cleverness or stupidity; we do not know whether he is an enormous idiot or an enormous philosopher; we know only that he is enormous, like a hill. These great, grotesque characters are almost entirely to be found where Dickens found them—among the poorer classes. The gentry only attain this greatness by going slightly mad. But who has not known an unfathomably personal old nurse? Who has not known an abysmal butler? The truth is that our public life consists almost exclusively of small men. Our public men are small because they have to prove that they are in the common-place interpretation clever, because they have to pass examinations, to learn codes of manners, to imitate a fixed type. It is in private life that we find the great characters. They are too great to get into the public world. It is easier for a camel to pass through the eye of a needle than for a great man to enter into the kingdoms of the earth. The truly great and gorgeous personality, he who talks as no one else could talk and feels with an elementary fire, you will never find this man on any cabinet bench, in any literary circle, at any society dinner. Least of all will you find him in artistic society; he is utterly unknown in Bohemia. He is more than clever, he is amusing. He is more than successful, he is alive. You will find him stranded here and there in all sorts of unknown positions, almost always in unsuccessful positions. You will find him adrift as an impecunious commercial traveller like Micawber. You will find him but one of a batch of silly clerks, like Swiveller. You will find him as an unsuccessful actor, like Crummles. You will find him as an unsuccessful doctor, like Sawyer. But you will always find this rich and reeking personality where Dickens found it—among the poor. For the glory of this world is a very small and priggish affair, and these men are too large to get in line with it. They are too strong to conquer.

It is impossible to do justice to these figures because the essential of them is their multiplicity. The whole point of Dickens is that he not only made them, but made them by myriads; that he stamped his foot, and armies came out of the earth. But let us, for the sake of showing the true Dickens method, take one of them, a very sublime one, Toots. It affords a good example of the real work of Dickens, which was the revealing of a certain grotesque greatness inside an obscure and even unattractive type. It reveals the great paradox of all spiritual things; that the inside is always larger than the outside.

Toots is a type that we all know as well as we know chimney-pots. And of all conceivable human figures he is apparently the most futile and the most dull. He is the blockhead who hangs on at a private school, overgrown and underdeveloped. He is always backward in his lessons, but forward in certain cheap ways of the world; he can smoke before he can spell. Toots is a perfect and pungent picture of the wretched youth. Toots has, as this youth always has, a little money of his own; enough to waste in a semi-dissipation, he does not enjoy, and in a gaping regard for sports, in which he could not possibly excel. Toots has, as this youth always has, bits of surreptitious finery, in his case the incomparable ring. In Toots, above all, is exactly rendered the central and most startling contradiction; the contrast between a jauntiness and a certain impudence of the attire, with the profound shame and sheepishness of the visage and the character. In him, too, is expressed the larger contrasts between the external gaiety of such a lad's occupations, and the infinite, disconsolate sadness of his empty eyes. This is Toots; we know him, we pity him, and we avoid him. Schoolmasters deal with him in despair or in a heartbreaking patience. His family is vague about him. His low-class hangers-on (like the Game Chicken) lead him by the nose. The very parasites that live on him despise him. But Dickens does not despise him. Without denying one of the dreary details which make us avoid the man, Dickens makes him a man whom we long to meet. He does not gloss over one of his dismal deficiencies, but he makes them seem suddenly like violent virtues that we would go to the world's end to see. Without altering one fact he manages to alter the whole atmosphere, the whole universe of Toots. He makes us not only like, but love; not only love, but reverence this little dunce and cad. The power to do this is a power truly and literally to be called divine.

For this is the very wholesome point. Dickens does not alter Toots in any vital point. The thing he does alter is us. He makes us lively where we were bored, kind where we were cruel, and above all, free for an universal human laughter where we were cramped in a small competition about that sad and solemn thing, the intellect. His enthusiasm fills us, as does the love of God, with a glorious shame; after all, he has only found in Toots what we might have found for ourselves. He has only made us as much interested in Toots as Toots is in himself. He does not alter the proportions of Toots; he alters only the scale; we seem as if we were staring at a rat risen to the stature of an elephant. Hitherto we have passed him by; now we feel that nothing could induce us to pass him by; that is the nearest way of putting the truth. He has not been whitewashed in the least; he has not been depicted as any cleverer than he is. He has been turned from a small fool into a great fool. We know Toots is not clever; but we are not inclined to quarrel with Toots because he is not clever. We are more likely to quarrel with cleverness because it is not Toots. All the examinations he could not pass, all the schools he could not enter, all the temporary tests of brain and culture which surrounded him shall pass, and Toots shall remain like a mountain.

It may be noticed that the great artists always choose great fools rather than great intellectuals to embody humanity. Hamlet does express the æsthetic dreams and the bewilderments of the intellect; but Bottom the Weaver expresses them much better. In the same manner Toots expresses certain permanent dignities in human nature more than any of Dickens's more dignified characters can do it. For instance, Toots expresses admirably the enduring fear, which is the very essence of falling in love. When Toots is invited by Florence to come in, when he longs to come in, but still stays out, he is embodying a sort of insane and perverse humility which is elementary in the lover.

There is an apostolic injunction to suffer fools gladly. We always lay the stress on the word suffer, and interpret the passage as one urging resignation. It might be better, perhaps, to lay the stress upon the word gladly, and make our familiarity with fools a delight, and almost a dissipation. Nor is it necessary that our pleasure in fools (or at least in great and godlike fools) should be merely satiric or cruel. The great fool is he in whom we cannot tell which is the conscious and which the unconscious humour; we laugh with him and laugh at him at the same time. An obvious instance is that of ordinary and happy marriage. A man and a woman cannot live together without having against each other a kind of everlasting joke. Each has discovered that the other is a fool, but a great fool. This largeness, this grossness and gorgeousness of folly is the thing which we all find about those with whom we are in intimate contact; and it is the one enduring basis of affection, and even of respect. When we know an individual named Tomkins, we know that he has succeeded where all others have failed: he has succeeded in being Tomkins. Just so Mr. Toots succeeded; he was defeated in all scholastic examinations, but he was the victor in that visionary battle in which unknown competitors vainly tried to be Toots.

If we are to look for lessons, here at least is the last and deepest lesson of Dickens. It is in our own daily life that we are to look for the portents and the prodigies. This is the truth, not merely of the fixed figures of our life; the wife, the husband, the fool that fills the sky. It is true of the whole stream and substance of our daily experience: every instant we reject a great fool merely because he is foolish. Every day we neglect Tootses and Swivellers, Guppys and Joblings, Simmerys and Flashers. Every day we lose the last sight of Jobling and Chuckster, the Analytical Chemist, or the Marchioness. Every day we are missing a monster whom we might easily love, and an imbecile whom we should certainly admire. This is the real gospel of Dickens; the inexhaustible opportunities offered by the liberty and the variety of man. Compared with this life, all public life, all fame, all wisdom, is by its nature cramped and cold and small. For on that defined and lighted public stage men are of necessity forced to profess one set of accomplishments, to rise to one rigid standard. It is the utterly unknown people, who can grow in all directions like an exuberant tree. It is in our interior lives that we find that people are too much themselves. It is in our private life that we find people intolerably individual, that we find them swelling into the enormous contours, and taking on the colours of caricature. Many of us live publicly with featureless public puppets, images of the small public abstractions. It is when we pass our own private gate, and open our own secret door, that we step into the land of the giants.

CHAPTER XI

ON THE ALLEGED OPTIMISM OF DICKENS

In one of the plays of the decadent period, an intellectual expressed the atmosphere of his epoch by referring to Dickens as " a vulgar optimist." I have in a previous chapter suggested something of the real strangeness of such a term. After all, the main matter of astonishment (or rather of admiration) is that optimism should be vulgar. In a world in which physical distress is almost the common lot, we actually complain that happiness is too common. In a world in which the majority is physically miserable we actually complain of the sameness of praise; we are bored with the abundance of approval. When we consider what the conditions of the vulgar really are, it is difficult to imagine a stranger or more splendid tribute to humanity than such a phrase as vulgar optimism. It is as if one spoke of " vulgar martyrdom " or " common crucifixion."

First, however, let it be said frankly that there is a foundation for the charge against Dickens which is implied in the phrase about vulgar optimism. It does not concern itself with Dickens's confidence in the value of existence and the intrinsic victory of virtue; that is not optimism but religion. It is not concerned with his habit of making bright occasions bright, and happy stories happy; that is not optimism, but literature. Nor is it concerned even with his peculiar genius for the description of an almost bloated joviality; that is not optimism, it is simply Dickens. With all these higher variations of optimism I deal elsewhere. But over and above all these there is a real sense in which Dickens laid himself open to the accusation of vulgar optimism, and I desire to put the admission of this first, before the discussion that follows. Dickens did have a disposition to make his characters at all costs happy, or, to speak more strictly, he had a disposition to make them comfortable rather than happy. He had a sort of literary hospitality; he too often treated his characters as if they were his guests. From a host is always expected, and always ought to be expected as long as human civilization is healthy, a strictly physical benevolence, if you will, a kind of coarse benevolence. Food and fire and such things should always be the symbols of the man entertaining men; because they are the things which all men beyond question have in common.

But something more than this is needed from the man who is imagining and making men, the artist, the man who is not receiving men, but rather sending them forth.

As I shall remark in a moment in the matter of the Dickens villains, it is not true that he made every one thus at home. But he did do it to a certain wide class of incongruous characters; he did it to all who had been in any way unfortunate. It had indeed its origin (a very beautiful origin) in his realization of how much a little pleasure was to such people. He knew well that the greatest happiness that has been known since Eden is the happiness of the unhappy. So far he is admirable. And as long as he was describing the ecstasy of the poor, the borderland between pain and pleasure, he was at his highest. Nothing that has ever been written about human delights, no Earthly Paradise, no Utopia has ever come so near the quick nerve of happiness as his descriptions of the rare extravagances of the poor; such an admirable description, for instance, as that of Kit Nubbles taking his family to the theatre. For he seizes on the real source of the whole pleasure; a holy fear. Kit tells the waiter to bring the beer. "And the waiter, instead of saying, 'Did you address that language to me?' only said, 'Pot of beer, sir; yes, sir.' " That internal and quivering humility of Kit is the only way to enjoy life or banquets; and the fear of the waiter is the beginning of dining. People in this mood "take their pleasures sadly"; which is the only way of taking them at all.

So far Dickens is supremely right. As long as he was dealing with such penury and such festivity his touch was almost invariably sure. But when he came to more difficult cases, to people who for one reason or another could not be cured with one good dinner, he did develop this other evil, this genuinely vulgar optimism of which I speak. And the mark of it is this: that he gave the characters a comfort that had no especial connection with themselves; he threw comfort at them like alms. There are cases at the end of his stories in which his kindness to his characters is a careless and insolent kindness. He loses his real charity and adopts the charity of the Charity Organization Society; the charity that is not kind, the charity that is puffed up, and that does behave itself unseemly. At the end of some of his stories he deals out his characters a kind of out-door relief.

I will give two instances. The whole meaning of the character of Mr. Micawber is that a man can be always almost rich by constantly expecting riches. The lesson is a really important one in our sweeping modern sociology. We talk of the man whose life is a failure; but Micawber's life never is a failure, because it is always a crisis. We think constantly of the man who if he looked back would see that his existence was unsuccessful; but Micawber never does look back; he always looks forward, because the bailiff is coming to-morrow. You cannot say he is defeated, for his absurd battle never ends; he cannot despair of life, for he is so much occupied in living. All this is of immense importance in the understanding of the poor; it is worth all the slum novelists that ever insulted democracy. But how did it happen, how could it happen, that the man who created this Micawber could pension him off at the end of the story and make him a successful colonial mayor? Micawber never did succeed, never ought to succeed; his kingdom is not of this world. But this is an excellent instance of Dickens's disposition to make his characters grossly and incongruously comfortable. There is another instance in the same book. Dora, the first wife of David Copperfield, is a very genuine and amusing figure; she has certainly far more force of character than Agnes. She represents the infinite and divine irrationality of the human heart. What possessed Dickens to make her such a dehumanized prig as to recommend her husband to marry another woman? One could easily respect a husband who after time and development made such a marriage, but surely not a wife who desired it. If Dora had died hating Agnes we should know that everything was right, and that God would reconcile the irreconcilable. When Dora dies recommending Agnes we know that everything is wrong, at least if hypocrisy and artificiality and moral vulgarity are wrong. There, again, Dickens yields to a mere desire to give comfort. He wishes to pile up pillows round Dora; and he smothers her with them, like Othello.

This is the real vulgar optimism of Dickens; it does exist, and I have deliberately put it first. Let us admit that Dickens's mind was far too much filled with pictures of satisfaction and cosiness and repose. Let us admit that he thought principally of the pleasures of the oppressed classes; let us admit that it hardly cost him any artistic pang to make out human beings as much happier than they are. Let us admit all this, and a curious fact remains.

For it was this too easily contented Dickens, this man with cushions at his back and (it sometimes seems) cotton wool in his ears, it was this happy dreamer, this vulgar optimist who alone of modern writers did really destroy some of the wrongs he hated and bring about some of the reforms he desired. Dickens did help to pull down the debtors' prisons; and if he was too much of an optimist he was quite enough of a destroyer. Dickens did drive Squeers out of his Yorkshire den; and if Dickens was too contented, it was more than Squeers was. Dickens did leave his mark on parochialism, on nursing, on funerals, on public executions, on workhouses, on the Court of Chancery. These things were altered; they are different. It may be that such reforms are not adequate remedies; that is another question altogether. The next sociologists may think these old Radical reforms quite narrow or accidental. But such as they were, the old radicals got them done; and the new sociologists cannot get anything done at all. And in the practical doing of them Dickens played a solid and quite demonstrable part; that is the plain matter that concerns us here. If Dickens was an optimist he was an uncommonly active and useful kind of optimist. If Dickens was a sentimentalist he was a very practical sentimentalist.

And the reason of this is one that goes deep

into Dickens's social reform, and like every other real and desirable thing, involves a kind of mystical contradiction. If we are to save the oppressed, we must have two apparently antagonistic emotions in us at the same time. We must think the oppressed man intensely miserable, and, at the same time, intensely attractive and important. We must insist with violence upon his degradation; we must insist with the same violence upon his dignity. For if we relax by one inch the one assertion, men will say he does not need saving. And if we relax by one inch the other assertion, men will say he is not worth saving. The optimists will say that reform is needless. The pessimists will say that reform is hopeless. We must apply both simultaneously to the same oppressed man; we must say that he is a worm and a god; and we must thus lay ourselves open to the accusation (or the compliment) of transcendentalism. This is, indeed, the strongest argument for the religious conception of life. If the dignity of man is an earthly dignity we shall be tempted to deny his earthly degradation. If it is a heavenly dignity we can admit the earthly degradation with all the candour of Zola. If we are idealists about the other world we can be realists about this world. But that is not here the point. What is quite evident is that if a logical praise of the poor man is pushed too far, and if a logical distress about him is pushed too far, either will involve wreckage to the central paradox of reform. If the poor man is made too admirable he ceases to be pitiable; if the poor man is made too pitiable he becomes merely contemptible. There is a school of smug optimists who will deny that he is a poor man. There is a school of scientific pessimists who will deny that he is a man.

Out of this perennial contradiction arises the fact that there are always two types of the reformer. The first we may call for convenience the pessimistic, the second the optimistic reformer. One dwells upon the fact that souls are being lost; the other dwells upon the fact that they are worth saving. Both, of course, are (so far as that is concerned) quite right, but they naturally tend to a difference of method, and sometimes to a difference of perception. The pessimistic reformer points out the good elements that oppression has destroyed; the optimistic reformer, with an even fiercer joy, points out the good elements that it has not destroyed. It is the case for the first reformer that slavery has made men slavish. It is the case for the second reformer that slavery has not made men slavish. The first describes how bad men are under bad conditions. The second describes how good men are under bad conditions. Of the first class of writers, for instance, is Gorky. Of the second class of writers is Dickens.

But here we must register a real and somewhat startling fact. In the face of all apparent probability, it is certainly true that the optimistic reformer reforms much more completely than the pessimistic reformer. People produce violent changes by being contented, by being far too contented. The man who said that revolutions are not made with rose-water was obviously inexperienced in practical human affairs. Men like Rousseau and Shelley do make revolutions, and do make them with rose-water; that is, with a too rosy and sentimental view of human goodness. Figures that come before and create convulsion and change (for instance, the central figure of the New Testament) always have the air of walking in an unnatural sweetness and calm. They give us their peace ultimately in blood and battle and division; not as the world giveth give they unto us.

Nor is the real reason of the triumph of the too-contented reformer particularly difficult to define. He triumphs because he keeps alive in the human soul an invincible sense of the thing being worth doing, of the war being worth winning, of the people being worth their deliverance. I remember that Mr. William Archer, some time ago, published in his interesting series of interviews, an interview with Mr. Thomas Hardy. That powerful writer was represented as saying, in the course of the conversation, that he did not wish at the particular moment to define his position with regard to the ultimate problem of whether life itself was worth living. There are, he said, hundreds of remediable evils in this world. When we have remedied all these (such was his argument), it will be time enough to ask whether existence itself under its best possible conditions is valuable or desirable. Here we have presented, with a considerable element of what can only be called unconscious humour, the plain reason of the failure of the pessimist as a reformer. Mr. Hardy is asking us, I will not say to buy a pig in a poke; he is asking us to buy a poke on the remote chance of there being a pig in it. When we have for some few frantic centuries tortured ourselves to save mankind, it will then be "time enough" to discuss whether they can possibly be saved. When, in the case of infant mortality, for example, we have exhausted ourselves with the earth-shaking efforts required to save the life of every individual baby, it will then be time enough to consider whether every individual baby would not have been happier dead. We are to remove mountains and bring the millennium, because then we can have a quiet moment to discuss whether the millennium is at all desirable. Here we have the low-water mark of the impotence of the sad reformer. And here we have the reason of the paradoxical triumph of the happy one. His triumph is a religious triumph; it rests upon his perpetual assertion of the value of the human soul and of human daily life. It rests upon his assertion that human life is enjoyable because it is human. And he will never admit, like so many compassionate pessimists, that human life ever ceases to be human. He does not merely pity the lowness of men; he feels an insult to their elevation. Brute pity should be given only to the brutes. Cruelty to animals is cruelty and a vile thing; but cruelty to a man is not cruelty, it is treason. Tyranny over a man is not tyranny, it is rebellion, for man is loyal. Now, the practical weakness of the vast mass of modern pity for the poor and the oppressed is precisely that it is merely pity; the pity is pitiful, but not respectful. Men feel that the cruelty to the poor is a kind of cruelty to animals. They never feel that it is injustice to equals; nay, it is treachery to comrades.

This dark, scientific pity, this brutal pity, has an elemental sincerity of its own; but it is entirely useless for all ends of social reform. Democracy swept Europe with the sabre when it was founded upon the Rights of Man. It has done literally nothing at all since it has been founded only upon the wrongs of man. Or, more strictly speaking, its recent failures have been due to its not admitting the existence of any rights or wrongs, or indeed of any humanity. Evolution (the sinister enemy of revolution) does not especially deny the existence of God; what it does deny is the existence of man. And all the despair about the poor, and the cold and repugnant pity for them, has been largely due to the vague sense that they have literally relapsed into the state of the lower animals.

A writer sufficiently typical of recent revolutionism—Gorky—has called one of his books by the eerie and effective title "Creatures that Once were Men." That title explains the whole failure of the Russian revolution. And the reason why the English writers, such as Dickens, did with all their limitations achieve so many of the actual things at which they aimed, was that they could not possibly have put such a title upon a human book. Dickens really helped the unfortunate in the matters to which he set himself. And the reason is that across all his books and sketches about the unfortunate might be written the common title, " Creatures that Still are Men."

There does exist, then, this strange optimistic reformer; the man whose work begins with approval and yet ends with earthquake. Jesus Christ was destined to found a faith which made the rich poorer and the poor richer; but even when He was going to enrich them, He began with the phrase, " Blessed are the poor." The Gissings and the Gorkys say, as an universal literary motto, " Cursed are the poor." Among a million who have faintly followed Christ in this divine contradiction, Dickens stands out especially. He said, in all his reforming utterances, " Cure poverty "; but he said in all his actual descriptions, " Blessed are the poor." He described their happiness, and men rushed to remove their sorrow. He described them as human, and men resented the insults to their humanity. It is not difficult to see why, as I said at an earlier stage of this book, Dickens's denunciations have had so much more practical an effect than the denunciations of such a man as Gissing. Both agreed that the souls of the people were in a kind of prison. But Gissing said that the prison was full of dead souls. Dickens said that the prison was full of living souls. And the fiery cavalcade of rescuers felt that they had not come too late.

Of this general fact about Dickens's descriptions of poverty there will not, I suppose, be any serious dispute. The dispute will only be about the truth of those descriptions. It is clear that whereas Gissing would say, " See how their poverty depresses the Smiths or the Browns," Dickens says, " See how little, after all, their poverty can depress the Cratchits." No one will deny that he made a special feature a special study of the subject of the festivity of the poor. We will come to the discussion of the veracity of these scenes in a moment. It is here sufficient to register in conclusion of our examination of the reforming optimist, that Dickens certainly was such an optimist, and that he made it his business to insist upon what happiness there is in the lives of the unhappy. His poor man is always a Mark Tapley, a man the optimism of whose spirit increases if anything with the pessimism of his experience. It can also be registered as a fact equally solid and quite equally demonstrable that this optimistic Dickens did effect great reforms.

The reforms in which Dickens was instrumental were, indeed, from the point of view of our sweeping, social panaceas, special and limited. But perhaps, for that reason especially, they afford a compact and concrete instance of the psychological paradox of which we speak. Dickens did definitely destroy—or at the very least help to destroy—certain institutions; he destroyed those institutions simply by describing them. But the crux and peculiarity of the whole matter is this, that, in a sense, it can really be said that he described these things too optimistically. In a real sense, he described Dotheboys Hall as a better place than it is. In a real sense, he made out the workhouse as a pleasanter place than it can ever be. For the chief glory of Dickens is that he made these places interesting; and the chief infamy of England is that it has made these places dull. Dulness was the one thing that Dickens's genius could never succeed in describing; his vitality was so violent that he could not introduce into his books the genuine impression even of a moment of monotony. If there is anywhere in his novels an instant of silence, we only hear more clearly the hero whispering with the heroine, the villain sharpening his dagger, or the creaking of the machinery that is to give out the god from the machine. He could splendidly describe gloomy places, but he could not describe dreary places. He could describe miserable marriages, but not monotonous marriages. It must have been genuinely entertaining to be married to Mr. Quilp. This sense of a still incessant excitement he spreads over every inch of his story, and over every dark tract of his landscape. His idea of a desolate place is a place where anything can happen; he has no idea of that desolate place where nothing can happen. This is a good thing for his soul, for the place where nothing can happen is hell. But still, it might reasonably be maintained by the modern mind that he is hampered in describing human evil and sorrow by this inability to imagine tedium, this dulness in the matter of dulness. For, after all, it is certainly true that the worst part of the lot of the unfortunate is the fact that they have long spaces in which to review the irrevocability of their doom. It is certainly true that the worst days of the oppressed man are the nine days out of ten in which he is not oppressed. This sense of sickness, and sameness Dickens did certainly fail or refuse to give. When we read such a description as that excellent one—in detail—of Dotheboys Hall, we feel that, while everything else is accurate, the author does, in the words of the excellent Captain Nares in Stevenson's "Wrecker," "draw the dreariness rather mild." The boys at Dotheboys were, perhaps, less bullied, but they were certainly more bored. For, indeed, how could any one be bored with the society of so sumptuous a creature as Mr. Squeers? Who would not put up with a few illogical floggings in order to enjoy the conversation of a man who could say, "She's a rum 'un, is Natur'. . . . Natur' is more easier conceived than described"? The same principle applies to the workhouse in "Oliver Twist." We feel vaguely that neither Oliver nor any one else could be entirely unhappy in the presence of the purple personality of Mr. Bumble. The one thing he did not describe in any of the abuses he denounced was the soul-destroying potency of routine. He made out the bad school, the bad parochial system, the bad debtors' prison as very much jollier and more exciting than they may really have been. In a sense, then, he flattered them; but he destroyed them with the flattery. By making Mrs. Gamp delightful he made her impossible. He gave every one an interest in Mr. Bumble's existence; and by the same act gave every one an interest in his destruction. It would be difficult to find a stronger instance of the utility and energy of the method which we have, for the sake of argument, called the method of the optimistic reformer. As long as low Yorkshire schools were entirely colourless and dreary, they continued quietly tolerated by the public, and quietly intolerable to the victims. So long as Squeers was dull as well as cruel he was permitted; the moment he became amusing as well as cruel he was destroyed. As long as Bumble was merely inhuman he was allowed. When he became human, humanity wiped him out. For in order to do these great acts of justice we must always realize not only the humanity of the oppressed, but even the humanity of the oppressor. The satirist had, in a sense, to create the images in the mind before, as an iconoclast, he could destroy them. Dickens had to make Squeers live before he could make him die.

In connection with the accusation of vulgar optimism, which I have taken as a text for this chapter, there is another somewhat odd thing to notice. Nobody in the world was ever less optimistic than Dickens in his treatment of evil or the evil man. When I say optimistic in this matter I mean optimism, in the modern sense, of an attempt to whitewash evil. Nobody ever made less attempt to whitewash evil than Dickens. Nobody black was ever less white than Dickens's black. He painted his villains and lost characters more black than they really are. He crowds his stories with a kind of villain rare in modern fiction—the villain really without any "redeeming point."

There is no redeeming point in Squeers, or in Monck, or in Ralph Nickleby, or in Bill Sikes, or in Quilp, or in Brass, or in Mr. Chester, or in Mr. Pecksniff, or in Jonas Chuzzlewit, or in Carker, or in Uriah Heep, or in Blandois, or in a hundred more. So far as the balance of good and evil in human characters is concerned, Dickens certainly could not be called a vulgar optimist. His emphasis on evil was melodramatic. He might be called a vulgar pessimist.

Some will dismiss this lurid villainy as a detail of his artificial romance. I am not inclined to do so. He inherited, undoubtedly, this unqualified villain as he inherited so many other things, from the whole history of European literature. But he breathed into the blackguard a peculiar and vigorous life of his own. He did not show any tendency to modify his blackguardism in accordance with the increasing considerateness of the age; he did not seem to wish to make his villain less villainous; he did not wish to imitate the analysis of George Eliot, or the reverent scepticism of Thackeray. And all this works back, I think, to a real thing in him, that he wished to have an obstreperous and incalculable enemy. He wished to keep alive the idea of combat, which means, of necessity, a combat against something individual and alive. I do not know whether, in the kindly rationalism of his epoch, he kept any belief in a personal devil in his theology, but he certainly created a personal devil in every one of his books.

A good example of my meaning can be found, for instance, in such a character as Quilp. Dickens may, for all I know, have had originally some idea of describing Quilp as the bitter and unhappy cripple, a deformity whose mind is stunted along with his body. But if he had such an idea, he soon abandoned it. Quilp is not in the least unhappy. His whole picturesqueness consists in the fact that he has a kind of hellish happiness, an atrocious hilarity that makes him go bounding about like an indiarubber ball. Quilp is not in the least bitter; he has an unaffected gaiety, an expansiveness, an universality. He desires to hurt people in the same hearty way that a good-natured man desires to help them. He likes to poison people with the same kind of clamorous camaraderie with which an honest man likes to stand them drink. Quilp is not in the least stunted in mind; he is not in reality even stunted in body—his body, that is, does not in any way fall short of what he wants it to do. His smallness gives him rather the promptitude of a bird or the precipitance of a bullet. In a word, Quilp is precisely the devil of the Middle Ages; he belongs to that amazingly healthy period when even the lost spirits were hilarious.

This heartiness and vivacity in the villains of Dickens is worthy of note because it is directly connected with his own cheerfulness. This is a truth little understood in our time, but it is a very essential one. If optimism means a general approval, it is certainly true that the more a man becomes an optimist the more he becomes a melancholy man. If he manages to praise everything, his praise will develop an alarming resemblance to a polite boredom. He will say that the marsh is as good as the garden; he will mean that the garden is as dull as the marsh. He may force himself to say that emptiness is good, but he will hardly prevent himself from asking what is the good of such good. This optimism does exist—this optimism which is more hopeless than pessimism—this optimism which is the very heart of hell. Against such an aching vacuum of joyless approval there is only one antidote—a sudden and pugnacious belief in positive evil. This world can be made beautiful again by beholding it as a battlefield. When we have defined and isolated the evil thing, the colours come back into everything else. When evil things have become evil, good things, in a blazing apocalypse, become good. There are some men who are dreary because they do not believe in God; but there are many others who are dreary because they do not believe in the devil. The grass grows green again when we believe in the devil, the roses grow red again when we believe in the devil.

No man was more filled with the sense of this bellicose basis of all cheerfulness than Dickens. He knew very well the essential truth, that the true optimist can only continue an optimist so long as he is discontented. For the full value of this life can only be got by fighting; the violent take it by storm. And if we have accepted everything, we have missed something—war. This life of ours is a very enjoyable fight, but a very miserable truce. And it appears strange to me that so few critics of Dickens or of other romantic writers have noticed this philosophical meaning in the undiluted villain. The villain is not in the story to be a character; he is there to be a danger—a ceaseless, ruthless, and uncompromising menace, like that of wild beasts or the sea. For the full satisfaction of the sense of combat, which everywhere and always involves a sense of equality, it is necessary to make the evil thing a man; but it is not always necessary, it is not even always artistic, to make him a mixed and probable man. In any tale, the tone of which is at all symbolic, he may quite legitimately be made an aboriginal and infernal energy. He must be a man only in the sense that he must have a wit and will to be matched with the wit and will of the man chiefly fighting. The evil may be inhuman, but it must not be impersonal, which is almost exactly the position occupied by Satan in the theological scheme.

But when all is said, as I have remarked before, the chief fountain in Dickens of what I have called cheerfulness, and some prefer to call optimism, is something deeper than a verbal philosophy. It is, after all, an incomparable hunger and pleasure for the vitality and the variety, for the infinite eccentricity of existence. And this word "eccentricity" brings us, perhaps, nearer to the matter than any other. It is, perhaps, the strongest mark of the divinity of man that he talks of this world as "a strange world," though he has seen no other. We feel that all there is is eccentric, though we do not know what is the centre. This sentiment of the grotesqueness of the universe ran through Dickens's brain and body like the mad blood of the elves. He saw all his streets in fantastic perspectives, he saw all his cockney villas as top heavy and wild, he saw every man's nose twice as big as it was, and every man's eyes like saucers. And this was the basis of his gaiety—the only real basis of any philosophical gaiety. This world is not to be justified as it is justified by the mechanical optimists; it is not to be justified as the best of all possible worlds. Its merit is not that it is orderly and explicable; its merit is that it is wild and utterly unexplained. Its merit is precisely that none of us could have conceived such a thing, that we should have rejected the bare idea of it as miracle and unreason. It is the best of all impossible worlds.

CHAPTER XII

A NOTE ON THE FUTURE OF DICKENS

THE hardest thing to remember about our own time, of course, is simply that it is a time; we all instinctively think of it as the Day of Judgment. But all the things in it which belong to it merely as this time will probably be rapidly turned upside down; all the things that can pass will pass. It is not merely true that all old things are already dead; it is also true that all new things are already dead; for the only undying things are the things that are neither new nor old. The more you are up with this year's fashion, the more (in a sense) you are already behind next year's. Consequently, in attempting to decide whether an author will, as it is cantly expressed, live, it is necessary to have very firm convictions about what part, if any part, of man is unchangeable. And it is very hard to have this if you have not a religion; or, at least, a dogmatic philosophy.

The equality of men needs preaching quite as much as regards the ages as regards the classes of men. To feel infinitely superior to a man in the twelfth century is just precisely as snobbish as to feel infinitely superior to a man in the Old Kent Road. There are differences between the man and us, there may be superiorities in us over the man; but our sin in both cases consists in thinking of the small things wherein we differ when we ought to be confounded and intoxicated by the terrible and joyful matters in which we are at one. But here again the difficulty always is that the things near us seem larger than they are, and so seem to be a permanent part of mankind, when they may really be only one of its parting modes of expression. Few people, for instance, realize that a time may easily come when we shall see the great outburst of Science in the nineteenth century as something quite as splendid, brief, unique, and ultimately abandoned, as the outburst of Art at the Renascence. Few people realize that the general habit of fiction, of telling tales in prose, may fade, like the general habit of the ballad, of telling tales in verse, has for the time faded. Few people realize that reading and writing are only arbitrary, and perhaps temporary sciences, like heraldry.

The immortal mind will remain, and by that writers like Dickens will be securely judged. That Dickens will have a high place in permanent literature there is, I imagine, no prig surviving to deny. But though all prediction is in the dark, I would devote this chapter to suggesting that his place in nineteenth century England will not only be high, but altogether the highest. At a certain period of his contemporary fame, an average Englishman would have said that there were at that moment in England about five or six able and equal novelists. He could have made a list, Dickens, Bulwer-Lytton, Thackeray, Charlotte Brontë, George Eliot, perhaps more. Forty years or more have passed and some of them have slipped to a lower place. Some would now say that the highest platform is left to Thackeray and Dickens; some to Dickens, Thackeray, and George Eliot; some to Dickens, Thackeray, and Charlotte Brontë. I venture to offer the proposition that when more years have passed and more weeding has been effected, Dickens will dominate the whole England of the nineteenth century; he will be left on that platform alone.

I know that this is an almost impertinent thing to assert, and that its tendency is to bring in those disparaging discussions of other writers in which Mr. Swinburne brilliantly embroiled himself in his suggestive study of Dickens. But my disparagement of the other English novelists is wholly relative and not in the least positive. It is certain that men will always return to such a writer as Thackeray, with his rich emotional autumn, his feeling that life is a sad but sacred retrospect, in which at least we should forget nothing. It is not likely that wise men will forget him. So, for instance, wise and scholarly men do from time to time return to the lyrists of the French Renascence, to the delicate poignancy of Du Bellay: so they will go back to Thackeray. But I mean that Dickens will bestride and dominate our time as the vast figure of Rabelais dominates Du Bellay, dominates the Renascence and the world.

Yet we put a negative reason first. The particular things for which Dickens is condemned (and justly condemned) by his critics, are precisely those things which have never prevented a man from being immortal. The chief of them is the unquestionable fact that he wrote an enormous amount of bad work. This does lead to a man being put below his place in his own time: it does not affect his permanent place, to all appearance, at all. Shakespeare, for instance, and Wordsworth wrote not only an enormous amount of bad work, but an enormous amount of enormously bad work. Humanity edits such writers' works for them. Virgil was mistaken in cutting out his inferior lines; we would have undertaken the job. Moreover in the particular case of Dickens there are special reasons for regarding his bad work as in some sense irrelevant. So much of it was written, as I have previously suggested, under a kind of general ambition that had nothing to do with his special genius; an ambition to be a public provider of everything, a warehouse of all human emotions. He held a kind of literary day of judgment. He distributed bad characters as punishments and good characters as rewards. My meaning can be best conveyed by one instance out of many. The character of the kind old Jew in "Our Mutual Friend" (a needless and unconvincing character) was actually introduced because some Jewish correspondent complains that the bad old Jew in "Oliver Twist" conveyed the suggestion that all Jews were bad. The principle is so lightheadedly absurd that it is hard to imagine any literary man submitting to it for an instant. If ever he invented a bad auctioneer he must immediately balance him with a good auctioneer; if he should have conceived an unkind philanthropist, he must on the spot, with whatever natural agony and toil, imagine a kind philanthropist. The complaint is frantic; yet Dickens, who tore people in pieces for much fairer complaints, liked this complaint of his Jewish correspondent. It pleased him to be mistaken for a public arbiter: it pleased him to be asked (in a double sense) to judge Israel. All this is so much another thing, a non-literary vanity, that there is much less difficulty than usual in separating it from his serious genius: and by his serious genius, I need hardly say, I mean his comic genius. Such irrelevant ambitions as this are easily passed over, like the sonnets of great statesmen. We feel that such things can be set aside, as the ignorant experiments of men otherwise great, like the politics of Professor Tyndall or the philosophy of Professor Haeckel. Hence, I think, posterity will not care that Dickens has done bad work, but will know that he has done good.

Again, the other chief accusation against Dickens was that his characters and their actions were exaggerated and impossible. But this only meant that they were exaggerated and impossible as compared with the modern world and with certain writers (like Thackeray or Trollope) who were making a very exact copy of the manners of the modern world. Some people, oddly enough have suggested that Dickens has suffered or will suffer from the change of manners. Surely this is irrational. It is not the creators of the impossible who will suffer from the process of time: Mr. Bunsby can never be any more impossible than he was when Dickens made him. The writers who will obviously suffer from time will be the careful and realistic writers; the writers who have observed every detail of the fashion of this world which passeth away. It is surely obvious that there is nothing so fragile as a fact, that a fact flies away quicker than a fancy. A fancy will endure for two thousand years. For instance, we all have fancy for an entirely fearless man, a hero: and the Achilles of Homer still remains. But exactly the thing we do not know about Achilles is how far he was possible. The realistic narrators of the time are all forgotten (thank God); so we cannot tell whether Homer slightly exaggerated or wildly exaggerated or did not exaggerate at all, the personal activity of a Mycenæan captain in battle: for the fancy has survived the facts. So the fancy of Podsnap may survive the facts of English commerce: and no one will know whether Podsnap was possible, but only know that he is desirable, like Achilles.

The positive argument for the permanence of Dickens comes back to the thing that can only be stated and cannot be discussed: creation. He made things which nobody else could possibly make. He made Dick Swiveller in a very different sense to that in which Thackeray made Colonel Newcome. Thackeray's creation was observation: Dickens's was poetry, and is therefore permanent. But there is one other test that can be added. The immortal writer, I conceive, is commonly he who does something universal in a special manner. I mean that he does something interesting to all men in a way in which only one man or one land can do. Other men in that land, who do only what other men in other lands are doing as well, tend to have a great reputation in their day and to sink slowly into a second or a third or a fourth place. A parallel from war will make the point clearer. I cannot think that any one will doubt that, although Wellington and Nelson were always bracketed, Nelson will steadily become more important and Wellington less. For the fame of Wellington rests upon the fact that he was a good soldier in the service of England, exactly as twenty similar men were good soldiers in the service of Austria or Prussia or France. But Nelson is the symbol of a special mode of attack, which is at once universal and yet specially English, the sea. Now Dickens is at once as universal as the sea and as English as Nelson. Thackeray and George Eliot and the other great figures of that great

England, were comparable to Wellington in this, that the kind of thing they were doing,—realism, the acute study of intellectual things, numerous men in France, Germany, and Italy were doing as well or better than they. But Dickens was really doing something universal, yet something that no one but an Englishman could do. This is attested by the fact that he and Byron are the men who, like pinnacles, strike the eye of the continent. The points would take long to study: yet they may take only a moment to indicate. No one but an Englishman could have filled his books at once with a furious caricature and with a positively furious kindness. In more central countries, full of cruel memories of political change, caricature is always inhumane. No one but an Englishman could have described the democracy as consisting of free men, but yet of funny men. In other countries where the democratic issue has been more bitterly fought, it is felt that unless you describe a man as dignified you are describing him as a slave. This is the only final greatness of a man; that he does for all the world what all the world cannot do for itself. Dickens, I believe, did it.

The hour of absinthe is over. We shall not be much further troubled with the little artists who found Dickens too sane for their sorrows and too clean for their delights. But we have a long way to travel before we get back to what Dickens meant: and the passage is along a rambling English road, a twisting road such as Mr. Pickwick travelled. But this at least is part of what he meant; that comradeship and serious joy are not interludes in our travel; but that rather our travels are interludes in comradeship and joy, which through God shall endure for ever. The inn does not point to the road; the road points to the inn. And all roads point at last to an ultimate inn, where we shall meet Dickens and all his characters: and when we drink again it shall be from the great flagons in the tavern at the end of the world.

THE END

Printed in the United States
134597LV00003B/98/A

9 781432 610432

Preface

Considering the size of the word, sex is a big topic. It is said, and I have no reason to disbelieve it, that men think about sex every nine minutes. Judging by the letters to Carlton's *The Good Sex Guide Late,* this seems a gross underestimation. Over 80 per cent of the letters were from men. What became very obvious was the amount of confusion out there when it came to sex. Some of the letters were funny, many were sad and each was unique. Even though there was often a common theme running through them, every person had their own interpretation. Working with Toyah Wilcox, Suzie Hayman and Christine Webber reassured me that empathy and understanding are not confined to a doctor's surgery. The fact that so many people – Carlton received over two hundred letters per week – chose to write to a television programme rather than see their own doctor has a message for the medical profession. If the sheer volume of mail is anything to go by, we are not training our doctors adequately to handle psychosexual problems. This is a shame. Sex is a fundamental part of our existence. If a patient has sufficient trust in their doctor to talk about their innermost sexual frustrations and problems, they will rate very highly any other medical advice offered.

What is particularly wonderful about these letters is their inherent honesty. Our answers might not always have been the most useful contribution to pyschosexual medicine but at least they were empathic. Human situations are rarely totally devoid of humour, as is evident from these letters, and fun was the cornerstone of the programme, which had to entertain as well as inform. The laughter was never directed at the people who had the courage to write in but rather at the way we treat sexual matters. Sex requires a sense of humour at the best of times; when things are not going quite so well, it really helps to be able to laugh. There are bits of ourselves in these letters. We are allowed to laugh at ourselves occasionally.

In search of the Big O

with apologies to David Devlin and Christine Webber

Nothing is better guaranteed to generate letters than the orgasm. What it is, how you have one, how many is normal and how to pronounce it are constant themes in my mail. Part of the interest is artificial and in direct response to media portrayal of sex. But at the end of the day, and they usually are, orgasms are nice things to have around the house – or anywhere else for that matter. Most letters fall into two camps: too little and too much. While one load of people are driven crazy trying to have even one, another lot are worrying in case they are abnormal having so many.

Somewhere in the middle there are people who couldn't care less. One thing is certain, orgasms are big business. Aphrodisia has been around for a long time despite little or no evidence that such potions exist. Rhinos are keen to stress this point. Three thousand years ago the Chinese emperor Chou Hsin was faced with impotence. Bad news for anyone, but this guy would balance a naked woman on his erect penis for the entertainment of his court. To restore his prowess he resorted to an aphrodisiac containing rhino tusk. Bad news for rhinos. Worse news for naked women doing their act as balancing plates, as rhino horn doesn't work – a fact self-evident by the near-extinction of the species.

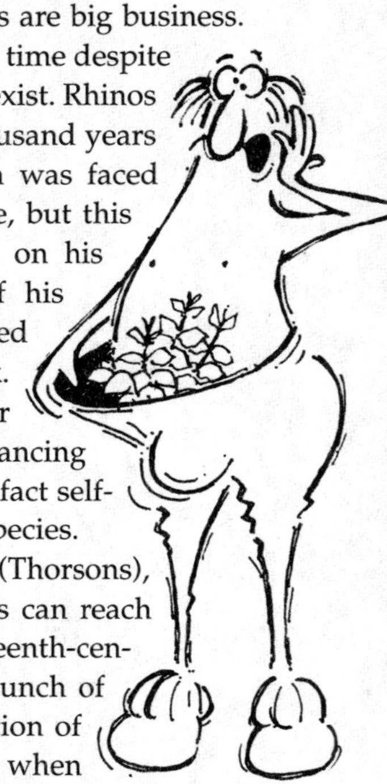

In her book *A to Z of Aphrodisia* (Thorsons), Diana Warburton reckons even nettles can reach those places lagers also reach. Seventeenth-century gallants were advised to put a bunch of nettles in their codpiece, 'for the erection of the yeard to synne'. All this at a time when man-sized paper tissues hadn't even been invented.

If you don't happen to have a codpiece, stew a handful of carefully washed nettles in milk. Alternatively, glaze a chopped onion in butter, add three large handfuls of nettles and steam for

three minutes. Add a pint of milk and nearly boil then liquidise. Cooking destroys the sting. Tastes delicious, honest.

Spanish fly is well known and acts by irritating the mucous membrane lining the urethra in the penis. It is derived from crushed cantharis beetles. Unfortunately, the itch persists after orgasm, often driving the user to distraction. Men have died from this stuff, but usually with a smile on their face. Like the rhino, cantharis beetles are at pains to point out to humans that there is no evidence that their crushed bodies act as an aphrodisiac. For the sake of science, however, they are prepared to give it a try the other way about.

Encore

> I am twenty-five and although while I'm having sex everything is fine, soon afterwards my penis becomes erect again without any stimulation and hurts intensely. So I have to have sex for a second or third time, which is painful, until eventually I become flaccid. Because of the pain, I try to get it over with as soon as possible. Why is this? Would painkillers help?
>
> G.Y.

Painkillers will do very little. What you are experiencing is the so-called aphrodisiac effect of urethral irritation. With an excess of hanky-panky, the urethra, the duct running through the penis, along with the glands and muscles which surround it, become slightly inflamed. This acts as a stimulant and so away you go again. Unfortunately, it becomes increasingly painful. Some sexually transmitted diseases can have a similar effect. Get yourself checked out at your local genito-urinary clinic if there is any discharge or rash.

Shelling out for pleasure

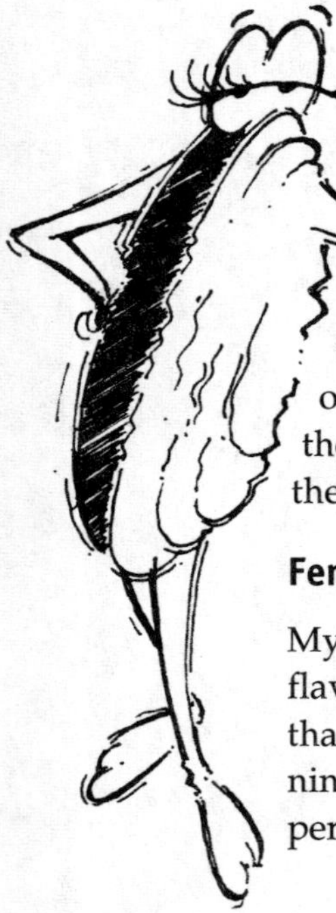

Oysters resemble female genitalia, according to Diana Warburton. Greeks and Romans knew their value and enormous quantities were transported from Colchester to Rome. The emperor Vitellius ate up to a thousand at each sitting. *Up Pompeii* might not be too far from the truth after all. For the sake of science I once ate twenty-three live oysters. I counted them going in and I counted them coming back and it was the same number.

Female orgasm

Myth surrounds the female orgasm and it is heavily flavoured by romantic fiction. The most common myth is that the female orgasm is always both effortless and stunningly pleasurable. There are also minor myths which are perpetuated in the media, such as:

- Climax follows climax.
- They are always easy to achieve and require no foreplay or romance.
- Penetrative sex is always necessary to achieve orgasm and the woman's climax should always happen simultaneously with that of her partner.
- Female ejaculation, where something is released during the climax, is commonly cited in erotic books but can be difficult to establish as fact.

The truth of the matter is quite different. Although the myths at first appear more attractive, by understanding the enjoyment of your partner and yourself, fact can be better than fiction.

Fact

- Most women do not find it easy to achieve orgasm. But it generally gets easier as you get older. Techniques and short cuts are learnt and used to greater effect.
- Foreplay is important. Yes, some people can climax very quickly but for most women it takes around ten to fifteen minutes.
- Physical stimulation is important. Few people can climax just by thinking about sex.
- While it is very pleasant for both parties to climax at the same time, most people do not.

The media would have us believe that you are a failure if you cannot have multiple orgasms. Worse still, you are a complete and utter failure if you cannot have any kind of orgasm at all. Mind you, there are people out there who are determined to examine gift horses in the mouth, as this letter so clearly shows.

Checking gift horses in the mouth

> Recently I've been having great sex with a very close friend of mine. We aren't going out as a couple even though I'm trying my hardest. My problem is that I have between five and twenty orgasms each time we make love. I'm not joking. My friends tell me I'm the luckiest woman in the world because they don't have nearly as many as me. That's why I'm worried. Is it normal to have as many orgasms as I do, or am I abnormal? Is it because this friend of mine's penis is about eight inches long when fully erect and it gets right to the G spot? He is the most gorgeous man I have ever seen and just the sight of him as well as the feel of him turns me on. Please help me. I am desperate to know if I am normal.
>
> J.B.

Who cares. I'm already jealous, along with half the population of the world. There is no such thing as a 'normal' number of orgasms during intercourse. Personally, I wouldn't worry too much about G spots, penis size or whether you are normal. I would just lie back and enjoy it, although it does explain your jerky handwriting.

Getting to know you, too well

Just to prove that this is not always the case, here's a letter from someone who is most definitely looking for a gift horse.

Familiarity breeds but not as much

> I cannot achieve an orgasm with my present boyfriend, a condition which is a repeat of the situation which existed in my previous two long-term relationships, including my marriage. I have never experienced any sensation on vaginal intercourse but initially, at the beginning of these relationships, achieved mini-orgasms from clitoral contact during heavy petting with my partners. However, this always tends to decrease as the relationship continues. It is precisely because I love my partner so much and I feel too embarrassed to go to my doctor.
>
> L.Y.

Men are often driven distracted and to near-exhaustion trying to bring about a climax for their partner. We tend to lay an enormous emphasis on the orgasm and often fail to recognise that many women do not have an orgasm; orgasms vary in number from woman to woman and for the same woman with different partners. It is unlikely that there is anything medically wrong with you. Familiarity tends to

bring in boredom and predictability. You find that your sexual stimulation declines as you get to know your partner. This is part of the predictability which unfortunately tends to take over as time goes by. Longer and more adventurous foreplay along with experimentation will help you keep your sex life exciting. There is no shortage of erotic literature which you can use with your partner to spice up your relationship. *The Big O*, by David Devlin and Christine Webber, is full of good suggestions.

Age, the great leaning post

Not being able to have a half-decent sex life can be caused by a whole battery of things. Generally speaking, if there was a problem at the onset it will take some work from both partners to improve matters. This is often easier said than done.

Excuses not reasons

> I am writing to you in sheer desperation, hoping you can help. I am sixty-one years of age and my husband and I have been married for forty-one years. Sex has never been very great and, although he is generous in many ways, he shows me very little love and affection. I did leave for five months a couple of years ago but we got together again. He can't seem to let himself go or talk to me when we're having sex (about five times this year so far). The

other night when I got undressed I stood naked for a short time and he just lay there. I said, 'You don't take any notice of me nowadays, do you?' and he said, 'Well, you've got so fat.' I am 5′ 2″ and twelve stone, and, yes I struggle, but I don't consider myself too bad. I cry myself to sleep and when I ask him to make love his answer is always, 'I will if you want me to.' I feel I have been denied a full love life and feel very angry. I've even taken HRT to remain sexy and moist for him. Perhaps at my age I shouldn't have these needs. What can I do?

B.T.

As the average life expectancy is now around ninety-two years, being sixty-one is not considered very old. You should still expect to have a good sex life if not the same as it was when you were younger. It is difficult to see both sides of the story when I have only your letter to explain what is happening. While I am not condoning your husband's behaviour, there may be reasons and explanations other than that he simply no longer cares about you. Boredom is a great killer of sexual play. Predictability, familiarity and lack of something new can lead to a stilted sex life. Perhaps you need to put some zing back into your relationship. Some men find women less sexually attractive naked than when they are dressed in provocative clothes. The fashion industry has not been slow to pick up on this. Obviously, the same applies to yourself and if he is not looking after his appearance you may also find him less attractive. Many men hide their impotence by blaming it on their partner. His saying you are too fat may mean he is scared to tell you that he can no longer sustain an erection. Communication is vital as these kinds of running sores can lead to a break-up in the relationship. At the end of the day, this may be all you can do if you wish to have a better life, and you are still young enough to do it.

Types of orgasm

A great deal of fuss is made about whether G spot orgasms are better than clitoral orgasms. Sigmund Freud, the father of psychoanalysis, reckoned clitoral orgasms were for teenagers while the vaginal versions were for mature women. I'm sure a great deal of practical experimentation went into this theory, which survived into the 1960s. We now consider it probable that women will be able to experience both at any stage of their sexual development. Named after its 'discoverer', Ernest Grafenberg, the G spot is located somewhere on the front wall of the vagina. It can be found by gently stroking the upper/front wall of the vagina with a well-lubricated finger. There is nothing to see. Don't expect a big sign with an arrow: G SPOT HERE. Women experience orgasm differently at different times of the month. This is often mirrored in the type of sex they would rather have. For some women, the days immediately before a period are the most exciting and they seek mad passionate sex. Others would rather have a cup of hot chocolate and wonder why their partners are reading the newspaper in the shower.

Male orgasms

Men are supposed to have the equivalent of the female G spot. It is found on the outside of the prostate. Now the only way of getting at this particular part of the male anatomy is either with a finger in the anus or by major surgery. I also have to say that as a doctor I have felt thousands of men's prostates using the anal route. To this day, not one man has fallen to the floor shouting, 'Be gentle with me, Big Boy.' I leave it to you to experiment and find out the truth for yourselves. What we do know is that men can have an orgasm without any physical stimulation – wet dreams were not a figment of your imagination, ask your mum. Generally speaking, however, men find it much easier if there is mechanical stimulation of the penis or anus. This can be achieved with sex toys, themselves or someone else. Being left-handed, I have no great belief in the old adage of using your left hand to masturbate 'as you think someone else is doing it'.

If you are a woman, never trust a man if he tells you that he can climax without actually ejaculating. This is the equivalent of having a baby without ever being pregnant – and you will find out just how true this is in about nine months' time.

Even vibration from travelling in a car can produce an erection and possibly orgasm. Long-distance lorry drivers call it Diesel Dong. As it happens, Rudolph Diesel, the designer of the engine that bears his name, committed suicide by throwing himself off a ship. Perhaps he knew what else his name was going to be attached to. Cynical women would say this just goes to show how much men can fall in love with their cars. Simple friction against an inanimate object will suffice, although the human variety works better. This is the basis for *frottage*, where men derive sexual pleasure from rubbing themselves against people in trains and buses. That guy standing next to you on the 79 bus is not smiling because he just got the joke. This next letter gives a whole new meaning to 'workouts in the gym'.

Weight training can be uplifting

> I am a sixteen-year-old male and recently I have taken up weight training, during which I have experienced something rather peculiar and unexpected. When I do the leg curl (lying face down on my weight lifting bench), after a minute or so I start to feel as if I'm having an orgasm! Sometimes it feels so good I feel as if I'm about to ejaculate. It's like another form of masturbating. Is this normal, or am I just lucky?
>
> A.B.

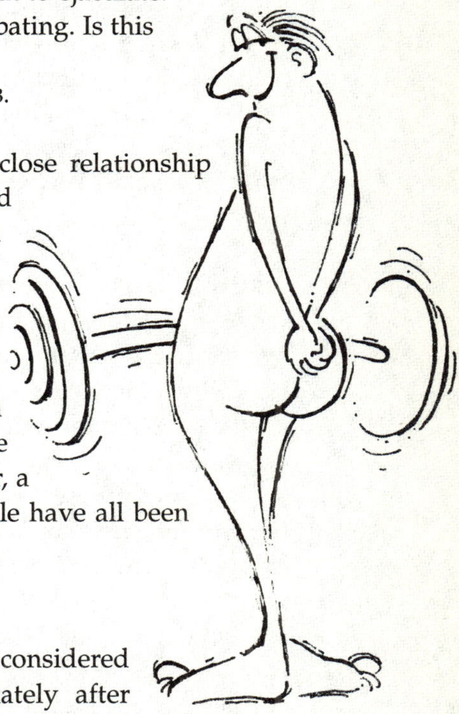

Forming such a meaningful and close relationship with your lifting bench is indeed lucky. All you are experiencing is a mixture of friction (it doesn't work if you lie on your back) and a poorly understood phenomenon where physical exercise translates into sexual pleasure. Endorphin release from the brain may be involved. Sitting on a tumble-drier, a bus, a washing machine and people have all been reported as having the same effect.

Deep sleep

Because it takes two to tango, it is considered bad form to fall asleep immediately after orgasm. Or at least it is if the man does it. Yet everything in the man's body is screaming, 'Whoa, boy.' The answer is more foreplay to allow the woman to have her pleasure as well. Unfortunately, for some men the lure of forty winks is more powerful than forty of a similar-sounding pleasure which has nothing to do with sleep.

Roll on, roll off

> I am a 24-year-old male and have a problem which I

> think is pretty common. Whenever I've had sex previously or when I make love to my girlfriend, after I have an orgasm I can't help but fall asleep. Whether it's me rolling off her, or her on top, within seconds I'm completely shattered and have gone to sleep. This has hurt the feelings of anyone I have done the deed with, because they always want for us to kiss and cuddle, hold each other, etc. I have tried all manner of things to prevent myself from nodding off – for example, splashing cold water on my face and holding my eyes open. Although this is a comical problem, it is an embarrassing one, and I would very much appreciate any suggestions you may have for keeping myself awake.
>
> N.T.

Sexual activity stimulates the release of endorphins from the brain. These hormones are responsible for the sensation of pleasure. Once the climax occurs, blood pressure, heart rate, adrenalin release and awareness all return to normal or even below normal levels. Sleep is a natural follow-up to the orgasm and masturbation is one way of getting off to sleep – you very rarely see this given as a technique for the treatment of insomnia but it works for a whole lot of people. A great deal depends upon how quickly you climax and whether your partner has reached those dizzy heights herself before you enter the Land of Nod. Rather than trying ways of staying awake, improve your foreplay so that your partner is satisfied. Falling asleep together can be fun and loving. You become responsive to stimulation fairly soon after the climax, unless it is late at night and you go into your normal sleep pattern. Ask her to wake you through playing with you in whatever way comes to mind. You might not wake up but I'll bet your dreams will be pretty interesting.

Hidden people

Recognition of the sexual needs and frustrations of disabled people received a boost with the formation of SPOD, the Association to Aid the Sexual and Personal Relationships of People with a Disability. For a long time it was considered reasonable that disabled humans would not have the same sexual desires as the able-bodied variety. The irony is that much of romantic and erotic literature is written by disabled people. An even greater irony is that many of the positions for sex and masturbation cited in the Kama Sutra, for instance, are utilised by disabled people for making love. Truly, there is nothing new under the sun when it comes to sex.

Good vibrations

> I am writing partly for advice but also to let your viewers know that we exist and need sex like anyone else. I am disabled from cerebral palsy. As it happens, I did not suffer from sexual frustration until I was eighteen. Then I realised that I was missing out on more than just freedom of movement and expression. Masturbation has been difficult. Most of the time I just rub myself against the bed. It works but is not very satisfactory. I have used vibrators but it can be even more frustrating trying to attach them and switch them on. My dream was to meet someone who would understand. My dream came true when I met my partner. Unfortunately, we are both disabled and find it difficult to use the 'normal' methods so we've invented a few of our own. I've heard of SPOD but never contacted them. Do you think it would help?
>
> A.M.

Many people with disabilities find that sexual intercourse in the traditional position (e.g. missionary – man on top, woman on her back, face to face – for heterosexuals) is often difficult, sometimes painful, or just plain impossible. A change to some other position can often help to solve this problem. Unfortunately, other positions are often considered to be kinky or abnormal. You are already experimenting. It is important to recognise that no position for sex is abnormal or kinky. What you will need, however, is a sense of humour. And a degree of patience. It may take a little time, and trial and error, to find a new position which is comfortable and satisfying for both partners but it will usually be worth it in the end. SPOD is an excellent source of hard-headed, no-nonsense advice. It gives practical hints and supplies contact addresses for equipment to help disabled people enjoy sex. More importantly, if there can be anything more important, SPOD provides a frank and open forum for debate about sex and personal relationships.

Lateral thinking

Forget about convention and the 'missionary' position. There is no good reason why the woman should not go on top, either lying on the man or straddling his hips in a kneeling or lying position. This is particularly true for older people who may have arthritis. Don't fall into the familiarity trap, where you can only make love in a certain way because 'that's the way you do it'. You don't always need to lie down, intercourse is possible in various ways with either or both partners standing, kneeling, crouching or sitting down. It is for this reason that you may have found yourself in a tall building waiting for a lift which seems to take for ever to arrive, only to discharge two slightly sweaty people when it does.

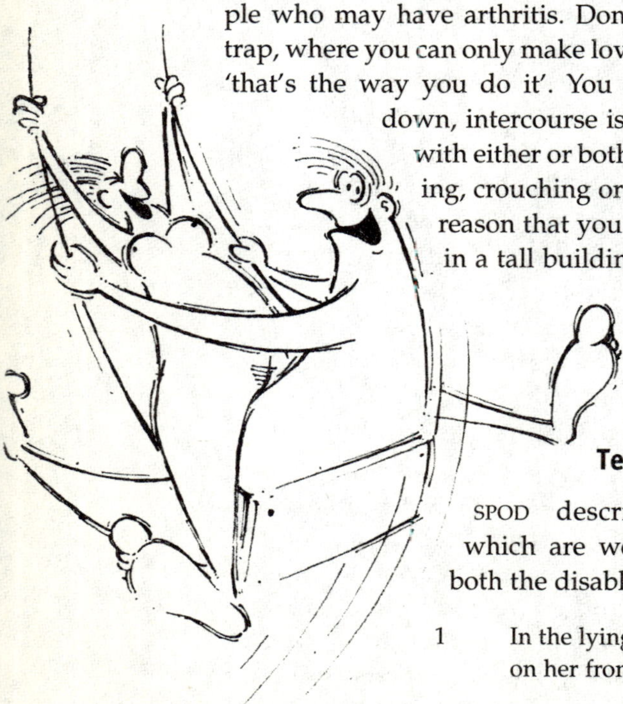

Teaching old dogs

SPOD describes various positions which are well worth considering by both the disabled and the able-bodied.

1 In the lying position, the woman lies on her front, with her buttocks slightly

raised, while the man lies on top of her or supports his weight on his elbows and knees.

2 Both may stand, the woman bending forward, preferably with some support.

3 If a disability allows, a number of kneeling and crouching positions can be used.

4 The rear entry position might be useful for a woman who is unable to bend her hips or knees.

5 If both partners are fairly slim, they can lie on their sides, either facing each other or with the man behind the woman.

In some of these positions, one partner may lie on a pillow to make up for their difference in breadth of hip.

Contact

Achieving any contact between the important bits of the individual partners' bodies creates difficulties. More to the point, some bits frankly get in the way. Getting around the problem may take some lateral thinking.

1 For example, the woman may lie across a bed (or washing machine/television/pool table) with her buttocks resting on its edge and her legs clear of support while the man enters her from any position which they find suitable. Jumping off the wardrobe is an optional extra.

2 Given a little practice, sex can also take place in a sitting position. The man sits with his partner straddling his legs, facing towards or away from him. This may require more movement by the woman, although the man may assist by placing his hands around or below her buttocks.

3 You can reverse the position, with the woman sitting in

an armchair, with her legs drawn up as far as possible. The man can then enter her from a position suitable to hers. The big plus is that the woman in this position does not have prolonged pressure on any of her joints. A woman who is unable to bend her hips and/or straighten her knees might find this position comfortable.

As in any relationship, shyness can often prevent couples from openly and freely discussing topics such as alternative positions. Instead of wishing your partner had the power of mind reading, tell them what you would love to happen.

SPOD can supply booklets on subjects such as:

- Disability and body image
- Physical handicap and sexual intercourse – positions
- Physical handicap and sexual intercourse – methods and techniques
- Devices to assist sex for people with physical disabilities
- Personal relationships and people with physical disabilities
- Sexuality and learning disability
- Sex and your child with a disability
- Sex and your partner with a disability
- Contraception for people with disabilities
- Sex and the person with an ostomy
- Multiple sclerosis and sex
- Disabled and homosexual
- Sex after your heart attack
- Sex and incontinence

Orgasms in later life

Although we do not like to admit it, it does get more difficult for men to achieve orgasm as they get older. We do not really know why, and it is difficult to separate physiological reasons from psychological. Some men are simply quite happy with one orgasm per month when they reach the age of seventy years. But others expect the same kind of sexual pleasure they had in their teens. In truth, most men develop better control over their orgasms, which is much appreciated by their partners (see p. 116).

There are ways of improving your chances of having orgasms later in life. Simply being fit and not overweight are important. Keeping boredom out of the equation is the single most important factor. Once sex becomes predictable and too familiar, it can be difficult to have so many orgasms as when you first met your partner.

Not the real thing

It is not surprising that some men will actually fake an orgasm in order to appear more sexually charged. What is surprising is that this happens quite often among young men as well as older men. This gives some idea of the pressures men find themselves under when it comes to fitting the media image of the macho male. For some men, faking a climax is necessary if they are not going to exhaust themselves. Alcohol has a profound effect upon a man's ability both to produce an erection and to achieve a climax. Rather than admit to 'brewer's droop', some men will simply fake their climax and usually go straight into thankful, if noisy, sleep. This letter gives some insight into the dilemma of faking a climax to maintain appearances and self-respect, not to mention keeping your heart pumping blood in the right direction.

So close and yet so far

I am in my sixtieth year and have had a very good sex life with my wife for many years. However, of

> late, I have had difficulty in reaching a climax even though I have very little problem in achieving an erection. My penis does not seem to have the same sensitivity and I have great difficulty in ejaculating, in some cases there is very little or no ejaculation of fluid, and I feel that I am drying up. By the time I have reached a climax I am absolutely exhausted. Twice recently I've had to fake a climax (I thought only women did this) to avoid complete exhaustion and loss of erection. Is this the start of the end of my love life? Could this be prostate trouble and should I seek help from my GP?
>
> G.E.

It is actually more common for men to fake an orgasm than most women realise. Most will do so for exactly the same reasons as yourself. Because of the emphasis we put on reaching a climax, some men feel they are failures if they do not achieve one. Tiredness, alcohol abuse, anxiety and predictability are all causes of the problem. The production of semen is fairly constant and limited so you can deplete your stores by multiple ejaculations. It is unlikely that there is any medical problem but if you are concerned about your prostate you should see your doctor. As time goes by, sexual play can become so familiar that it becomes predictable. It would be a good idea to introduce some excitement and variation. The use of erotic literature and videos can have a dramatic effect upon people's jaded sex lives.

Allergy amore

Being allergic to the one you love sounds like science fiction. Yet numerous letters and phone calls confirm that some people appear to have some sort of reaction to their partner. It is difficult to imagine this being a normal response to sex as the human race would have died out years ago. Soap and body sprays are a common cause. When sex is anticipated, a lorry-load of deodorant, soap, aftershave and perfume gets dumped in those regions with natural smells completely different to Chanel No. 5. It is not surprising that some reaction will take place in some people.

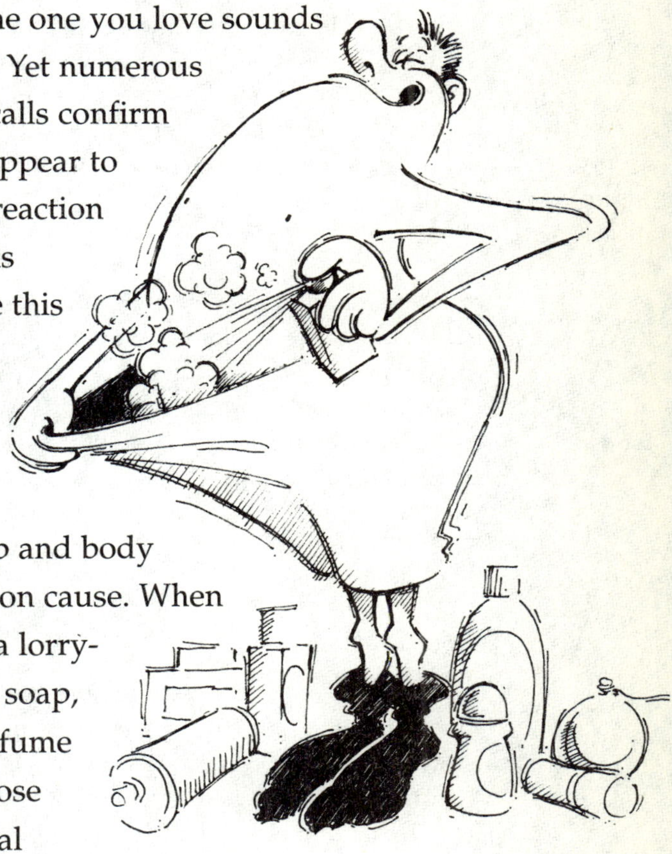

Soap is particularly irritant. Deodorants and perfume have their own vehicles in which the active ingredients are mixed. Most aftershaves contain alcohol as an astringent which tightens the skin. Little imagination is required to predict the effect on the wobbly red bits of the body.

Prickly on heat

> I am twenty-three years old, and after making love with my girlfriend I come out in a rash which covers my whole body and it itches like mad. This stops me from giving loving kisses in the aftermath of our lovemaking. It has never happened with any other girlfriend. Could it be to do with the fact that I do a lot of exercise?
>
> N.S.

It sounds as though you need the exercise. The rash you describe is almost certainly a simple heat rash which would respond well to showering or as a last resort anti-histamine tablets. You might just have some sort of allergy to your girlfriend's body spray, the washing powder the sheets are cleaned in or her soap. On the other hand, you might just be working too hard, if you follow my drift, and just like after hard exercise, the skin can tingle and drive you crazy, you lucky, lucky man.

Rash decisions

> My boyfriend and I decided one year into our relationship that we wanted to spend the rest of our lives together. So we decided to make love for the first time. It was so marvellous, we even came together and now we make love all the time. At first we used the pill and condoms together, but one night we used just the pill and I felt a painful stinging when he ejaculated inside me. I had to have a cold shower and direct the spray inside me to cool the burning sensation down. The next day a red rash

appeared. We have been to a clinic and neither of us has any infections. Am I allergic to my boyfriend's sperm?

B.R.

Such a shame. A truly romantic story ruined. It is interesting that you chose to use both the oral contraceptive pill and condoms. The pill will prevent unwanted pregnancies but not sexually transmitted diseases. Condoms provide protection from both. It was only when you stopped using condoms that your problems started. There are undoubtedly cases of allergy to sperm, and it may be part of the normal response to foreign bodies. Unless the woman has some reaction to sperm, pregnancy may be difficult to achieve. The answer could lie in your boyfriend's occupation. Farmers' wives, for instance, often complain of vaginal irritation, usually caused by the chemicals used on the farm. Even thorough washing before making love is not enough as it takes only traces of these chemicals to cause a reaction in such sensitive areas. Preventing the substances getting on the penis in the first place makes good sense, so adequate protective clothing is essential. Some of these chemicals are linked with cancer so it's worth checking out.

Handy tips – masturbation

The list of euphemisms for male masturbation is almost endless – five-knuckle shuffle, Ham Shank, J. Arthur Rank, Barclay's Bank and so on. Women do not have the same range of vocabulary in this area. This probably reflects two things:

- It is only relatively recently that female masturbation has been recognised and accepted.

- Men are less able to discuss psychosexual matters and commonly use different expressions to describe sex organs, masturbation and intercourse itself.

This causes confusion as the correct medical terms are either unknown or linked to some other activity. The old joke that cunnilingus was an Irish airline is not so far from the truth. While 'fellatio' may be recognised, 'sixty-nine'

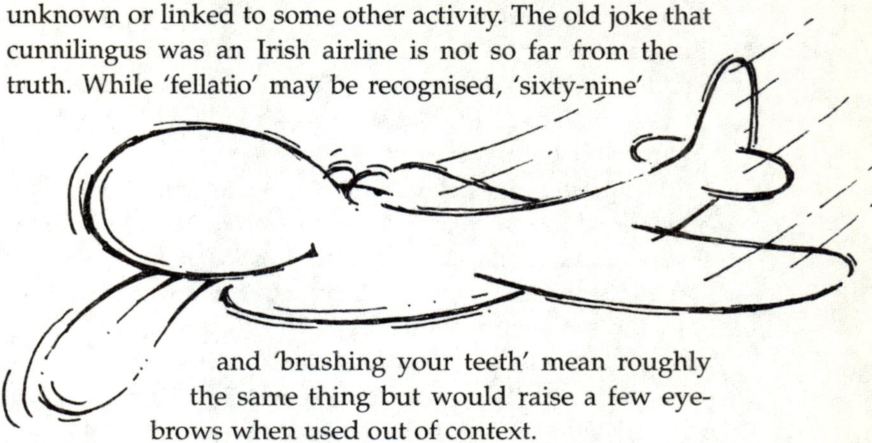

and 'brushing your teeth' mean roughly the same thing but would raise a few eyebrows when used out of context.

Masturbation is normal. It is difficult to explain why a perfectly normal body function should raise such alarm. Trying to have a sensible conversation about cleaning out earwax is bad enough but dinner table small talk rapidly trails off when this topic pops up, excusing the turn of phrase. Things are changing but there still lingers a taboo over body functions which are pleasurable.

Taboo

Although still bad at present, things were worse – much, much worse – in the recent past. Victorian boys found masturbating had long safety pins pushed through their foreskins. Not only did this make erections extremely painful, it made even thinking about masturbation a bad idea. Population control is a recent phenomenon. Most societies used to actively encourage large families with tax incentives or prizes. Wasting sperm, and perhaps more to the point the sexual act, was seen as more than just being antisocial. The Talmud clearly states, 'Thou shalt not practise masturbation either with hand or foot.' God knows how you are supposed

to get good at it otherwise. Mind you, the Bible comes down pretty hard on more than just a knuckle-shuffle. Corinthians just hates waste: 'Be not deceived. Neither fornicators, nor effeminates, nor abusers of themselves . . . shall inherit the Kingdom of God.' Well, at least we know it won't be standing room only up there.

Masturbation was closely linked to insanity. Even worse, it heralded the end of civilisation as we knew it. In 1850 the *New Orleans Medical and Surgical Times* reckoned it was a danger to be rooted out: 'Neither plague, nor war, nor smallpox, nor a crowd of similar evils have resulted more disastrously for humanity than the habit of masturbation. It is destroying the element of civilised society.' The very last person you talked to about masturbation was your doctor – not unless you wanted a dirty great nappy pin stuck in your pink bits.

Do-it-yourself courses

> We had a discussion at our college about sexuality and were surprised to find a high incidence of masturbation among the girls here. The boys are surprised because they thought girls did not do this since they have no reason to masturbate. Boys have to masturbate regularly because of the build-up of seminal fluid. Girls do not have this problem.
> Two questions:
>
> 1 Is female masturbation common?
> 2 Why do we girls need to masturbate?
>
> K.B.

If ever there was a golden excuse for having a five-knuckle shuffle, the dreaded 'build-up of seminal fluid' has to be the best yet. Sperm are produced by the testes and are carried by the vas deferens to the prostate at the base of the penis. The bulk of material actually ejected comes from the prostate, epididymal and Cowper's glands, not from the testis. Sperm are produced at a more or less constant rate and stored for a short while in the epididymis. Any that are not ejected are reabsorbed and recycled, similarly for the rest of the secretions. The testicles of boys not masturbating on a regular basis will not explode, showering your classmates with genetic material. The reason why men and women masturbate is simple. It's great fun. Deafness and poor vision are not recognised complications of masturbation. On the other hand, painful ears when your dad finds you with his 'adult' magazines most definitely are. As Woody Allen said in *Annie Hall*, 'Don't knock masturbation. It's sex with someone I love.'

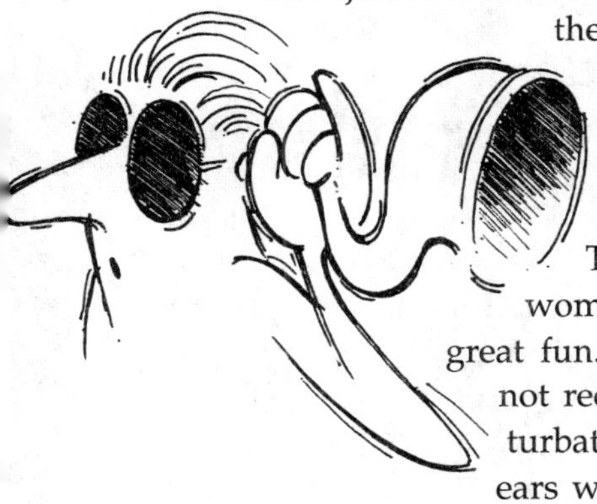

Stimulation

Men use different stimuli to women. Most men use visual stimulants while most women use fantasies instead. These can involve all kinds of weird and wonderful combinations that most people would never normally admit to – sex with multiple partners, well-known figures, partners of the same sex and especially film or television personalities. Politicians will be pleased to hear that they also figure in the ratings, which must be worth a vote or two.

Vibrators

If you work in the construction industry, a vibrator means a machine which weighs a few hundredweight and violently shakes the ground. Men using these machines often experience a pleasurable sensation which has nothing to do with the foreman coming round with the pay packets. Fortunately, you can buy a much smaller machine which reaches those parts the 3-cwt versions fail to reach. Around 15 to 20 per cent of women routinely use these gadgets, which are available from most sex shops or building suppliers. They are invariably battery-driven. Two hundred and twenty volts passing through the nether regions will certainly take your breath away – for a very long time too. Shapes vary. Fairly obvious designs loosely fashioned on the penis are still popular but torpedo-shaped vibrators with warty protuberances are gaining ground. Even round ball-shaped machines can be purchased. Plonking one of these on the dinner table and asking who's for tennis will secure your reputation as a host. It will widen your circle of acquaintances too.

Although the risk is less than with penetrative sex, it is possible to pass on sexually transmitted diseases through a shared vibrator. Either cover it with a condom or wash it thoroughly between each person. It might be a good idea to switch it off before trying to slip the condom on as it can shake your partner's confidence watching you crawling round the bedroom on all fours after an escaping vibrator.

Sex on the back boiler – libido

Letters from women about lack of sexual drive were common but usually had a unique quality about them which gave the clue to their individual problems. Part of our problem with sex is expectation. The media portray sex as always having an orgasm, which is usually pretty noisy. When things don't happen quite like this, women (and men) can feel inadequate and a vicious circle is established. The greater the feeling of not being a 'normal sexual being', the harder it becomes to attain enjoyment. Most problems are psychological and environmental. Being constantly tired is not a good recipe for sex.

Having kids constantly barging in just at the juicy bits doesn't help much either.

Hormone deficiency, particularly of thyroxine, the thyroid's chemical messenger, can drastically reduce libido. This can be checked by your GP.

At the end of the day, sex is pretty complicated. We know the result when smouldering eyes meet thundering chest. But we don't know how or why. More to the point, we have yet to work out why people are turned on by individuals others find unattractive. Despite all the attempts by the media to tell us what is and is not sexually attractive in people, we still have an enormous range of preferences – which is quite handy for the survival of the human race.

Female impotence

> I often wonder if there is such a thing as female impotence. I am a woman aged twenty-seven and I've been having difficulty coming to terms with my problem, which is lack of sexual appetite, so to speak. This problem started long before I can remember. A couple of years back I informed my GP, who recommended a psychosexualist, but after a couple of sessions and advice on masturbation I opted out as my situation didn't improve. I have had casual relationships but I simply cannot feel any emotion and therefore do not get aroused. I remember feeling the adrenalin flowing through me in my teen years. In those days I was very sexually active and responsive. My current situation has made me promiscuous in the hope that I'd finally break through the 'barrier'. I wonder if it is a mental or a physical problem. Am I incapable of love, or impotent – if there is such a thing – or more likely sexually dead? Please help me.
>
> P.S. I can assure you I'm heterosexual and would never consider myself even a bisexual.
>
> S.K.

Libido is not constant throughout life. Nor is it the same in every person. The good news is you once were easily sexually aroused so all the equipment appears to be in working order. Most problems with sexual appetite are caused by tiredness, alcohol abuse, anxiety or poor stimulation. All of these can be helped once the problem has been identified. Work often gets in the way of sex. Worries over promotion, redundancy or friction between you and colleagues can all directly affect your sex drive. At the end of the list comes physical problems. Hormone deficiencies, particularly those that influence metabolic rate such as thyroxine, can adversely affect your desire for sex. You may be confusing 'love' with sexual desire. Equally, you may be trying too hard and be having sex with men you don't find in the least bit attractive. Sexual play from someone who really turns you on is worth two in the bush, as it were. Keep the dangers of casual sex at the front of your mind and always insist they wear a condom. There are female versions available (see p. 170). If you are happy about all of the other possible causes, you can ask your GP for a simple blood test to check the levels of these hormones. Boy George once said he would rather have a cup of tea than sex. Great news for the plantations if nothing else.

Earth-moving equipment

Whoever coined the phrase 'and the earth moved' has a lot to answer for. Losing your virginity is portrayed as a great mind-boggling event which leaves you panting in orgasmic shock. Actually, most people think, 'Is that it?' after their first penetrative sex. It is usually, if you will excuse the expression, a big anticlimax. Some people are lucky. For them the earth really did move, or had they simply forgotten to apply the handbrake on the Mini? It's not only the casual one-off affair either. Some people, more often women, wait until they have met the 'right' person only to be bitterly disappointed with their first sex. Well, the good news is, it gets better. But like playing the piano, practice helps.

Scary things can happen in relationships. Bullying, blackmail and selfishness are signs of a one-sided affair. Desperate people will act desperately and allow things they would never normally accept. This only adds to the feeling of self-disgust which makes further sex even more unpleasant. The only way to break this kind of vicious circle is to get out of the relationship. Often easier said than done.

Feeling vulnerable and unprotected

> I'm forty years old and have had only two sexual partners. The first was six years ago, at which time I lost my virginity. I waited for thirty-four years only to be very disappointed. This relationship lasted only a few days. My only first, real boyfriend was four years ago and I went out with him for two months. We had sex within the first week. I was so naive. Because my partner would not wear a condom, I allowed him to have unprotected sex. I thought it was love and became really hooked on this man but I later learnt that he only went out with me because of my large chest. I think I maybe only went out with him because I was pleased that he had asked me out. I worry that I may never have a real, normal relationship. I'm not really bothered about sex – I don't really enjoy penetration – but I would like companionship, love without sex. Am I

> normal? I would also like to add that I feel socially awkward and find it difficult to make friends with either men or women, in fact I am quite a loner.
>
> S.H.

You are perfectly normal. One of the problems with our hyped society is everyone is expected not only to want sex desperately every minute of the day but to be able to provide it as often. In truth, people's sexual appetite varies considerably. People are attracted to other people for lots of reasons and it would be difficult to say what is 'right' or 'wrong'. You are quite correct to be concerned over unprotected sex with people you know little about. Vaginal sex is not so hazardous as anal sex but still carries a significant risk. Non-penetrative sex can be every bit as exciting and is far less risky. If your boyfriend wants penetrative sex and so do you, make sure he uses a condom. Either that or a cold shower.

Rhythm sticks – S & M

People get awfully upset about sadomasochism, rightly so when it involves people who do not want anything to do with it. The European Court recently upheld a British court decision against men who subjected themselves and each other to some form of 'torture'. In truth, we all dabble with S & M. Sex is a form of sadism and masochism. All kinds of games take place behind those net curtains that nobody likes to admit to. The spectrum is considerable, from verbal pain to physical.

The old joke about the masochist asking the sadist to inflict pain and being refused is so much a reflection of our realisation of pleasure. Being 'hurt' in a controlled fashion with the ability to see the need or stop the process is fundamental to human behaviour. 'Adventure' is often just another word for near self-inflicted torture. Who in their correct mind wants to be spun around, shaken up and down and subjected to horrific visual displays? Nip down to your local 'funfair' and see them queuing up for 'joyrides' which are guaranteed to shake your ear lobes off, or anything else which is hanging down for that matter. Pain is relative. The following letters are a tribute to people's honesty. They also show how confused we all can get when it comes to balancing society's expectations against personal pleasure. That fine line between what is acceptable and ethically correct and personal gratification can be easy to step over. Freedom comes at a price.

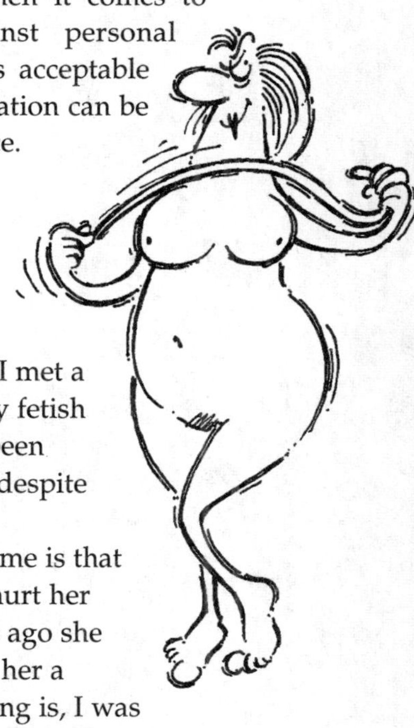

Botty spanking

I am a forty-year-old man and admit to liking having my bottom spanked. I understand that this is not uncommon among men. Not long ago I met a woman about my age and admitted my fetish to her. She then told me how she had been slippered at school on her bottom and despite the pain, it had not been an altogether unpleasant experience. What concerns me is that she wants me to take this further and hurt her quite severely. For instance, a few days ago she produced a cane and asked me to give her a number of hard strokes with it. The thing is, I was caned across my bare bottom at school and it's not something I would want to subject a woman to. Is this something I should put a stop to, or is it harmless? Also, is it common for women to like this sort of thing?

B.P.

You have obviously met someone who is fairly close to your way of thinking when it comes to enjoying sex. She, however, wants to go a bit further than you are prepared to go. This is very common when it comes to matching each other's sexual expectation. So long as neither of you is mentally or physically injured and you both recognise the danger of physical excess, then there should be no problem. Make sure that you have a code word which you both recognise as marking the end of the session. It is difficult to give you strong advice and it really does depend upon what you both feel about your expectations. You need to talk to her and explain your worries. Point out that you are unhappy when it comes to actually hurting her and that you find it difficult to fulfil her wishes.

I'm tied up at the moment

> I have been with my boyfriend for almost a year. I love him very much and I know he loves me and our sex life is really great. However, something happened recently which really shocked me. I called at his flat unexpectedly after finishing work early and as I have my own key I let myself in. To my amazement I discovered my guy lying on the floor, his wrists and ankles tied with my stockings and a pair of my panties in his mouth. I thought for a moment he had been attacked and robbed. Then I saw he had a huge erection and had been masturbating himself. I untied him and he was very embarrassed and confessed that he had a fantasy that I tied him up and then used him as my sex slave. I never had an inkling that he was into this sort of thing and, quite frankly, I do not know exactly where our relationship is heading. I would welcome your advice.
>
> S.S.

This is the basis behind all answerphones, 'Sorry, I'm tied up at the moment. I'll get back to you.' This fantasy is common.

He may well have wanted to be 'found out' so he could live his fantasy for real. He is basically offering you a chance to enter into this sex dream. If you find the idea repulsive and cannot in any way take part, then say so. I suspect his ego and your relationship may well be a little crushed. Some fantasies can dominate all sexual play. If you are willing to take part, make it clear that you want your enjoyment too. Sex is a great bargaining tool. Make sure he washes your panties afterwards.

Habit-forming

> My boyfriend and I have been together almost a year and love each other very much. We plan to get engaged at Christmas. I am rather worried as I think that I may have started him on a bondage fetish. To explain: we were larking about on the bed together and I was sitting on his back, the cord of his dressing gown was beside me and for a joke I pulled his arms behind him and tied his hands with it. He was struggling and yelling and I have to confess I was teasing him a lot. I even tied my tights over his mouth as a gag. I noticed that he had an enormous erection and, without going into the more sordid details, we had sex. Since that time, however, he has asked me to tie him up whenever we have sex and when I have refused he has got very upset. I am not a prude, but I would not be happy with our future lovemaking being dependent on me trussing him up every time. I blame myself as, quite innocently, I did it for a joke, but it seems to have backfired on me. Is there anything I can do?
>
> S.S.

Sex can get pretty boring at the best of times. Doubly so if there is only one way to do it. Experimentation keeps sex lively but any form of sexual play, no matter how exotic, runs the risk of familiarity. Where the fun is unequal, as in your case, one partner is bound, if you will forgive the expression, to get fed up. You need to shout, 'Wot abaht the workers?' very loudly in his ear, preferably while he is gagged. Using tights for partial strangulation is a dangerous manoeuvre, they can actually kill. Do not use tights or nylons as gags either, they ladder easily unless your partner has taken his false teeth out first.

Mummy's little boy

> I have a rather peculiar and obsessive fetish which I think might be the reason for me not getting a girlfriend. This fetish is a strong form of bondage called mummification and not a single day goes past without a fantasy about being stripped naked by strict naughty nurses and then wrapped up in an infinite amount of bandages until my entire body is tight, white and completely immobile. How weird is this fantasy, and what does it say about my sexuality?
>
> T.C.

Resisting the temptation to discuss an Oedipus complex, I'll tell you that this type of fetish is actually common. It represents the ultimate in submission and most people will experience minor variations on this theme, particularly as children. Being tied up is a childhood delight which also has its place in adult sexual play. Many transvestites prefer clothes which are ridiculously tight. They will tolerate bodices and corsets few women would entertain for a minute. It may all have a basis in the tradition of wrapping babies up very tightly. This may not have been very comfortable but it went with a lot of cuddles from mum or dad. There is a theory that mummification bondage may decline as parents are encouraged not to overheat their babies. Your difficulty in finding a girlfriend is perhaps understandable. I would suggest reading the contact pages of erotic magazines for a like-minded partner. You would need to take turns, otherwise your bedroom would very quickly resemble the British Museum Egyptology department – with about as much sex too. Unless you have a particularly understanding GP, it is unlikely you will get your bandages on the NHS. On a very serious note, never bind your chest, throat or mouth too tightly. Over-tight bandages will cause swelling, which then tightens them even more. People, often young men, die from this form of sexual stimulation.

You're in for a big surprise

> My younger sister, who is eighteen, recently moved in with me and as the big sister I had to promise my mother that I would watch out for her and look after her. She's a student and sometimes she brings friends home, which is fine by me. The other evening I left her alone with her boyfriend, but I returned home unexpectedly early as I had a migraine. I was in for a shock. My sister and her boyfriend were on the floor of the living room. He was tied hand and foot and was gagged. My sister was astride him, she was wearing my leather boots and very little else and they were having sex. I expect my sister to have boyfriends as she is a very attractive girl but I was disgusted with the nature of their sex act. I regard bondage as a perversion, not to say dangerous, and the result was an almighty row. I would ask her to leave but my mother would want to know the reason so I am in a very awkward position. I have tried talking to her but she just ignores me.
>
> M.E.

You were quite right to be outraged. How dare she wear

your leather boots without asking! You have a problem here: the conflict of guardian with free will. Your sister is over eighteen and bondage between consenting adults is not illegal. If you find her behaviour unacceptable you have every right to ask her to leave, and you can find plenty of explanations for your mother. Sexual play is such a cause of discomfort for some people yet most of it is harmless and personal. I doubt she did this deliberately to offend you. At the end of the day, the most serious thing you have to worry about is verrucas.

Trouser press

> Why should an otherwise macho male need pain to get a good orgasm? I like to be hurt by being painfully crushed by my girlfriend's legs and this always gives me a full-blooded orgasm. I can't consider myself a masochist as I'm not otherwise into pain, only in this special way. It's so important to me that I've given up some previous girls because they were not strong enough to really hurt. Is this unusual?
>
> S.N.

Pain is relative. Getting your tackle squeezed by a pair of thighs is relatively painful. You are not actually doing anything different from most men, just more so. Pain is actually part of sexual play. Having your back scratched with sharp fingernails goes down well during a steamy night's fun. You are not quite so sure when you have a bath or shower and you think someone has flayed your back with a cat-o'-nine-tails.

During any enjoyable or intensive act, pain is either disregarded or transformed into pleasure. How this happens is not certain, and a lot of S & M addicts would pay good money to find out, but endorphins may play a role. These hormones are released from the brain and are involved in the perception of pleasure. Most people would be afraid of hurting their partner so I suspect you will continue to have problems finding a suitable partner. Cock rings are said to give a similar sensation. See p. 43 for more information.

Bed bound but not gagged

> I wonder if you can help me. The other night, after having sex, my wife and I started to discuss our fantasies. We shared lots of the same desires and want to try them, but my wife then said she wanted to be handcuffed to the bed while we made love. Is this normal? Should I go along with it? Personally I'm not too sure.
>
> C.G.

Bondage is great fun so long as it doesn't get out of hand. There is an element of bondage in all sexual play. Fantasy about rape is common but has no connection with the real thing. Men and women brutalised by rape suffer scars long after their tormentors have ceased attracting attention from the law. Between consenting adults, tying each other up allows an element of release from responsibility for their actions. There is a fine line between enjoyment and fear. Even close, loving relationships can be brought into question when this line is crossed. If you find this hard to accept, try looking very closely at yourself in the mirror and make threatening faces. Unless you have a different type of mirror from mine, it can scare the pants off you. Only use ropes which can be broken, handcuffs which have an emergency breakage built in, and never, ever, tie anything around the neck, not even in fun. We humans suffer badly from having our brains on the end of our necks and all the blood supply has to go through it to keep us from going cold.

Strangulation is unfortunately not rare during sexual play. Agree on a code word which will instantly stop all bondage. There must be no confusion over the meaning of the word. 'Stop' is not the best choice as it tends to be muttered during the fun bits. Use the name of your car. Shouting 'Bubble car!' at the top of your voice will probably reduce the most ardent handcuffist to tears of laughter anyway.

Hit me with your rhythm stick, more often

> I am having serious sexual incompatibility problems with my wife. We've been married eleven years and I absolutely adore sex, while her sex drive is comparatively low. Consequently, I have to make do with making love only when she wants, maybe two or three times a month. Added to this, I have an obsession with bondage and S & M – my wish is to be on the receiving end as the submissive rather than dominant partner. However, my wife views this kind of behaviour as perverted and unnatural and refuses to co-operate. As much as I love my wife, I am considering divorce as the only step towards sexual satisfaction. Can you offer any help or advice?
>
> K.K.

If only we had some sort of viewers' guide before we get hooked up to one person. Part of the problem is our innate inability to communicate better about areas we think of as embarrassing. Sexual preferences also change with time. Talking things through will often allow some kind of compromise. Finding something that she enjoys as well can allow you both to enjoy sex without it becoming the only way. Her concern will be that you will eventually want only one form of sexual pleasure, sadism and masochism. By convincing her that this should be only part of a much wider spectrum of sexual activity, you might be able to experience what you desire. Her upbringing may also shade her view of such activity and imposing your wishes will only produce an equal and opposite reaction. At the end of the day, compromise is the only way. Divorce seems a sad way to end eleven years of marriage because of a lack of one aspect of sexual play which may be obtainable, if only in fantasy, through films or books without being unfaithful to your wife. Dwell on the thought that her refusal to take part in being sadistic to you is the ultimate sadistic act. Smile next time you ask.

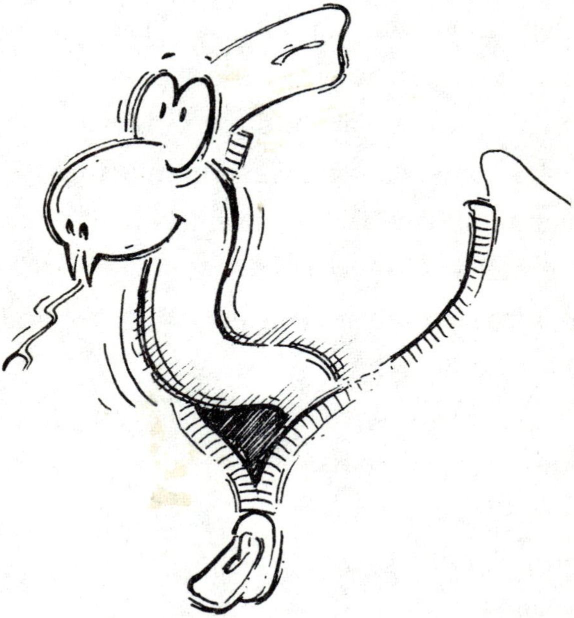

Games people play

Sex toys are as old as sex itself. I am constantly referred to as a sex toy, or was it a vexed boy? We get so moralistic about such devices yet will happily use other machines to make our lives more pleasant in other ways. Look around the modern kitchen with its toasters, washing machines and blenders. One of my patients admitted to getting great satisfaction out of sitting on the spin-drier. While kitchen machinery may be put to alternative use such as this, I recommend caution when it comes to the blender.

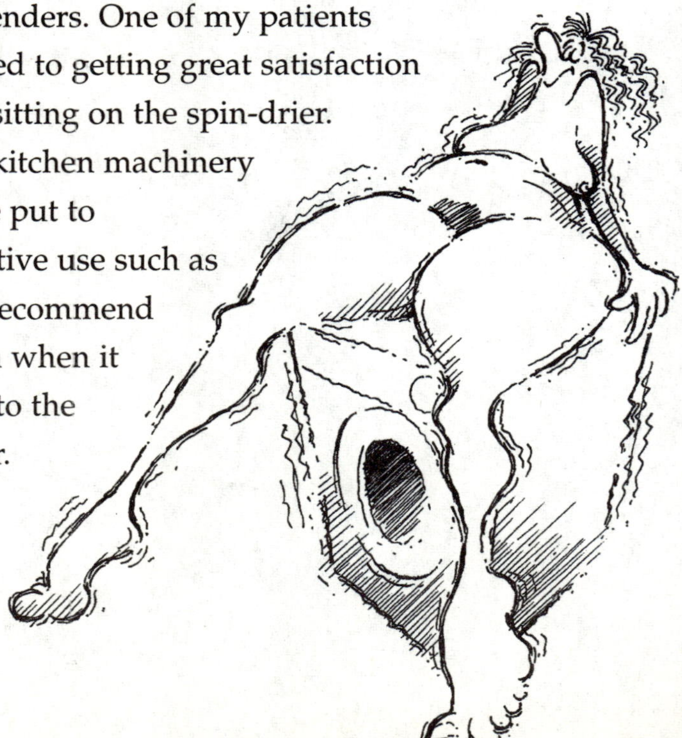

A cock and bullring story

> I don't know if this is a problem, but I like to use a cock ring while making love or even when I masturbate. I am forty-five now and have been doing this for quite some time – I tried to stop but the feeling is so nice that I just can't. Is this normal and more importantly is it harmful? Can it damage my penis or my sperm? Should I make more effort not to use one or to try other toys?
>
> D.D.

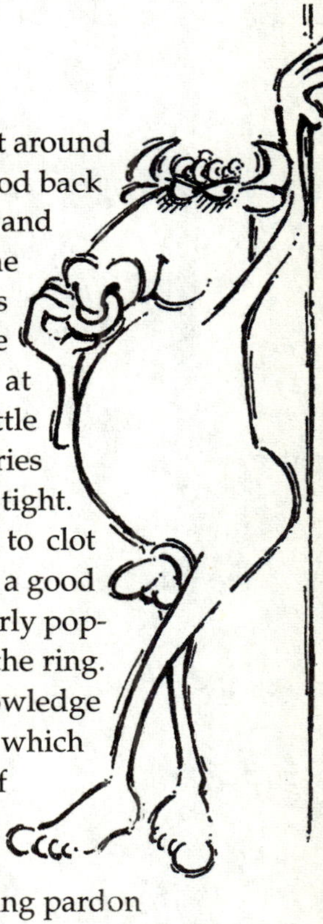

Cock rings, for the uninitiated, are bands which fit around the base of the penis. They restrict the flow of blood back out of the penis, thus making the erection firmer and more durable. Exotic variations on the theme include those with spikes, fur or leather thongs which attach around the waist or neck. It can be tricky getting through the metal detectors at Heathrow airport while wearing one – not a little embarrassing too. Only people with good memories should wear them, particularly if they are very tight. Leaving them on too long can cause the blood to clot inside the penis, which doesn't so much give you a good erection as a very long black pudding. A particularly popular steel version has tiny needle points around the ring. The faint-hearted or those without any prior knowledge of their blood group should avoid these types, which would not look out of place in the Tower of London's dungeons. No evidence is at hand to suggest they will put any strain on your sperm, excluding the need to jump through hoops, begging pardon for the play on words. If you enjoy wearing them, and your partner has no objections, then there is little to lose from continuing to benefit from their use.

Mind expansion

Nature seems to let us down at times. Things are not there

when you need them and when they are they aren't big enough. Dildos are mentioned in ancient texts. Tired men may have had recourse, not to mention frustrated women. They can also have interesting lateral uses not envisioned by the manufacturers of contact lenses.

Dildos can affect your vision

> After reading an erotic story in a magazine which she said turned her on, my girlfriend has expressed the desire to penetrate me using a strap-on dildo. She is often willing to help me with my fantasies so I am willing to give it a try. However, I am worried about the possibility of damage to my anus – the strap-on dildos that I have seen look enormous, and appear to be designed exclusively for female-to-female use. I have suggested that she could use a small dildo by hand, but she says that this wouldn't be the same at all, as the fantasy that she has in mind would not work for her that way. Please can you advise me about this? Are there any such devices on the market that are safer than others, and would my anus be permanently stretched by this type of penetration?
>
> R.R.

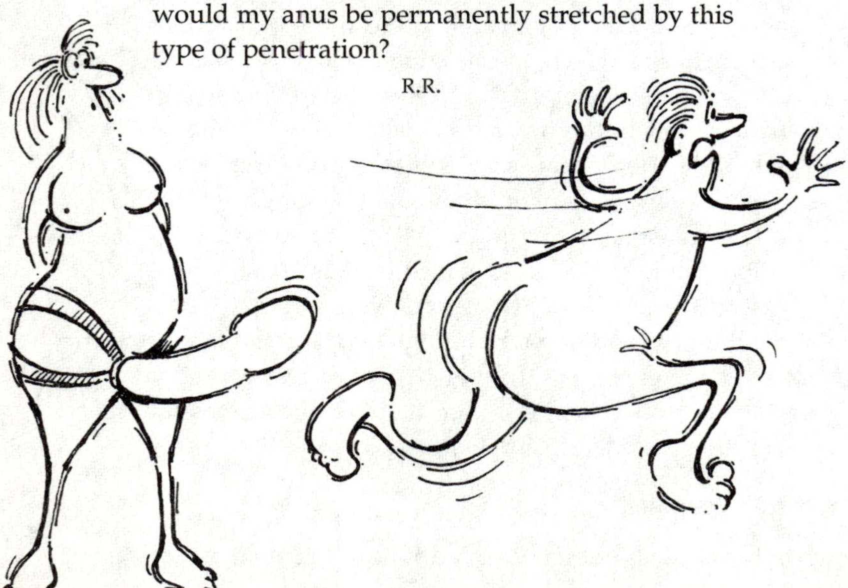

It won't be your anus that will be stretched so much as your sense of humour. When the anal ring was designed, poo of enormous dimensions had to be catered for. I am constantly amazed at the size of motion three-year-kids can produce when they really try. Unfortunately, they also suffer occasionally from tiny anal tears, which are painful when the next motion comes along. Repeatedly using a very large dildo could also damage the muscles surrounding the anal ring. Even so, gay men use this form of sex and there are few complaints of lax anal rings. Interestingly, we use large dilators to treat recurrent anal fissures. Mind you, most people ask for a general anaesthetic before the operation is carried out. Perhaps you might happen to know a friendly anaesthetist who has been struck off recently. My advice is to use plenty of lubrication and take your contact lenses out in case your eyes pop.

The written word

Not all toys are mechanical. In a sense, literature and videos are a form of sex toy. There is a fine line between a healthy use of such forms of erotic stimulation and harmful perversion which damages either the subject for examination or the person who is reading about or watching them. We wrestle constantly with this in society. Sometimes simply reading can cause conflict between couples, as this letter shows.

Pornographic pen pals

> I have been married for six years to a wonderful man. Last year I accidentally found some very explicit photos and videos that he'd obviously sent for and kept hidden from me. We discussed it and I said I didn't understand his need to look at these things. I agreed that he could have them, but I didn't want to know about them. Now recently, I've found more explicit photos along with a letter from a woman he's obviously been corresponding with for

> a long time. He is sending her money and she is posing for him and sending the photos. It hurts more now because it's personal and I feel as if he's having an affair. Am I responsible for driving him into this? I don't want to share him with anyone and I'm not giving up on the marriage.
>
> K.Y.

Men seem to have a different view of erotic literature. Most men would not see a copy of *Playboy* as a co-respondent in a divorce trial. Women find it more degrading and threatening. When men are asked about the same type of magazines for women, they suddenly adopt all the attitudes displayed by women. It is not too late to sort things out. It is unlikely that your husband sees his relationship with someone supplying photographs as being unfaithful. He essentially is looking for excitement in his sexual relationship about which he fantasises regularly. Your confrontation convinced him that you would not be prepared to take part in his fantasies. Give and take is the order of the day when it comes to marriage or any form of relationship. Perhaps you should talk about your fears and inhibitions and let him explain his needs. Somewhere there has to be compromise, particularly if you are determined not to let your marriage crumble. On the plus side you could get him to pay you to pose for photographs for his personal use. Few charities would refuse this money should you wish to go non-profit-making. This is a serious suggestion.

Enabling disabled people

Like a bolt of clear light, SPOD comes on the scene. The Association to Aid the Sexual and Personal Relationships of People with a Disability has for ever broken the myth about sex aids. If they help, use them is its motto.

Part of the reason that such devices are so emotive is the popular image of them as 'dirty' or 'kinky', yet sex aids are simply aiding people to do things in their sex life that they can no longer easily do for themselves. Those who are having trouble with their sight use 'seeing aids', usually called spectacles. A hearing aid may be used if someone is having trouble hearing, or artificial teeth by those who need help with eating and talking. It would therefore seem quite a natural progression to the idea of using a sex aid for those who need some help.

Many of the items advertised in sex aid catalogues are primarily for the purposes of titillation and some may find the catalogues offensive, but there are five or six devices which do have a prosthetic or therapeutic value.

The energising ring is made of ebonite and fits behind the man's penis and testicles. The ring is usually made to measure, and therefore fits comfortably and is unobtrusive when the man is clothed. The snug fit sets up a tiny charge of static electricity, which cannot be felt, and which has the effect of enlarging the minute blood vessels on which an erection depends. It can nearly always improve an erection which is otherwise incomplete but does depend on the man being able to obtain more than a reflex erection. A secondary benefit is the assurance that the ring is individually made and in place, which can reduce anxiety, often a cause of erectile problems.

SPOD has received very positive feedback from men who have used the energising ring. SPOD can provide a catalogue and order form. There is a cheaper alternative to the energising ring which is a small loop or tube of latex rubber that fits around the base of the penis. This may help to improve a rather limp erection or help to maintain an erection which would otherwise be rapidly lost. If it is not possible for a man to get and maintain an erection, there is a range of artificial penises for use by the man when penetration is desired. This imitation penis, which straps on to the man's body with an elastic harness, may be solid, or hollow so that the flaccid penis can fit inside. The more sophisticated models can even squirt a warm fluid to simulate ejaculation if this is thought important; some even have a built-in vibrator. A lubricating jelly should be applied before the artificial penis is inserted.

For women who are unable to have sexual intercourse, e.g. after radical surgery, an artificial vagina may be useful. These devices are made of latex and most models have a built-in vibrator. The artificial vagina is held between the thighs and produces the desired effect for those requiring to simulate intercourse. Men who have difficulty in sustaining masturbation to completion may also find this device helpful. The aid is designed so that it can be washed thoroughly.

If both partners can happily accept their use, the artificial penis and vagina can provide satisfaction to the non-disabled partner and allow the disabled partner to have sex in the 'usual' way when this might otherwise be difficult or impossible. Many disabled people find this very important but such aids are not always acceptable to both partners and there should be mutual agreement about their use. For those who are not happy with a vibrator which is penis-shaped, there are circular massagers, available from most chemists, which have a similar effect. The body usually provides its own lubricating fluids to make intercourse smooth and pleasant. However, where these are reduced or lacking, and especially when sexual aids are used, a water-based lubricating jelly such as KY can be enormously helpful,

SPOD warns about useless 'aids': 'Don't be conned by smart suppliers into buying useless articles at fancy prices.' If in doubt, ask SPOD, who will be happy to provide you with advice, information and, if necessary, a mail-order catalogue.

Rubber duck – fetishes

One person's fetish is another person's perversion. Have you ever wondered why there are so many fetishes? Why do people get so upset over things that turn other people on? It is pointless even trying to define a fetish because you will inevitably run into conflicts of interest. One man told me he could not make love unless there was a picture of the Queen in the same room.

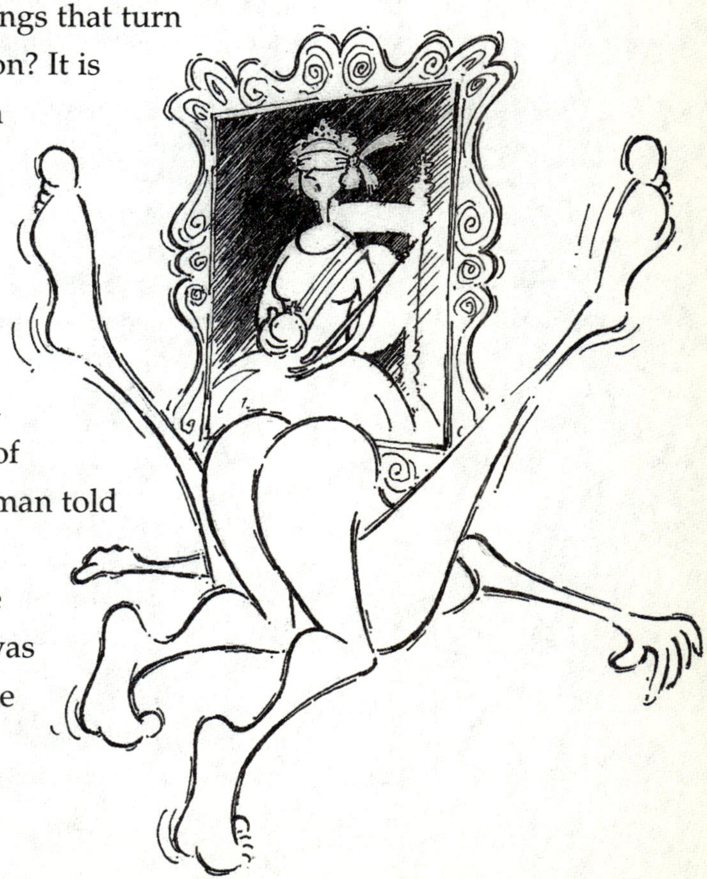

Paradoxically, another man said he could not make love with a 'bleeding heart' icon in the room. Perhaps we should stop trying to analyse what turns people on and simply lie back and enjoy it. The letters which follow are but a small sample of 'fetishes' from people who are more honest than the rest of us. I suspect everyone has something which acts as a powerful sex stimulant, an object, smell or scenario. That's what makes the entertainment industry go round. It's a pity we can't be more honest with each other. Sex would be more interesting.

Hot-water bottle

Please help. I have a problem which has been bugging me for ages. I love sex, but I really love sex dressed head to toe in rubber. It started when I was working in London and I met a girl who introduced me to the pleasures of rubber. I thought I'd found heaven and we often indulge in sex in rubber which includes threesomes with women and men. I never thought of being gay, but when we're all dressed up I don't care who I'm making love with. Am I a freak to want to wear rubber suits and masks during sex?

M.L.

A fetish is only abnormal when it harms the person or those around them. Rubber fetishes are so common they can hardly be called abnormal but rather one end of a spectrum most people would consider unusual. This attraction towards rubber is so strong it has almost superseded your attraction to people themselves. As you say, you don't really care what sex the person is so long as they are dressed in rubber. This will limit your choice of sexual partners because making love looking like Jacques Cousteau is not everybody's idea of a good night out. When sex becomes so fixated and frenetic, safer sex can go to the wall. Mixed couples for casual sex are potentially lethal without taking the correct precautions. Consider covering yourself all over with rubber, and I do mean all over. Please remind me never to accept a cheque off you.

Rubber knickers

> My boyfriend and I are in what I suppose you could call a sub/dom relationship. He dominates me, which I really enjoy because it's in a very loving way and even when he punishes me, he does it with care and never oversteps the limits we've both agreed on. We both like rubber and PVC and he's bought me several skirts and dresses to wear, but now he's decided I should wear rubber panties during the day and PVC ones at night. I dust them with medicated powder before I put them on but they still get very hot and sticky. I've always been very concerned with personal hygiene and never suffered from any vaginal infections. Is wearing these rubber knickers permanently likely to cause me to suffer from infections? If so, would wearing a panty liner help or what can I do to reduce the risks?
>
> J.T.

Establishing the ground rules for domination is important. You appear to have worked out a safe way of doing so. Code words can help. Once you say them, your partner knows that it is time to stop. Rubber will not allow fluid to escape, hence its unrivalled success as a condom. Unfortunately, it also stops perspiration from evaporating and, as you say, causes overheating. With attention to hygiene and regular washing with simple soap and water, you will be unlikely to suffer from infections. Cystitis is the curse of women. Make sure the underwear is well washed regularly to prevent bacteria from the anus travelling in the wrong direction. Avoid sending them to the dry cleaners as they invariably come

back with holes and the assistants smile far too much when you go to pick them up. Don't use talcum powder. It is made from chalk and fish scale and you can do without either of these smells.

Happy nappies

A few months ago I went around to my boyfriend's flat to give it a clean and tidy. While I was in his bedroom I discovered a holdall containing large-size nappies, rubber pants, a feeding bottle and a dummy. There were also some magazines with letters and photographs from people who dress up in this way. I was shocked, to say the least. He'd never even hinted that he found such things a turn-on. I confronted him and eventually he admitted the truth, that he'd been dressing up as a baby since his late teens. We talked it through and came to a compromise, so now once a week I bathe him, put him in a nappy and rubber pants and bottle-feed him. My problem is I've begun to enjoy mothering him and find myself looking forward to having him as my baby. Surely that can't be right? Do you think I should stop? I would appreciate any advice you can give me.

L.A.

Along the spectrum of sexual pleasure you will find just about everything which turns people on. So long as it harms no one and takes place between consenting adults, there is no problem. Your boyfriend is enjoying one of the 'fringe benefits' of sex. Being a baby is the ultimate in submission. You are totally dependent upon your mother or carer. For some men this is linked to the only real happiness they can remember. As they grew up, life became more challenging and harsh. They were not allowed to express their emotions by crying, for instance. Dressing as a baby is predominately a male preserve, probably because of the way we bring men up to be dominant, expressionless and never admitting they have a problem. Successful businessmen are among those who find this type of sexual behaviour a form of release from the straitjacket of conformity imposed upon them by society. If you enjoy the sexual play then fine. You may find it becoming tiresome and questions may come into your mind about the future should you wish to have children. If only for these reasons it would be best to continue to limit the amount of time spent in this form of sexual activity and to experiment with other, less personally demanding sexual attention. A great danger is to lose sight of the person you are so fond of in favour of your natural instincts as a potential mother. Be careful where you stick that nappy pin. You may both regret it.

In love with hairy armpits

> I have always been sexually attracted to hirsute women. I find thick eyebrows, hairy legs and excessively hairy vaginas a turn-on. I have spoken to many men who share this sexual turn-on. Is this normal?
>
> P.L.

I once met a man who, according to his medical notes, owned a hairy suit. Dictating notes is not always a good idea. Hairiness is predominately a genetically inherited trait. Some ethnic groups tend to be very bushy, with hairy ears and noses. Western fashion has decreed that hair should be found only in certain places and most of us go around worrying about lack of scalp hair while plucking our noses frantically. In truth, it is impossible to say what is normal hairiness. Women are driven by the media to shave their armpits, legs, eyebrows, face, arms, noses, ears and even the pubic area to conform with what is 'acceptable'. I suspect if men had to do the same there would be a dramatic shift in media presentation in a very short time. If humans secrete sex attractants, pheromones, it would be from the hairy bits as the hair allows for free distribution of the smell as the wind whistles through. Did you know that men's kneecaps are actually hairy? Only the constant friction against trousers removes the hair as it grows. When trapped in a plaster of Paris cast, men's legs develop hairy kneecaps which would make a passable toupee.

Team efforts

Ever since I was a child I remember I have worn football shorts under my ordinary trousers. I only ever have sex with myself, pulling down the shorts slowly and watching myself in the mirror. I am forty now – what has happened to me? A woman I did some wallpapering for seduced me once and I had sex with her but I hated the whole experience and I could not climax. When I fantasise I think about women and when I see women football players I am happy for the rest of the day! Please sort my problem out. Thank you.

B.A.

Clothes are a powerful sexual stimulant. It is possible to 'fix' on some article of clothing which enhances sexual pleasure. Shoes, underwear, hats, ties, belts, you name it and for some people they act like an aphrodisiac. If this fix becomes too powerful, it is impossible to have sex unless they are present. Some men, for instance, cannot sustain an erection unless their partner is wearing boots. Your sexual experience has been limited and has revolved around masturbation stimulated by your shorts. It is easy to see why your first sexual encounter was so unenjoyable. You were probably wishing the whole time that the woman was also wearing shorts. This is why you find female football players so sexually attractive. As you do not mention anything to do with male football players, I suspect you are not gay. This fetish for shorts is not abnormal. It is simply one of the many things which makes sex more interesting. Perhaps if you were to meet a woman and explain your pleasure in her wearing shorts during sex play, you may be able to have enjoyable sex. This could lead you on to other ways of having sex. You would be surprised how many people have the same attraction and it is quite harmless.

Downtrodden male

> I have been with my boyfriend for some months. We seem to hit it off very well and when we have sex he is very gentle and considerate. But I have recently discovered he has a shoe fetish. We had been out to a disco and on our return I went to make some coffee, leaving him watching the TV. As the door was ajar, I glanced into the living room and was stunned to see him with one of my boots over his nose. I could not fail to see that he had a huge erection, which he was masturbating furiously. I tackled him immediately and to say he was embarrassed is putting it mildly. I managed to drag it out of him that he had a thing about my footwear and especially my boots. As I really like him, I agreed that I would wear my boots when we have sex

although I feel foolish wearing my boots and very little else. On the plus side I have to admit that our sex has improved a lot. I have been considering asking him to consult a sex therapist but quite honestly I don't know how he would take my suggestion. I would not like to give him up as I have very strong feelings for him.

R.W.

This is quite common among men – if you don't believe me, watch *A Fish Called Wanda*. Shoes are a powerful attractant for men, which explains why women hobble around on otherwise illogical stiletto heels. We also know that pheromones, the sex attractants, are probably secreted through the feet. Feet are actually very sexy. Toe sucking is considered a major turn-on, not least by some former members of the British royal family. It's called 'shrimping' after the appearance of the little toe. Toe sucking probably has its roots in infancy, when your parents pretended to bite your toes off or subject them to 'This little piggy . . .' Shoes simply enhance the allure. You don't need to worry. Your boyfriend is not going to ditch you in favour of a pair of crocodile shoes, particularly if previously worn by Jimmy Nail.

Bums on seats – anal sex

It always tickles me reading advice from 'counsellors' when they become very pious over anal sex between heterosexuals. Despite changes and fluctuations in laws all over the world, people have been practising anal sex for countless generations and it is well described in the literature. Similarly, warnings of dreadful things which befall people who indulge in this form of sexual play have not yet brought the human race to its knees.

Paradoxically, it is used as a form of birth control in many cultures, which may explain its abhorrence by some religions. More liberated experts are quite happy when it comes to homosexual relationships as if gay men somehow are gifted with extra-durable anuses. Common sense dictates that it is safe so long as simple hygiene and safer sex are employed. Without putting too fine a point on it, the anus is full of things you would not want on your cornflakes. At the same time, oral sex involves some pretty intimate contact with places not a million miles away. Its a safe bet that the anus was not designed by evolution for sex. But then few people get pregnant by oral sex either. If you like it, and not all of us do, then fine. Keeping clean and using safer sex makes sense for all modes of entry, as it were.

Getting to the bottom of things

I have lived with Robert for eighteen months and we have a very good sex life. However, because of the publicity given to anal sex, Robert now wants us to try it and I thought I would write to you for your advice. I can see that from a man's point of view anal sex is probably not very different from vaginal sex except that perhaps the anus may be a tighter fit and more pleasurable. But I would like to know what sexual satisfaction I will get. For example, can I have an orgasm? Also should Robert use a condom? Furthermore, is it likely to be harmful to Robert if he does not use a condom?

J.E.

Trying to describe what anal sex is like to someone who has never experienced it is rather like explaining what it is like in a maze to someone with a similar lack of experience. It is impossible to issue a realistic answer as you may find the experience unpleasant, painful and/or humiliating. On the other hand, it may be one of the most sexually exciting experiences you have ever had. Judging from its popularity within the gay community, there is unlikely to be any danger. You should, however, practise safer sex, and using a condom makes good sense anyway because it can prevent the transmission of bacteria from the anus to your vagina. Use plenty of lubricant and the eternal phrase 'Be gentle with me.'

From the bottom up

> My wife and I practise anal sex all the time and we both really enjoy it. However, am I really being fair to her to want sex in this way all the time? We always use a condom and so all I'm really doing is checking if what we are doing is OK and won't do any harm.
>
> M.K.

Anal sex is now legal between consenting heterosexual adults. It was previously made legal for consenting gay men and the law for heterosexuals has been brought into line. As a sexual practice, it has been around for ever. It is favoured by some groups as a form of contraception and during menstruation. Gay men have anal sex with relatively little physical harm done so long as safer sex is practised. If your partner is happy with the relationship, then fine, but I do suspect that she would like some vaginal sex if only to relieve the boredom. You are using an organ which gives you great pleasure while she is not using hers. The simple answer is to ask her without applying pressure one way or the other, if you will excuse my turn of phrase.

Pick a number, any number

Is it possible to be faithful yet unfaithful? For centuries, men have rationalised that it is quite reasonable to employ the services of a prostitute while away from their partners. Few women would subscribe to this philosophy. Yet there are couples who find the idea of group sex, 'controlled infidelity', very exciting.

Judging by the number of letters on the subject, it is more common than most people think. My fear is that one of the two who are about to tango is not quite so sure about it all. Judge for yourself from these letters.

Three's a crowd and four is even better

> My wife and I have been together now for eight years and we share the most fantastic love life. We often reveal our fantasies and act some of them out, bringing ecstatic and mutual pleasure. For some time now, my wife has desired group sex and this idea turns me on. Is this abnormal or is it healthy to have such thoughts? Obviously, we would take precautions against diseases, but we both wish to see one another in the act with a total stranger just once in our lives.
>
> N.T.

The catch comes in your last sentence 'just once in our lives'. What generally happens is one partner enjoys it more than the other and wants to continue. Jealousy starts to creep in and then comes the full-blown row. You are over eighteen and can make up your own mind, and it is not a matter of morals. Do whatever you both want to do so long as nobody gets hurt. There are clubs which cater for couples, although I suspect most people go along as spectators. If you can survive this experimentation, you have an extremely stable relationship. Most marriages and relationships eventually crumble. As you say, safer sex is vital. And don't forget where you leave your socks – verrucas are such a nuisance.

Added punch

With many letters it can be difficult to untangle wishful thinking from reality. Watching two women fight is a constant theme, however, which seems to excite some men. My personal anxiety would be that they would turn on me. I've only got little legs.

Fatal attraction

I am a happily married man who has enjoyed a very varied, experimental sex life with my wife, but what happened recently blew my mind. A few weeks ago my wife and I went to a party and during the evening we both danced and flirted with other people, as we usually do. However, one woman I was talking to took it completely the wrong way and became persistent to the point of wanting me to take her home. My wife became angry and we both left. To my amazement, the woman followed us and halfway across the park on our way home, my wife stopped and confronted her. They both stood face to face and within seconds and without warning, this other woman struck out and hit my wife full in the face. My wife retaliated and then they got embroiled in a full fight. I was glued to the spot because I found the whole spectacle of two women fighting a major turn-on. In fact, I got an erection and ejaculated without even touching myself. Eventually, I intervened and stopped the fight and went home with my wife and had fantastic sex. She too found the whole thing exciting and now we both want to find her another opponent to fight with, this time with them both being naked. How strange are we?

P.L.

Strange? Not at all. Most people are looking for someone to have a fight with, but not necessarily naked. You are falling for the 'lesbian fantasy'. It crops up in various formats in most male daydreams. Two women fighting features in many films. As a gypsy girl, Sophia Loren did her bit for male eroticism by fighting another woman. Fighting is not a million miles away from sex. Good news for your wife: the Amateur Boxing Association has opened its doors to women, though I'm not too sure how it will take to the idea of boxing naked as it is difficult to gauge a blow below the belt.

Leap out of the dark

Some couples video themselves in action. This is not new. Many a bedroom has been built with a mirror over the bed and many a book has been written about them. We are fascinated by the sexual antics of both ourselves and our partners. This can spill over to wanting the voyeur's view of the action. Unfortunately, this can go horribly wrong when one or other of the couple like what they see too much.

You might not like what you find

> I accidentally came across a book in my husband's possession which featured letters from husbands and wives who got turned on by the husbands watching their wives performing with other men. I was shocked, and when I confronted him he admitted that he'd often fantasised about this. We are both dark-haired and my husband said he would really get turned on at the sight of me giving oral sex to a very blond man. I am totally confused! Does my husband really love me? Could he be bisexual? Should I please him by fulfilling his fantasy? I could just about do so, I think, provided the person was a total stranger, clean and very attractive! Help!
>
> L.M.

No, he is neither gay nor abnormal. Such fantasies are popular as shown by the book you accidentally found belonging

to your husband. One of the truisms of any long-standing relationship is that you need to work at it. Familiarity begins to equate with boredom. Finding new and exciting things to keep the sparkle in your love life is one of the keys to a successful sexual relationship. In these days of sexual liberation it can sound prudish to advise caution. Even so, fantasy turned into reality can be a great disappointment. The single biggest danger is jealousy, as you find yourself willing to 'just about do it' again. It sounds as though it will not take much arm-twisting for you to give it a whirl. Some couples appear to survive these experiments but for some it is the last straw and they drift apart. You may find it better to help him enjoy the fantasy rather than the reality. Talking through such an encounter can provide great sexual stimulation without the hassle of divorce. Either that or get him to buy a blond wig.

When is adultery not adultery?

Sometimes it is difficult to work out what is going on in a relationship. There can be a mixture of frustrated desires, mixed emotions and self-doubt. This letter shows that all is not as it seems at first sight.

Puppy love

Please help me, I feel so isolated. I am twenty-six and engaged to a guy of twenty-three. I have two

> problems. I have a long-standing desire to commit adultery with boys around sixteen years old. I have actually done this already. I am never attracted to mature males. I feel so guilty as I have been with my boyfriend for seven years and really love him. My other problem is that my boyfriend likes me to masturbate in front of him but I am very uncomfortable with this. Please can you help me as I feel abnormal with these two problems.
>
> S.Y.

Relationships, particularly sexual relationships, are never straightforward. Often one person wants to dominate while the other is submissive. Problems occur when both people want to take the lead role or both be submissive. Forget about men always being the master. Many happy relationships occur where this traditional view of sex is reversed. Similarly with gay men and lesbian women. It may well be that you wish to be dominant but your boyfriend is making demands of you that make you more submissive than you really like. 'Teaching' a younger man the art of sex is a fantasy of both men and women. Where would *The Graduate* be without Mrs Robinson? You say you want men 'around' sixteen. Be very careful. The legal age of consent in Britain is sixteen and not a day younger. Northern Ireland's age for consent is seventeen. I have often wondered whether you can be arrested on the boat from Liverpool exactly midway across the Irish Sea. You are not married so you cannot commit adultery in the legal sense of the word although a seven-year relationship with one person gives a certain moral claim irrespective of the law. Many men are really turned on by watching their partners masturbate. Like all sex play, you need to come to an agreement over what is and is not acceptable to both of you. Talking through your fantasies and sexual needs is the first step towards real understanding between sexual couples.

Pregnant pauses

Although the myth and mystery is being taken out of pregnancy to the extent that even men are beginning to understand it, there is still fear that sex is taboo. Strict rules used to be enforced over sex during pregnancy, but as the baby is virtually immune from harm during lovemaking, sex is safe at all stages, right up to the date the baby is due. A too liberal interpretation of this general observation can provide no end of entertainment for the labour ward staff.

There are some important exceptions requiring caution and advice and possibly abstinence from penetrative sex:

1. If there have been repeated miscarriages
2. If there has been a series of premature labours
3. If there is placenta praevia (where the placenta lies close to or over the opening of the womb)
4. If there is any bleeding during intercourse
5. If the waters have already broken

You should seek the advice of your obstetrician.

In late pregnancy, because of the growing foetus, women may find the 'man on top' position uncomfortable and be more relaxed, happy and comfortable with the side-by-side or rear-entry positions. Many women are more comfortable when they lie on top. There are of course other ways of showing and making love than penetrative sex. It may be that your partner has no desire for sex during the pregnancy. It is always best to talk about this as you can often find ways of helping each other.

Sexual desire

Male attitudes vary towards the appearance of their partner as pregnancy changes her shape. Some men find it very attractive, while others confess, often guiltily, that they find it a big turn-off. However, the phenomenon cannot be ignored. There is no rule that says you must find your pregnant partner attractive and equally you are not a pervert if it makes the hormones race.

During pregnancy, changes in a woman's sexual desire and in her sexual responses are usual. Some pregnant women have a reduced sexual interest in the first half of pregnancy, which continues, with considerable individual variation, through the second half of pregnancy. Reduced sexual appetite can be misinterpreted as rejection. Spending a longer time in body contact with each other, without being demanding, will help maintain confidence in your relationship.

I was never really sure why I stopped having sex. It certainly was not from [my partner's] side, she was more keen than ever. I can remember thinking about what would happen if I was made redundant from work, or if the baby was unhealthy. I also have to say that I was attracted to [my partner] in the first place because she was so slim, all my fantasies revolved around that. Isn't that pathetic to say. (New father)

I felt as though someone had given me an injection of something. I couldn't keep my hands off her. I loved the idea of having a little me inside her. (New father)

Myths

1 *Penetrative, vaginal sex causes an abortion.* Untrue. The penis cannot enter the womb. Your doctor will advise you if there are any good medical reasons not to do so.
2 *Sex can damage the baby.* Untrue. The baby is well out of harm's way during intercourse. It is possible to introduce sexually transmitted diseases such as HIV which could affect your partner and possibly your baby but you can be tested for these complaints. Meanwhile, use condoms, male or female.
3 *Sex can lead to premature labour.* There is no evidence for this although there are some conditions in which caution should be exercised (see above).
4 *An orgasm when pregnant will injure the baby or start labour prematurely.* Untrue. An orgasm can bring on contractions which are normally present towards the end of pregnancy called 'Braxton Hicks' contractions. They will settle on their own in a short time. Previous premature labours may require caution and your doctor will advise you.

We couldn't have sex in the 'normal' way because

[my partner] had placenta praevia. I read a book on sex play without having to enter her. So long as we both climaxed it was great. Even if one of us didn't it was still better than nothing. It made a big difference to our sex life after the baby was born too. [My partner] confessed to me that it had been getting a bit predictable.
(Father of four children)

It was me who was the most scared. I couldn't do it for fear of hurting the baby. We tried playing with each other instead. It worked and we also felt a bond between us, as if we were looking after the baby, like.
(New father)

Normal part of life

It is always worth remembering, because some doctors can forget, that pregnancy is not the same as being sick. Pregnant women are not 'patients'. Most women are healthier during pregnancy than at any other time in their lives. Pregnancy is a normal part of life and is remarkable for the lack of problems that actually occur.

Rabbit, rabbit, rabbit

I am in my early twenties and had a baby three months ago. To be honest, I used to be like a bunny when it came to sex but now, since I gave birth, I hate my boyfriend looking at any bits of my skin – I have stretch marks all over my stomach, thighs and breasts – and it upsets me that sex isn't as comfortable as it was before. I used to have a fit,

> healthy, slim body – not any more! I went from eight and a half stone to thirteen stone. Is the painful sex psychological or physical? Is there anything I can do to make the stretch marks go away?
>
> P.S. One positive thing – I have a beautiful baby!
>
> C.S.

Having a baby can take its toll on the body. Many of the changes are temporary and can be reversed with some simple exercises and diet. It helps if you are fit and exercise regularly before having your baby. Strict diets while pregnant are dangerous but so is simply allowing the weight to go on without any control as it is so much more difficult to reduce your weight afterwards. If your weight remained much higher after your baby was born it may be because you are less active than before. There is also a tendency to eat more both during and after pregnancy. If you reduce your calorie intake and increase your activity, your weight should return to normal. There is no good physiological reason why it should stay markedly higher after delivery.

Stretch marks are areas of altered skin. Collagen, which maintains skin elasticity, is reduced with ageing or by scarring. The skin loses its normal pigmentation. The marks are more noticeable if you are overweight so losing some pounds will make them smaller, like writing on a balloon. Creams containing vitamin E and A derivatives are said to help return skin to its normal condition.

Passing something the size of a rugby ball, and twice as hard, through your pelvis is bound to have some effect on your vagina. Some women find their vagina is too loose after having a baby. If this is a major problem it can be solved with relatively simple surgery. Episiotomies, cutting the perineum to avoid tearing during birth, are controversial and avoided whenever possible. The repair can be remarkably good at restoring normal service but some women still find sex uncomfortable afterwards. These repairs used to be performed by the most junior doctors or even medical students. Now only senior staff and highly trained midwives under supervision, if necessary, are allowed to put together those parts no man should let asunder. You could make use of lubricants to ease the friction as you may be too dry. This causes a vicious circle of anxiety which causes dryness leading to pain and round again to anxiety over the next attempt at making love. Foreplay and relaxation are essential.

Sexual persuasion

Most letters came from men. This cannot simply reflect the ratio of gays to lesbians. Women appear to come to terms with their sexuality far better than do men. More to the point, they are able to talk to other women far more easily than men can talk about being gay to other men. Some men agonise for ages before opening the closet door. Few are sorry they ever did.

Which way to turn?

> I have been thinking about having sex with another man for a couple of years now and I wonder whether I should go through with it. I love sex with women but a guy at work is gay and for some reason I really fancy him. I think he knows it because he is always smiling at me and it turns me on. Should I go for it at least once and see if I like it and what precautions should I take before allowing penetrative sex?
>
> A.N.

It sounds as though you have already made up your mind and that it is a case of 'when' rather than 'if'. Sexuality is a broad spectrum and it is possible, indeed common, for heterosexual men and women to be attracted to members of their own sex. This increases in certain situations where only the one sex is present. This does not make it right or wrong, it is simply an expression of human sexuality. In the rest of the animal kingdom such behaviour is also common. Whales in particular are known to have sexual play with members of their own sex. As the penis of the blue whale is at least six feet long this may explain that great spout of water which comes out of their heads. You have probably noticed your attraction towards men from a relatively early age. Most men are aware of their sexuality by the age of sixteen years. There is nothing to be ashamed of in investigating and examining

your own sexuality. But be careful and use safer sex. No matter how attractive you find Willie the killer whale, do not attempt under any circumstances to approach him without a six-foot condom.

Can see both sides of the argument

> I'm really worried about my sexuality. Please help. I'm a nineteen-year-old male and I'm in a steady relationship with a woman. She is good-looking and the most wonderful person. We have excellent regular sex and get on very well. The thing is, I masturbate up to three times a day and always fantasise about sexy muscle-bound men and I often stimulate my anus with a vibrator while fantasising that it's a man. I also look in the mirror and masturbate and find my own body very sexy indeed! My sister is a lesbian and when she came out my parents went mad. I've had feelings of being bisexual for years but I can't open up because my girlfriend would be so hurt. I'd love to go with a man but don't know where to find gay or bisexual men. Please help me as I'm so confused.
>
> M.K.

I don't think you are really confused so much as scared to come to terms with your own sexuality. Your sister's experience with your parents doesn't help matters much either. It's fairly obvious that you are either bisexual or gay. So where is the problem? The problem is with other people, your girlfriend, your parents and possibly your employer. Well actually, that's really their problem, not yours, because you are what you are. Like many men and women who eventually come out, you may be pleasantly surprised at the reaction of your girlfriend when you tell her. She probably suspects anyway and may find you attractive for exactly this reason. Parents generally go through a fairly predictable grief reaction. Disbelief, anger, guilt (did they make you gay?) and then coming to terms with the reality. Many parents not only continue to love their gay or lesbian children, they become fiercely supportive. There are some very famous bisexual people around. In truth, for every famous bisexual person there are countless thousands of perfectly ordinary bisexual men and women living everyday lives.

Lesbian love

Many women, like some men, find that they can still love someone without 'normal' sexual play. This tends to become more like sisterly love than that of true lovers in the sexual sense. Unfortunately, for some women they confuse this with what is expected from a relationship without realising just how much they are missing. Awareness can then come gradually and not like a blinding flash of light. Recognising habit for what it is is important for future happiness and fulfilment.

A dawning awareness

> I am twenty-five years old and I've been with my boyfriend for three years. We love each other very much but we haven't had sex now for nearly eighteen months and this is worrying me a lot. When we did have regular sex it never really did anything for me physically. I used to do it more out of habit than anything else, but now I don't like it if my boyfriend touches me intimately. I really love him, so why do you think this is? We still cuddle and are emotionally close in all other ways. Sometimes I wonder what it would be like to make love to a woman and images of naked women do turn me on. Could I be a lesbian? Being with a man does appeal to me even though the sexual desire isn't there. Please help.
>
> P.Y.

Men are generally aware of their sexuality fairly shortly

after puberty and certainly around sixteen years of age. They will bow to pressure from family and friends and go through heterosexual relationships just to 'fit in'. They may even marry and have a family. For some women this can take longer and many find themselves married, with children sometimes, before they understand their true sexual persuasion. Man or woman, this can be devastating for a marriage and cause pain on all sides. I suspect you are starting to question your own sexuality. It is quite normal and common to have long-standing friendships, love included, with someone to whom you are not physically attracted. Lesbianism is not abnormal, nor is being a gay man. They are both part of the spectrum of human sexuality which simply make us richer in our human resource for love. Other people's morality is their own concern, not yours.

Keeping safe

Confusion can lead to strange forms of stimulation. After thousands of letters, nothing now surprises me when it comes to things that turn people on. Reality never quite lives up to its corresponding fantasy. It's making sure nobody is going to get hurt that is the main thing.

Snow White and her little helpers

> Over the past year or so I have found myself more and more attracted to short women – to be more precise, people who would normally be called midgets or dwarves. Maybe it's because I feel they need protecting but I can't help but fantasise about having sex with a midget. To make matters worse, about two weeks ago I began to masturbate while watching my little sister's copy of *Snow White*. I watch it quite a lot now and I believe my mother suspects something. Apart from this, I'm a normal twenty-year-old who has no real vices. I don't think that this is normal behaviour and I don't think I'm

> gay – even though the blokes in the cartoon excited me. I need some advice. Is there any way to stop this?
>
> D.W.

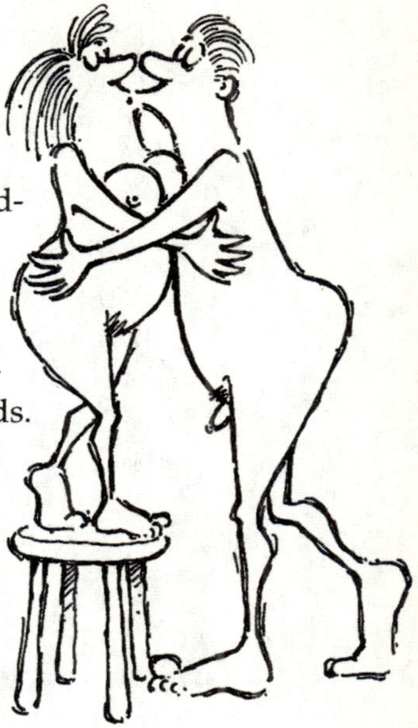

There is absolutely nothing wrong with finding people of short stature attractive. Ask anyone of short stature. Turn it on its head and ask is it abnormal for a person of short stature to be attracted to average-sized people. We all have the 'ideal' size in our heads. Generally speaking, this is not absolute and many of us end up with partners different from what we consider our perfect match. The problem comes when only one character is acceptable and becomes an obsession. People of short stature have as much right to a loving relationship with other people of whatever height. There is no law which says you must stick to people of your own physical build, thank goodness, or it would be a dull world indeed. It may well be that you like to feel protective and in charge. Many men choose smaller women than themselves for exactly this reason. You need to decide whether you like small adults or whether there is an attraction to small people because you perceive them as immature and childlike. This could be dangerous. I feel you may be terribly confused over your own sexuality as you denied gay feelings yet are attracted to short-stature men. I would suggest a trip to your GP, who could refer you for some psychosexual counselling.

Any excuse will do so long as it is a good one

Thanks to all the pressures from society, parents and the law, people will try to rationalise their sexuality in bizarre ways. Instead of simply saying to themselves, 'I just so happen to like people of the same sex and find them sexually attractive', they will make up 'reasonable explanations'. This is also true of parents and society, who will jump to conclusions such as upbringing or the person being dressed in the wrong colour as a baby. Men try these mental contortions more than women, but both sexes produce some pretty weird interpretations of reality.

The long and short of it

> I am in a very difficult situation. I am attracted only to hermaphrodite women. I have no idea where to find one. Do you know where they go and how I can meet them? I live in Ireland, by the way, and miles from the nearest big town. I know I'm not gay, and I never could be, but please can you shed any light on the mystery of my sex life?
>
> A.D.

I sense some confusion here. You basically cannot be either a male or female hermaphrodite as by definition they have the genital organs of both sexes. It is possible to be genetically male but have the appearance of a woman. Thankfully, these conditions are rare as these people have no uterus and a short vagina. As a cruel irony, they tend to be very attractive and live their lives as women, finding out only when their periods fail to begin. It may well be that you are, despite your denial, attracted to men. Some men who are gay but deny it are attracted to transvestites or transsexual men. It provides the subconscious rationale that they didn't *really* know about the true sex of the person. This is more likely if you have had a very strict upbringing with rigid guidelines about sexual behaviour.

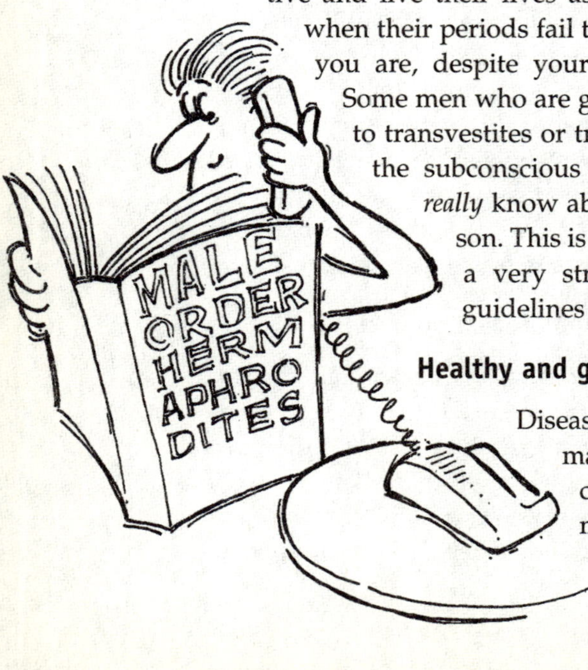

Healthy and gay

Disease has little concern for a man's sexual orientation. Life can be difficult for young men who are homosexual or unsure about their sexuality. Many feel like square pegs in round holes, driven by society, school, relatives and even the law. Some can become desperately lonely and depressed. Indeed the suicide rate is higher among gay teenagers. For most men, 'coming out' is a difficult decision, but most are surprised and relieved by the reception they get from friends and family.

If you are not sure, talk to someone you trust, a friend, teacher or parent.

Health

If you are not on a GP's list, you should get on to one. Ask your friends – it is usually very obvious which GPs make a special effort or are gay themselves. If you feel that your GP is not approachable over gay issues, choose another one whom you know to be better socially adjusted. Ask your local genito-urinary (GU) clinic or HIV unit. They will tell you which GPs in the area are 'gay-friendly'.

Anal sex

Anal sex is practised by many gay and straight men. Indeed it is a common form of 'contraception' in some cultures. Regular anal sex often leads to tiny cuts inside the rectum, which has a relatively thin lining. These cuts will often bleed, particularly during anal sex. It is essential, therefore, to take precautions and use a strong condom such as Durex Extra Safe, Mates Extra Strong, HT Specials or Gay Safe. This will protect both you and your partner.

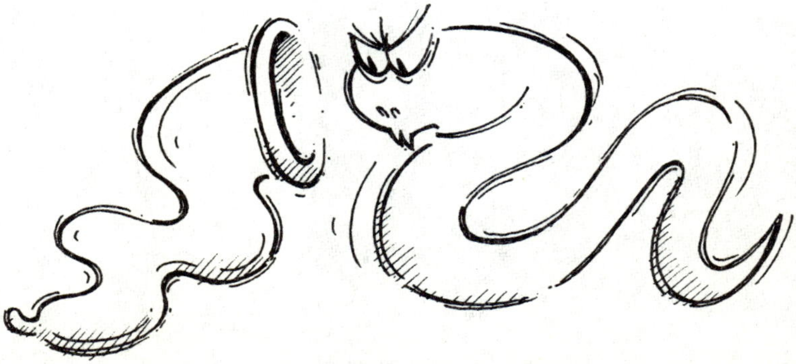

Although extra lubrication is often required, do not use an oil-based lubricant such as Vaseline, baby oil, margarine or butter. They will damage the condom. There are water-based lubricants available such as KY Jelly or Foreplay. If you are not sure, ask the chemist. They sell thousands of them and will not be embarrassed to give advice.

Greener grass – gender conflict

Television and newspapers are eternally fascinated by gender conflicts. Men wishing to be women is more common than vice versa. Nobody really knows why. When a GP or a teacher 'changes sex', it attracts media attention to the point of intrusiveness. But for every high-profile case, there are thousands of unhappy people who just get on with their lives. For them a sex change is impossible for either financial or personal reasons. They are often clinically depressed and seek psychiatric help.

It's from these people that these letters mainly originate. Many are confused about their sexual identity and what they can or should do about it. Humour is never far away but then neither is merciless ridicule from an unsympathetic and often vicious press. This is in contrast to the reactions of patients, students, pupils, workmates, colleagues and even spouses of these unhappy people. These are but a tiny fraction of the letters received, which is a measure of the misery bubbling beneath the surface.

Dressed to kill

> I am a 26-year-old male virgin and since I've lost my girlfriend six years ago I have lost all my self-confidence and my urge for sex. Since then I have started cross-dressing and I find that this relaxes me. My friends knew I was doing this for a while and now help me with my make-up and clothes. When I am dressed I look very convincing and raunchy. My problem is that I have met this girl who's interested in me but I don't know what to do or say to her. Should I tell her that I cross-dress or should I wait? I want to be totally honest with her.
>
> P.S. I'm also very shy. What should I do?
>
> B.M.

Your new girlfriend will probably recognise the way you feel most comfortable. Many women find this particular aspect of sexual enjoyment and personal fulfilment very attractive. You are very fortunate in having the support of your friends. Society can still be very harsh on people who commit the terrible crime of simply wanting to be who they are. If you feel more comfortable when you are dressed in this way then it gives a good insight into your personality and you should not suppress it unless it brings you into conflict with people who are less understanding than your friends. Being honest really is the best policy and you should tell your girlfriend how you feel. You may well be pleasantly surprised by the reaction.

Terminological inexactitude

Semantics often get in the way of understanding and simply increase confusion. In desperation, people look for terms or descriptions which best fit their perception of themselves. Unfortunately, there is often a great deal of overlap between medical terms. While it makes not a jot of difference to the individual what they are 'called', it compounds their unhappiness if misunderstanding creeps in and others condemn when there is no logical reason to do so. You won't read a more confused letter than this one.

The riddler

> I'm a hermaphrodite, or in today's terms 'intersexual', and while I was raised as a boy, I am intrinsically a girl and I love being feminine. When I reached puberty I began to dress normally as a girl and kept it secret from my parents. Now in my adult life, I am confused. I prefer to be a woman but I don't fancy men, so I'm not homosexual. I'm not heterosexual because I'm half-female; I'm not a lesbian because I'm half-male; I'm not bisexual because I don't fancy men! Please tell me, what am I?
>
> S.A.

At a good guess, confused. You are mixing terms up as if they are all mutually exclusive. Many transsexuals describe themselves as being trapped in a body of the opposite sex to their true sex. In other words, their appearance is opposite to the way they feel about themselves. True hermaphrodites are rare as by definition they have the sexual organs of both sexes. A transvestite is someone who prefers to wear clothes of the opposite sex but doesn't actually see themselves as being of that sex. Obviously, there is great overlap between these two. Sexual persuasion is also a spectrum with great overlap. You can be 'heterosexual' yet still find members of your own sex attractive. Similarly, you can be gay or lesbian and find the opposite sex attractive. Some people will be at one end or the other of this spectrum. Somewhere in the middle there is bisexuality, where you find both sexes equally attractive. I'm confused just writing this so I'm not in the least bit surprised you are finding it difficult to sort out your own feelings. If you really want to know what you are, I'll tell you – you are a person who wants to enjoy being what you feel you really should be. If you used this definition for anything else it would be called personal honesty and integrity. Just because when it comes to sex we like to box everything up in clever terminology makes no difference. Be what you are, not what everyone else wants you to be.

A fine line

Cynics will tell you that all the letters presented by agony doctors have been made up by themselves. In my experience, not only is there no shortage of letters – Carlton Television received over two hundred each week for *The Good Sex Guide Late* – but it would be impossible to have enough imagination to do this. On the other hand, there is no way of knowing just how true any particular letter actually is. Simply writing down a fantasy can be therapeutic. I suspect some of my answers are not. This letter could be one of those.

Puss in boots

> Mine is not so much a problem as a discovery. I am a 27-year-old male and have always looked upon the idea of working under a woman boss as a bit humiliating. However, recently I accepted the job of personal assistant to a 35-year-old self-employed business lady. She is smart, stylish and very attractive. She is also highly efficient and strict on timing and general office procedure. It really began after I'd been working for her for about a month,

when she invited me into her sitting room for a drink and started to lecture me on the benefits of good discipline, self-control and restraint. I thought this was strange since I had never made any advances towards her, nor had it entered my head to do so.

But there is just something about her – her perfume, her elegant demeanour, the swish of her clothes as she passes me. Anyway, I found myself agreeing with everything she said, and said I would be completely obedient – even accepting corporal punishment. There is no sex as such, but I am now required to wear shorts and whenever I make a mistake, however slight and trifling, I find myself bent across her desk and being soundly spanked. On Friday evening I am caned. It jolly well hurts too. I know this sounds bizarre, but I actually like it. I think it is wonderful and I wouldn't change my job for anything. I adore and respect her. She is magnificent. Is this masochism gone mad?

P.S. I think all women are gorgeous!

R.N.

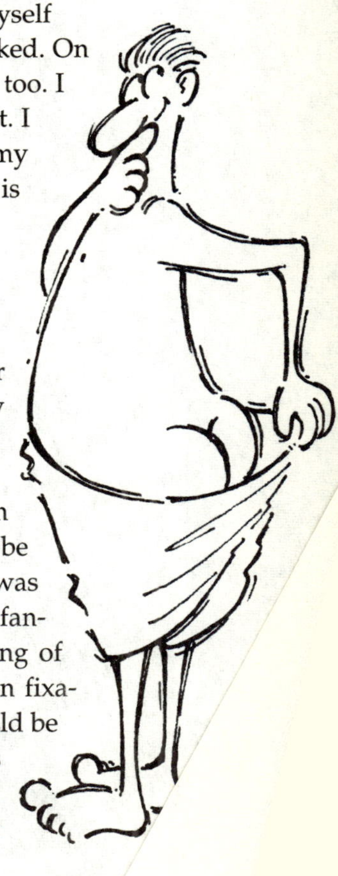

I would like to be a fly on the wall if this ever became a case at an industrial tribunal. Generally speaking, employers are not allowed to spank their employees no matter how much they ask for overtime. If you converted the boss into a man and you into a woman, I reckon there would be some questions asked in parliament, even if it was only to get her phone number. Either this is pure fantasy on your part and you are seriously thinking of going into erotic literature or you have a certain fixation on femininity. My suspicion is that you would be happier stepping into her shoes, literally. This has less to do with masochism and more to do with transvestism or even transsexualism. At some point she will suggest you try on her clothes. Or you might just find some of her underwear left behind, 'by accident'. When they are discovered to be missing the next day she will demand to know where they are, at which point you will guiltily admit that your admiration for her led you actually to put them on. Or perhaps I am seriously considering a career in erotic literature as well. Either way, lie back, or rather forwards, and enjoy it.

Powerful pressure

Such is the pressure from society to conform that parents will apply enormous blackmail tactics in a desperate attempt to 'normalise' their children. Marriages can become almost arranged affairs as part of this process. Most parents are aware of their children's sexuality but choose to ignore or suppress it. This letter tells a sad story, bordering on abuse. I trust there will come enlightenment and constructive sympathy and I will be able to stop reading such mail devoid of hope.

Cross over cross-dressing

> I am writing because I don't know what to do. When I was eight years old I started to dress up in my mum's clothes and one day I got caught. My uncle was very nasty to me because neither he nor my mum understood. My mum didn't speak to me for ages and threatened to tell everyone else if I didn't stop. I am now twenty-six years old. I have told my best friend and she is very understanding but I am very upset because I keep doing this bad thing and I can't stop. My friend asked me a lot of things about why I dress up, and I said I like to do it, I wish I was born a girl instead of a boy. I am very confused. I have thought of killing myself and just wish I could stop. I just want to wear women's clothes – is this such a crime? Please help me, I don't know what to do.
>
> S.K.

First of all, relax. You are in good company as cross-dressing is extremely common and is actually favoured in some societies. The use of austere clothes for men is a relatively recent phenomenon and when given half a chance men will be as flamboyant as women. This is not quite the same as wanting to wear female clothing. Sexuality is a sliding scale. Few men or women never have concerns and doubts over their sexuality. For some people, dressing as the opposite sex provides relief and sexual enjoyment. Transvestism is not the same as transsexualism. Women born in men's bodies are true transsexuals. They feel psychologically female but trapped within the male physique. Some transsexuals would go further and refute the psychological connection: they are simply women, full stop. The desire to cross-dress for a transvestite or transsexual is very strong and many men have suffered ignominy and humiliation from a society more tolerant of violence than such a harmless act as cross-dressing. Parents often overreact and try to 'normalise' their child. It rarely works, causing only frustration, bitterness and desperation. It is far more important for you to come to terms with yourself as you are. There is nothing immoral, illegal or socially dangerous in being a transvestite or transsexual.

Scale of misery – losing a partner

Psychologists often refer to a scale which rates life events in terms of the stress they can cause. The death of a spouse or child comes at the very top. Many people will not admit that part of their feeling of loss comes from the absence of physical contact and sex. It is hard for anyone who has not gone through the experience to realise just how bad this can feel. Worse still, thoughts of sex with someone else bring a whole basketful of mixed emotions to the surface, not least guilt. It helps to recognise the pattern that happens when a partner is lost.

On a much lower level, getting your car nicked will result in a similar, but obviously much less painful sequence of emotions.

Too mobile

If, for instance, you return to the car park and fail to find the car where you left it, you pass through a number of phases:

1. *Denial*: 'Can't be true, must have left it somewhere else.' You will probably hunt round the whole car park despite the fact that you know exactly where you left it. You may even 'see' the car in another parking place.

2. *Anger*: You will blame the car park attendant, the police, God, society, Liverpool FC and even the car itself for being stolen. 'Stupid car, can it not even look after itself, and in a car park for heaven's sake. That's the last wax and shine it gets from me.'

3. *Guilt*: The next emotion can be the most destructive – guilt. 'How could I be so idiotic? I should have taken all the wheels off before I left it.' People will find the most unlikely things with which to whip themselves unmercifully. It can last a long time, despite rationalising the cause of their misery.

4. *Acceptance*: After a certain amount of time there comes a period of acceptance. The length of time varies, and it can even depend upon the community. Thus if cars are stolen every night from the street, it is socially acceptable to nip out and buy a new one. People generally will profess to have come to terms with their loss before they actually have done so. 'It was only a car after all, even if it was a GTi.'

5. *Coming to terms*: Well-meaning folk will tell you that you will get over it. The truth is you never 'get over' a major life event. What does happen is that you come to terms with it, the pain diminishes gradually with time. This is not a smooth progression, however, and anniversaries,

> returns to places or even casual mention will release waves of heartache. 'Wasn't this where you bought the GTi? Why are you banging your head against the window?'

Obviously there is no comparison to the loss of a partner but the phases are more or less the same. Some people find it very difficult to break out of the vicious cycle of thinking about sex and the guilt it produces. These letters show all the stages of grief and how people come to terms with their loss. They are looking forward now, but not forgetting the past.

Just to help me sleep

Even masturbation can feel like a betrayal. Men and women find themselves enjoying company, lightly sprinkled with sexual attraction, then suddenly feel guilty. Television with its goodly dollop of sexual titillation may be a form of relief but can also raise guilty feelings. Like a medical equivalent of a cold shower, many will turn to sleeping tablets. This is no surprise. The bed represents everything to do with sexual comfort and loving. Buying a different bed can evoke a mixture of pain and relief.

Wide awake and standing to attention

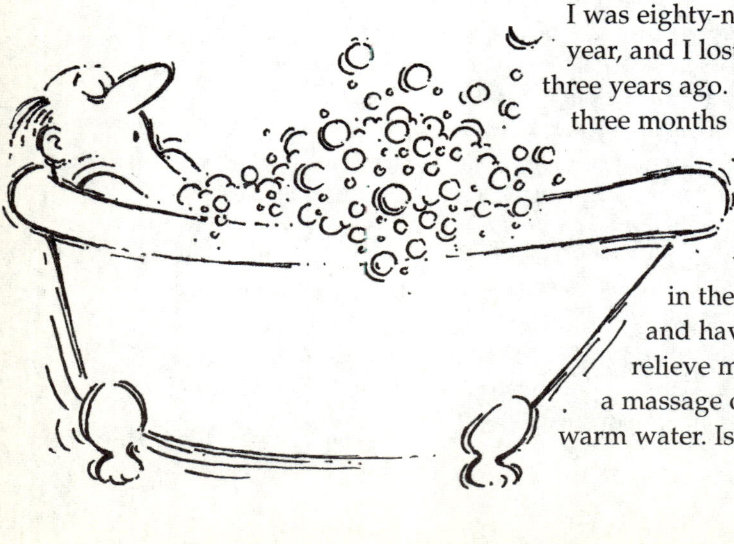

I was eighty-nine last year, and I lost my wife three years ago. For the last three months I get intense erections when waking up in the morning and have to relieve myself with a massage of soap and warm water. Is my

> hormone/testosterone out of order? I was sexually active since I was fourteen and since then sex played a big role in my life. However, since my wife died I find it very difficult to form new relationships as all my female companions say sex is out of the question.
>
> A.F.

For most men the problems start when they wake up in the morning with no erection. The prostate holds the only known G spot for men. Vibration or rubbing against this gland will cause arousal. During the night your bladder fills, putting increasing pressure on the prostate. This does a very nice job of causing an erection when you wake. You may find this happens more often after a few drinks the night before. Needless to say, it is normal and proves that all your tackle is in good working order. Age is no barrier to enjoying sex. Ageism, where men were dubbed 'dirty old men' if they as much as expressed any sort of sexual desire, is on the way out, not least because we are all living so much longer. It sounds as though you are surfacing from your grief over losing your wife. No one will ever replace her, but there are plenty of women who would be glad of male company and sexual relationships. As men die on average six years younger than women, you are heavily outnumbered by women. Change your female acquaintances if they all feel you are too old to enjoy sex, or that you need to remain 'loyal' to your wife. You are not asking anyone to step into her shoes.

Effects underestimated

Most people underestimate the effects of bereavement on a person, until it happens to themselves. The bereaved person often will not realise that the loss of interest in their job or family, constant pacing of the floor, spontaneous weeping or complete loss of appetite are all normal and common manifestations of grieving. People who are close to the bereaved person may also become impatient with them as time wears on, again underestimating the extent of the effects, and the length of time they can be felt by the person. It is at this point that true friends are worth their weight in gold. To know when to let the person alone and when to sit and listen, often to the same story over and over again without interruption, is a gift that few people have nowadays. Bereavement can even affect the memory and people will comment upon a 'complete blank' for a period following the death. Almost every facet of life can be affected, only the scale and duration varies between people. Being non-judgmental and supportive when the conversation inevitably turns to new relationships can be difficult, particularly for close relatives and children. Ageism also creeps in. Old men and women are expected to 'know their place' and not to behave in any sexually overt manner. How many poor sods have been threatened by their children with, 'What would Mummy think!' Thankfully, there are professional agencies who specialise in this form of counselling and they can be contacted through your GP. Nobody pretends that strangers are as good as friends or relatives, but they can often help a person who has difficulty coming to terms with their loss.

The greatest loss

> I am fifty-three years old. My husband and only sexual partner of over thirty-three years died suddenly. Marriage was not all a bed of roses. Like many couples, we had our ups and downs, but we stuck it out together, and the sexual side, in the early years, was absolutely terrific. Later on, menopause affected my needs and desires but we coped well and my husband was quite understanding. Over the past eighteen months I have missed his presence and companionship, but now I'm beginning to miss the physical sexual contact and the cuddles. I am not looking for a replacement for my late husband, but any advice you can offer towards 'filling the gap' would be of great help.
>
> A.E.

Grief and grieving take their toll. People grieve in different yet fairly predictable ways. After the disbelief, anger and slow realisation there comes the self-blame: 'If only I had bought those shoes he asked for he wouldn't have slipped.' There is no limit to the number of whips you will choose with which to beat yourself. Sexual desire is a very good example. Just thinking about sex is enough to start off a great waterfall of guilt. Even Scarlett O'Hara had trouble with the traditional grieving role in *Gone with the Wind*, but you can open the curtains and let the light in. Masturbation is a great comforter. You can use memories to supply the stimulus. Finding a replacement for your husband is impossible and undesirable. Few people will tolerate for long being compared to some former partner, and nobody will ever fill shoes that once trod paths special to you. These memories are yours and don't need to be diluted with surrogates. Look to the future. You are a young woman with a long life ahead of you. Only the most selfish of partners would wish their loved ones a life devoid of loving once they had gone for ever. Look for someone different, expect different compliments, fresh observations on common scenes. There will never be anyone the same as your partner. But that's better. Cuddles from someone new, sex with a different person is not the same as trying to pretend your partner still has you in his arms. Extend your circle of friends through social groups. One disaster for couples is the isolation they self-impose which excludes single people and friends. Don't let anyone kid you that you ever get over the death of a partner. You don't, but you do come to terms with it, and everyone does it in their own way. Let the tut-tutting classes tut. Life is so very short. Look for future happiness while remembering what went before.

Points to remember

- People have different ways of expressing grief, there is no 'normal way'.
- Talk about it, even if it hurts.

- Don't be afraid to seek support from friends, relatives or your doctor.
- Aggression is natural, even towards close relatives and well-meaning neighbours. Doctors are a common focus of anger.
- Allow yourself time to grieve, and avoid drugs, if in doubt .

We only rent this space and life is not a dress rehearsal, this is it.

Still lonely after all these years

I am seventy-five years old and throughout my long marriage until my wife died I never associated with any other women except those I met on a purely friendly basis. I love my wife so very much and bitterly regret losing her so what follows is in no way derogatory. Basically, although we had regular sex throughout our marriage it was always fairly unadventurous with one main position – the missionary position. I did on one occasion suggest we find alternatives but she just didn't want to know. I accepted this but always knew that sexually things could have been considerably better between us. Recently, I bought a newspaper in which women were offering sex in the guise of massage and my question to you is, do you think I could obtain from these women the kind of sex I would have enjoyed but never experienced with my wife?

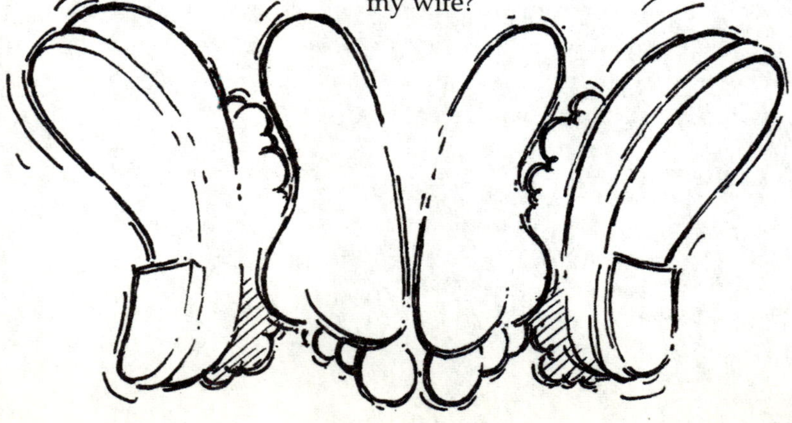

> Certainly, I would never have considered such a move while my wife was alive.
>
> P.K.

Grief differs in the way it affects people. There are, however, stages which are well recognised. People move through grief in the form of disbelief, anger, guilt and, finally, coming to terms with their loss. Wishing for what should have been is very common. The relationship with your wife was very special and cannot be replaced, but it is understandable that you miss the sexual part of your relationship along with the loving that you experienced. It is impossible for anyone else to replace the very special relationship that you two shared. However, men and women are living much longer. Women actually live longer on average than do men, and so the good news is that there are more women of your age than there are men. Without doubt there are women who will be able to supply your sexual needs but you may find it more satisfying to have a meaningful relationship with a woman which includes more than just sex. Replying to advertisements in magazines carries all the risks of exploitation on both sides, not to mention the danger of sexually transmitted diseases. Perhaps it would be better to make contact with someone new rather than take these major risks.

Points to remember – penises

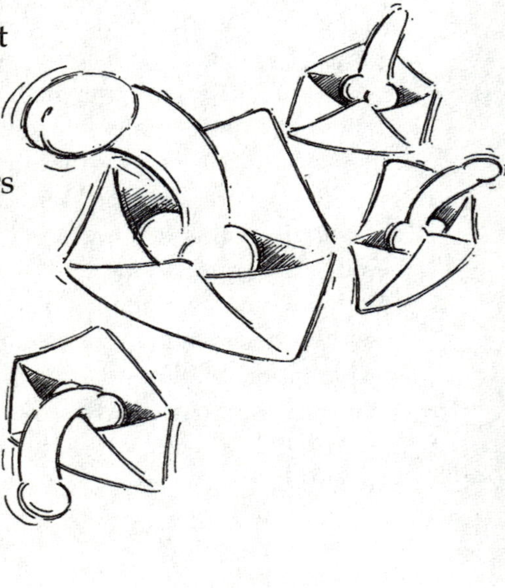

Most of the letters I get from men involve their penises. A fair proportion of the letters from women also deal with this subject. I can only conclude that penises are pretty important no matter which end of one you happen to find yourself.

Size is a perennial cause of concern. Most men compare themselves with the guy at the next urinal, which is a mistake as looking sideways on gives an impression of length which is lost when looking down. It's best to use a mirror.

Surgery can lengthen the penis and some famous men admit to subjecting themselves and their tackle to the knife. About 50 per cent of the penis is hidden inside the pelvis, held by ligaments. These help maintain the angle of dangle during erection. By cutting these ligaments a significant increase in size can be achieved but at a cost. Instead of the penis taking off like a Harrier jump jet, it will do so like a Lancaster bomber. Losing weight can also help. Roughly one inch of penis length is gained for every thirty pounds of excess weight lost. There is a law of diminishing returns operating here and once you get down to a total body weight of under seven stone you become either a jockey or a pole-vaulter.

Shape

Men worry about the shape of the penis more than their nose. Most will accept a nose bent sideways at ninety degrees with little hope of disguise yet want almost invisible kinks ironed out from their penis. The structure of the penis gives a clue to why it is the shape it is. There are three large tubes of spongy tissue, the cavernosa. By filling these with blood the penis will enlarge, both radially and in length. If one fills less than the others, or if scarring stops one from extending as it fills, the whole thing is pulled to one side. There may well be room here for creative surgery, particularly for wine lovers.

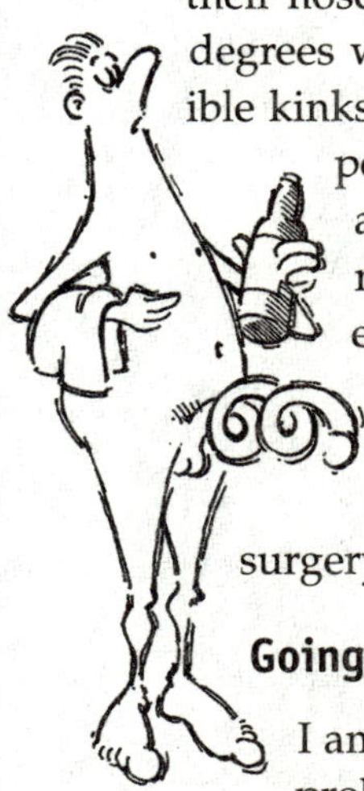

Going bananas

I am a 24-year-old man, with a very worrying problem. It has to do with the shape of my penis. When I become aroused, my penis grows in size and becomes hard, as normal, but it also bends quite severely downward so that it doesn't look like a full erection. I feel sexually inadequate because of this.

I've heard of something called Peyronie's disease. Could this be it? Also, I've read that vitamin E might help. Is this true? I am a virgin, and because of this problem I am reluctant to form a sexual relationship with a woman. Please help.

V.T.

Penises vary considerably in both size and shape. If we were to believe all the erotic or pornographic videos, your penis should be at least twelve inches long and as straight as an arrow. In truth, the range of size is from around three inches to six inches (7.5 cm to 15 cm). Most men do not have a perfectly straight penis but instead have bends in any direction. Severe angulation goes under the heading of Peyronie's disease but actually there is no single cause. We do know that trauma early on in life can produce thickened bands of tissue on one side of the penis shaft. This causes the penis to bend during erection and can make ejaculation painful. Surgery is available on the National Health Service and you should consult your general practitioner. Creams containing vitamin E have some success in improving skin quality in the area of scars. You may try this while you are waiting for an appointment with the plastic surgeon.

Insult to injury

Considering the way it sticks out, you would think there would be even more injured penises than there are. Even so, men manage to mangle, chop and burn their most prized possessions on a regular basis. Unfortunately, the embarrassment factor can delay treatment. One man was cooking while naked. He had wisely put a tea towel around his chest to protect himself from fat splashing from the frying eggs. No problem. No problem, that is, until he reached over to switch on the fan behind the electric cooker and his penis went under the grill. This is bad enough, you may say, but it gets worse. The element was the old type with uncovered wire. Not only did he burn his penis but he experienced 220 volts in those places not designed to conduct electricity. All this came to light only when he turned up at casualty with burns to his chest from two fried eggs.

Energetic lovemaking also causes casualties. Tears, fractures and even amputations occur when the red haze becomes too much, particularly if your partner has reason to believe that he or she is not the only person to have provided oral sex recently.

Broken arrow

> I have a real problem. When I was very young I fractured my penis (so young I don't remember how or when it happened). It makes it difficult to get close to the girls in my life, to the point where I cannot stay in a relationship much beyond the first intimate contact. I am still a virgin but I want a full relationship. Do I need surgery? If so, how much will it cost and is there any risk to the feeling in my penis?
>
> A.Y.

Generally speaking, most men know when they suffered a fractured penis – it's the kind of thing that tends to stick in a person's mind. Not many of us would look down, scratch our ear and mutter, 'Now I wonder how that happened.' Physiology-wise, you can fracture your penis only while it is fully erect. The spongy tissue is then filled under pressure with blood and is extremely firm. Most injuries occur, therefore, while making love and few men would fail to notice. The penile shaft actually does break and is held together only by the skin, urethra and blood vessels. Unfortunately, the blood tends to clot once blood flow becomes impossible. This makes surgery extremely difficult. With expert attention the penis can recover but it tends to have bends where once there were no bends. Plastic surgery can help and it is possible to insert a metal or plastic prosthesis which restores an 'erection'. (See p. 119 for more detail.) I suspect you never actually fractured your penis but are suffering from Peyronie's disease. The causes of Peyronie's are many and may involve minor trauma during childhood or during sexual play. This would explain your confusion. Tight bands of thickened tissue form on the shaft of the penis, causing it to bend in one direction and making erections either difficult or extremely painful. This can be treated surgically under the NHS.

Forewarned

You could be forgiven for thinking that the foreskin was an afterthought. It can be both a blessing and a curse. One man came into casualty with his foreskin neatly zipped up in his trouser fly. He refused, not without good reason, to sit in the waiting room and stood instead in the corridor. This was his undoing, literally. He fainted and while he was slumped on the ground unconscious an experienced nurse deftly pulled down his zip. He waddled off into the sunset a happier and less entangled man.

The foreskin is a thin layer of skin which normally sits over the head or glans of the penis. Its job is probably to protect the sensitive glans beneath and act as a valve along with the thickened ridge around the base of the glans preventing sperm from leaving the vagina. It has secretory glands producing substances which may act as pheromones or sex attractants. If it is not regularly pulled down and washed, a cheesy yellow smegma forms which reminds passing Dobermann pinschers of Grimsby fish market. You can run from a Dobermann pinscher but you cannot hide – not with four pounds of haddock down your trouser front anyway.

See pp. 107–8 for more information about circumcision.

That's why it's called a foreskin

> My problem is that when my penis is erect my foreskin remains over the helmet. When I try to pull it back it feels quite painful and I imagine that sex would also be quite painful. I have seen a couple of sex videos and all the men have their foreskin pulled back. I feel that I am abnormal in some way. Is there anything I can do about it? Do I need to be circumcised?
>
> S.W.

Yes. Stop worrying. The foreskin sits over the helmet or glans of the penis until it is pulled back. That's why it's called a foreskin. If you haven't been pulling it back regularly during masturbation or washing, then it is bound to be tight. For some men such tight pullovers can be painful when first having sex. They usually find it gets better each time although riding a bike becomes a whole new experience for a short while. You should really be retracting your foreskin regularly anyway if only for hygiene reasons. Do it when flaccid first, then partly erect, then, finally and excruciatingly, when fully erect. If it refuses to return, squeeze the helmet firmly after applying an ice compress for about ten minutes. It will eventually go back if you squeeze firmly enough. You do not need a circumcision.

Premature exasperation

> I suffer from premature ejaculation and have only a four-inch penis. I started masturbating when I was only thirteen and I am sure that this was when I stopped developing sexually. I have tried sex with quite a few women but have never satisfied any of them. This is because I cannot last more than one minute. I am very envious of people who have a normal sex life and am always depressed. Please do not say size doesn't matter, as I think it matters a

> great deal. Could it be some sort of hormone deficiency? If so, what can be done?
>
> P.K.

Average penis sizes range from around 7.5 cm to 15 cm (3 to 6 inches). There is no normal size as such but less than 6.5 cm would be considered on the small side. Old maxims such as 'it's not the size, it's what you do with it' have an element of inherent truth. Most women will admit, however, to preferring larger rather than smaller penises. Unfortunately, most men compare themselves in the wrong way. Looking sideways at another man's vital bits only to glance down at your own puts you at an unfair disadvantage. Looking straight down when comparing sizes makes the penis look even smaller. Stand beside a mirror and look sideways. Yes, that great horse clobber belongs to you. Avoid doing this in a public toilet as it only raises eyebrows, not to mention expectations. Hormone deficiency will influence penis size, particularly if the deficiency was present during puberty. Masturbation has no effect on penis size, which is sad considering the frenetic attention this organ gets from most men. Myths such as excessive masturbation causing mammoth-sized appendages are unfortunately old wives' tales, probably your mother's. Thankfully, masturbation will not cause a gradual disappearance of the same organ, a myth which is patently untrue as the human race continues to increase in numbers at an exponential rate.

Jelly fishy

> I have a very embarrassing problem which is starting to concern me more and more. I am a sexually healthy 24-year-old male with a wonderful caring girlfriend. The problem is that sometimes when I ejaculate, among the white semen is a largish jelly-like substance and I don't think it's normal or looks very nice. Even though my girlfriend doesn't mind and she'll still perform oral sex on me, she's also said that she's never seen anything like this

before with previous boyfriends. Am I normal? Am I producing bad sperm? Will it affect my chances of fathering children? I await your reply. Please can you help me?

S.M.

There is very little chance that you are abnormal or that the 'jelly' you are producing is abnormal sperm. Most of the ejaculate, the semen, is stuff to keep the sperm alive and to neutralise the acid environment of the vagina. Boozing too much will cause dehydration, which will affect the thickness of the semen. Similarly, the frequency of sex will have an effect on the consistency of semen. You sound as though your girlfriend is very understanding and someone to keep hold of. Many people actually find oral sex off-putting, particularly if they have to swallow the semen. Forcing someone to do so is the beginning of the end of a beautiful relationship, as Humphry Bogart nearly said in *Casablanca*. Infections of the testes and even cancer can also cause changes in semen consistency so if you are concerned go and see your doctor.

That's torn it, again

I have a problem of a tearing frenulum. It is a problem which I (and my wife) suffer from regularly and it is very painful. I have to stop immediately. The moment is then ruined and lost for both of us. I have been to my GP and he has prescribed a steroid cream which solves the problem for a couple of days. But what about the cause? Do I need to be circumcised? I do use a lubricant but I find that my wife does 'dry up' on me. I am fifty-three and my wife is fifty-four.

G.H.

I was once called out to a man who was absolutely distraught. He and his wife were having sex while she was seven months pregnant. Suddenly, blood was everywhere.

He thought he had caused an abortion, which is almost totally impossible through sex during a normal pregnancy. It transpired he had torn his frenulum, which is a thin ligament under the foreskin to the glans of the penis. Relief was not the word when I explained what had happened. Only then did he all at once notice the pain in his penis. Regular use of powerful steroid creams is not a good idea. They can actually cause a weakening of the ligament and the surrounding skin, making it more likely to break again. You most certainly do not need a circumcision. Many men are circumcised for the wrong reason. We perform more circumcisions in Britain than most countries in the EU, and need to look at why we are doing them. Once you stop using the steroid cream and use a good lubricant, things should improve. I suspect your partner is anticipating another 'disaster' and this is causing her to go dry. More foreplay will also help. If all else fails, you can have the frenulum removed by minor surgery. Either that or find a very large pencil sharpener.

Spotted dick

> I am twenty-two years old and my body has not changed and my scrotum has not enlarged in puberty. I suffered from terrific pain in the scrotum. Could this have been caused by antibiotics prescribed by the doctor for severe acne in my adolescence? I have had sexual relations with girls in the past but they have not been satisfying because I cannot maintain an erection and also suffer from premature ejaculation. I have had this problem for at least eighteen months and the doctor has prescribed testosterone injections, which I have had for a while. I am also going to sexual counselling but this doesn't seem to be working. It's making me so depressed – can you give me any advice?
>
> V.S.

It sounds as though your GP is trying very hard and the

problems with pain in the scrotum are unlikely to be related in any way to antibiotic treatment. Unfortunately, acne is often not treated vigorously enough, leaving young men even more self-conscious and sometimes badly scarred. Paradoxically, it is triggered to some extent by testosterone, the male sex hormone. Yet you were given testosterone injections, presumably to make good a shortfall. If your scrotum has not enlarged, you should make sure both testicles have descended. If you can't feel them both while lying in a warm bath, ask your doctor to check.

Knobbly nibblets

> They say doctors have heard it all, but have you heard this before? I love my boyfriend but I hate his willy. The ridge is covered with whitish, pimply bumps. He promised he hadn't had sex with anyone else and I believe him. The problem is I don't want to have oral sex with him. He won't go to the doctor. What are they? Can they be removed?
>
> C.B.

He probably doesn't need to see a doctor. Sweat glands and hair follicles stand out on the penis when it is erect, just like goose pimples. The skin is so thin they are pushed outward by the hard shaft immediately underneath. The only other things that could possibly be a cause are warts. Genital warts tend to be very small but may clump together like a tiny cauliflower. They are usually caught from someone else during intercourse but it is possible to develop warts anywhere on your body without such contact. If they are warts, they can be removed at a genito-urinary clinic. He shouldn't try to do this himself as it makes the eyes water terribly.

Cancer of the penis

Penile cancer is thankfully rare. One or two men per 100,000 will develop the cancer, with approximately 100 men dying each year in the UK. It is a disease of older men, usually over sixty-five years of age. If caught early it is eminently treatable, with a 90 per cent survival rate. Despite this, many men consult their doctor too late.

Causes

Smegma may be a culprit. Circumcised men rarely develop the tumour and it is almost unheard of in men circumcised at birth. Personal hygiene is considered important for the same reason.

Check it out

Carefully check the region between the glans and the foreskin.

- Look for small, often painless ulcers or warty nodules. Difficulty in retracting the foreskin may indicate tethering at this point.
- A persistent red velvet-like patch on the glans needs medical attention even if it is painless.

Safe but scary

- Tiny bumps all over the shaft are just sweat glands. The penile skin is so thin they stand out.
- Bleeding from beneath the foreskin after vigorous sex or masturbation is common – the skin between the foreskin and the glans is easily torn. If it persists, see your doctor.
- It is easy to bruise the skin in the same way with dramatic purple patches appearing the next day. They should disappear in a few days.

Treatment

Anti-cancer drugs can be applied as a paste to the tumour itself. Localised radiotherapy and laser surgery are also used. More advanced cases require partial amputation, a couple of centimetres back from the growth. Cosmetic surgery restores normal services in the sex and waterworks departments. Serious cases involve total amputation.

A chip off the old block

We have a strange, love-hate relationship with circumcision. As a society, we tolerate male circumcision yet the majority of us find female circumcision abhorrent. Words such as mutilation are commonly levelled at those who surgically remove a girl's clitoris yet medical and ritualistic circumcision of boys is commonplace. As a nation, the UK performs this operation for medical reasons twice as often as most other European countries. Either they are performing too few circumcisions or British doctors too many. It is possible to restore the foreskin, but it takes patience and perseverance. Weights are applied to a ring which sits around the base of the glans, progressively stretching the remains of the foreskin. The process is similar to that employed by some African tribes for extending their necks, lips or tongues. There are organisations which will give good advice, for example Norm UK

A good tip

> I had a circumcision six months ago to rid myself of a problem I've had for five years. Everything went fine and the old problem cleared up thanks to the operation. The only problem is I have been left with a very ugly scar and a ridge around my penis. It looks ugly and is obviously worrying me. Can you tell me if the scar will fade because it certainly doesn't look as if it will. And will the ridge surrounding the scar go down and disappear? Also, it's still very sensitive. Will this also get better with time?
>
> O.B.

Obviously, I don't know what your original problem was, possibly a phimosis or tight pullover, as it is called in the trade. Having your foreskin stuck in the retracted position is not good fun. One guy came into casualty unable to bear the pain after two days. His glans was the size of a small orange but quite different in colour. If you find your foreskin impossible to bring back into the normal position, place a plastic bag of ice over the glans for ten minutes, no longer. Then firmly grip the glans, squeezing the blood out and reducing its size. This takes a certain amount of courage and a goodly supply of paper tissues for your eyes. If you squeeze firmly enough for long enough, the foreskin will return over the glans. Lack of success means a trip to your local casualty department, sooner rather than later. Circumcision is the definitive answer but is not always necessary. With any surgery some scarring is inevitable. You can try ointments containing vitamin E, which promote normal skin healing. Unfortunately, once the scar is well established, success is limited. Further surgery to remove the scar only incurs the risk of making an even larger scar. Keloid is a type of scar tissue which resembles callus seen on trees after branches have been cut off. It is ugly and difficult to treat. Check with your GP. If your original operation was performed under the NHS you may be able to have plastic surgery to correct the problem.

The ups and downs in life

The old way of checking whether you were functionally impotent was to check for erections during the night. Obviously, if erections were happening, even if you were unaware of them, you could not, by definition, be impotent. Sticking a ring of postage stamps around the penis saved your partner sitting up all night on watch. If the perforations were broken the next morning an erection must have taken place. A word of caution – use only second-class stamps as they can be difficult to reuse on envelopes afterwards.

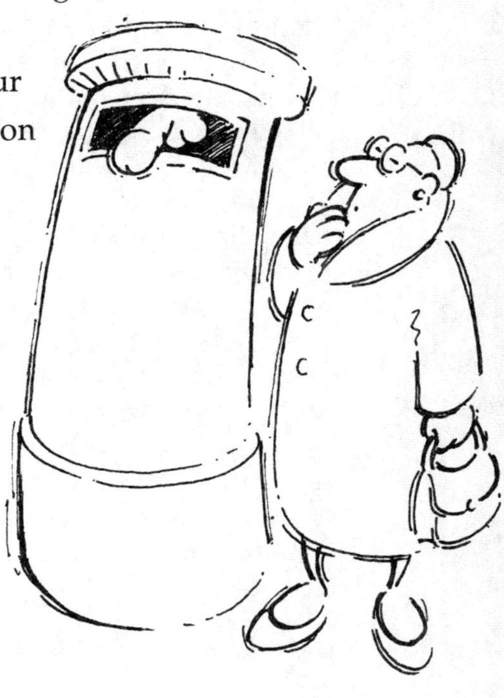

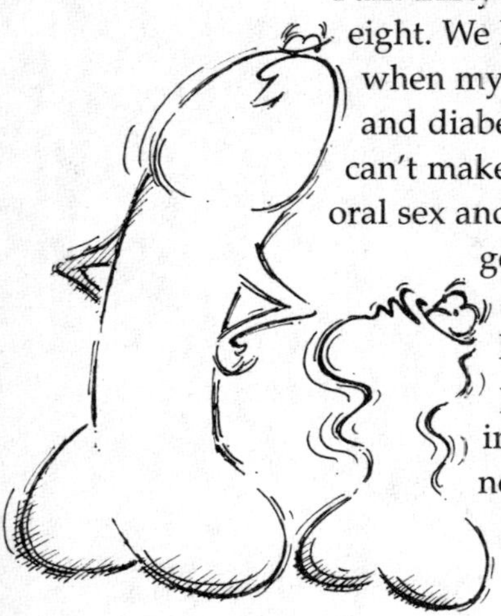

I am thirty-nine and my husband is forty-eight. We had a great marriage until last year when my husband contracted liver failure and diabetes. The trouble is my husband can't make a penetrating erection. We have oral sex and masturbation, but my husband gets very depressed. I don't mind so much as we love each other dearly. He has also lost three inches off his penis and he used to have an eight-inch erection. His GP says there is nothing he can do to help. But please, please, for my husband's sake let me know your views.

R.H.

Most causes of impotence are physical not just psychological, as we once thought. In your husband's case, however, it is fairly obvious that there is a problem with the normal way the penis has an erection. Both the liver and the pancreas play a part in normal bodily functions which influence the way an erection is brought about. While it may be very difficult to treat the effects of the liver and pancreas disease, it may still be possible to enable your husband to have an erection. You sound like the kind of couple who would have the sense of humour to be able to use the medication or devices which can bring this about. See pp. 118–19 for more information about Viagra, hormone replacement, vacuum devices and other ways of producing erections. Impotence is something most men do not like to admit to, yet it is extremely common, affecting around one in ten. Your husband should see your general practitioner and talk to him about alternatives. Some of these treatments can be obtained on the National Health Service.

Slow to rise to the occasion

I am a 54-year-old man, who is fit and healthy, but my ability to achieve erections has very slowly but surely declined. I now consider myself to be more or less impotent. My penis hardly increases in size at all until I actually ejaculate and then goes down almost instantly afterwards. I do not actually have a girlfriend of my own, but I always have had a heterosexual relationship with a younger couple whom I share sexual activity with by watching them as they have sex. Do you think I will ever be able to have sex of my own again?

K.B.

The vast majority of men will have suffered some form of erectile dysfunction at some time in their lives but it does become more common in later life. For some of us men, it's what's between our ears rather than between our legs that is the problem. Marital disharmony, anxiety, alcohol abuse, tiredness or just not being physically attracted to your partner are all frequent causes. Most of these can be addressed in some way or other. Better sexual foreplay can have a dramatic effect on 'impotence'. It seems sad that you can enjoy sex second-hand by watching others. For some people severely disabled, films and books are a great help for relieving sexual tension and providing stimulation. I suspect you are getting yourself into a rut and may become dependent on your friends for your sole source of sexual enjoyment. Break out of the circle and find some good sex for yourself.

High blood pressure – low penis

I am male and I'm in my late fifties. I wondered whether you would let me know if high blood pressure tablets would have any effect on reducing the size of the penis. I'm on a very heavy dose and since I started taking these tablets my penis, when it is erect, has reduced from seven inches to five inches.

J.D.

Drugs are a common and often overlooked cause of erectile dysfunction, particularly beta blockers such as propanalol. Erections are produced and maintained by raising the blood pressure within the shaft of the penis. Spongy tissue allows the blood to collect while its escape is prevented by muscles constricting the blood vessels leaving the penis. Anything which prevents the blood entering or allows it to leave will affect the penile erection. Atherosclerosis causes a hardening of the blood vessels and increases with age. This not only reduces the flow of blood into the penis, it prevents the outgoing blood vessels from constricting. Some blood pressure drugs act by dilating peripheral blood vessels, which is why they can cause 'flushing'. Unfortunately, they also dilate the blood vessels which should constrict to allow an erection. Not all men are affected in this way. Your doctor can often change your medication if this is a problem. Never fall into the trap of blaming it all on age until everything else has been checked out. Diabetes and some neuronal conditions will have the same effect. Although many men dismiss the psychological effects of impotence, it can wreck relationships and even self-esteem. It is possible to produce an erection with injections of papervine or a hormone called prostaglandin straight into the base of the penis. This has a remarkable effect on dry eyes too. While vacuum devices need a sense of humour to use, they work and don't involve drugs.

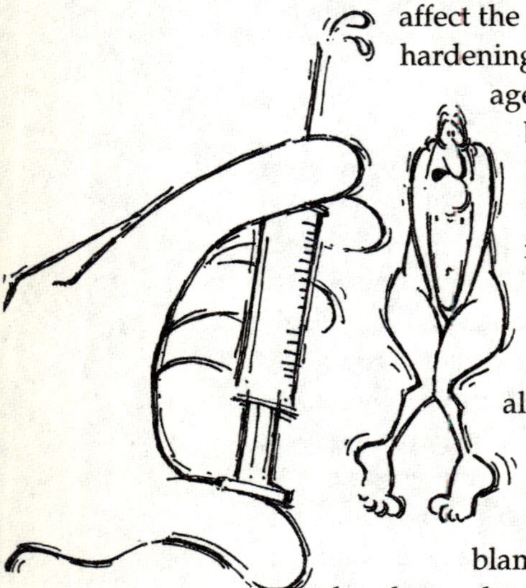

When the flesh needs convincing

While there is great variation in the actual size of the penis throughout the animal kingdom, humans come top of the list in their group, the Primates. Unlike some of the other Primates, we do not have a prehensile tail. The penis also appears to have a disproportionate influence over the everyday life of our species as few other animals give sex, as distinct from reproduction, the same level of priority. Similarly, the role of the human penis is complex and extends beyond simply being a means of transferring sperm to the female or even passing urine. Society places a certain importance on the size of a man's penis. The Central Intelligence Agency seriously considered supplying oversized condoms to villagers during the Vietnam/Cambodian war to enhance the 'prowess' of American troops in the eyes of the enemy.

No bone to pick

There is no bone in the penis. Its function depends upon hydraulic pressures. A balloon filled with water is more rigid than one without, and the erect penis works on the same principle, using blood rather than water as the stiffening medium. By allowing blood into spongy tissue within the penis, but restricting its exit, the penis can enlarge by around 5 cm during an erection. While valuable for placing sperm well into the vagina, an erection hinders the passing of urine. Indeed there is a one-way valve at the base of the penis which prevents urine being passed at the same time as sperm. Urine or sperm travel down the penis from the bladder or testes in a thin tube called the urethra. The thin skin of the penis is covered in small bumps which may be important in stimulation of the sexual partner. Unfortunately, they also cause a disproportionate amount of concern, particularly among young men. These are the sweat glands and hair follicles that are not normally felt on thicker skin. They are even more noticeable during an erection because the skin is stretched much thinner.

Average sizes

While men are prone to exaggerate, the average size of the human penis is around 16 cm (6.3 inches) erect and about 7.5 cm (3 inches) to 15 cm (6 inches) when flaccid. There are operations which lengthen the penis by up to 50 per cent.

Numerous studies, however, have shown that penile length is not the main factor for sexual pleasure in the female or male partner.

Penile erectile dysfunction (impotence)

Erectile dysfunction is not the same as infertility. A man can father children without being able to have an erection. Problems with erections are common. A study in 1994 showed that at least one in four British men have had some sort of erectile dysfunction at some stage in their lives. Furthermore, around one man in twenty has permanent erectile dysfunction problems. Misery on this scale is often masked by men's understandable reluctance to discuss these problems despite the fact that many of them can be overcome by relatively simple treatments. For most cases of erectile dysfunction there will be a varying mixture of physiological and psychological causes, along with adverse effects of medicines. Around one-third to one-half of all cases will be purely psychological and will often respond well to non-clinical treatments such as sex counselling. Generally speaking, if you have erections at any time other than during attempted intercourse, then you have a psychological rather than physiological problem. Whether you are having erections in the middle of the night, for instance, can often be discovered from your partner. Successful erections during television programmes, sexy videos or self-masturbation bode well for the future, although this is not a 100 per cent test. You can either ask your GP for advice or contact the addresses listed at the end of this book.

Psychological causes

Counsellors can help with this problem. You will need to be honest with yourself and your counsellor. They will want to know a number of important things.

1. Childhood experiences and your attitude to sexuality. This may well include the attitudes of your partner.
2. Your sexual experience during adolescence.

3 Your own body image and how you feel about your genitals.
4 How content you are with your sexual relationships.
5 'Bad trips'. Have you had some painful experiences which are flavouring your appreciation of sex.
6 Your feelings about sexual arousal. What is 'normal' or 'acceptable' practice.
7 How you rate yourself as a sexual being.

After looking into these areas they will want to know if these problems came on suddenly, and what preceded them. Psychological problems tend to come on quite abruptly whereas physiological causes tend to be more insidious. Your medical history will be examined. Some drugs (medicines) can cause erectile problems. Even homoeopathic treatments can be a factor. Some diseases which travel in families, such as diabetes, hypertension or depression, can also be an important clue to diagnosis. Obviously, details of drinking habits (remember 'brewer's droop'?) and even smoking, diet and exercise can all be important.

Examination

A number of tests can be performed to exclude physiological causes. These include tests for:

1 Diabetes.
2 Anaemia.
3 Liver problems.
4 Thyroid deficiency. The thyroid is a gland in the neck which acts as a thermostat for body metabolism. If it is set 'too low' then everything slows down, including erections.
5 Testosterone, prolactin and luteinising hormone levels. The balance between all three shows whether you are producing the right levels of hormone to make erections possible in the first place.

Your doctor will also check on your:

1 Blood circulation. Poor blood flow through arteries in your legs can also mean the same thing for your penis.

Your legs use bone to stay straight, your penis can use only the pressure of blood.

2 Loss of facial hair, large breasts or small testes. These all indicate a hormone problem.

Age, the great escape

If ever there was a universal scapegoat for things that go wrong with the human body, particularly sexual activity, it has to be 'too many birthdays'. Thankfully, we are realising that sex is not just for the young and the enjoyment of sex can go on indefinitely. Expressions such as 'dirty old man' are becoming less common as we all live longer and older people predominate in our society.

Age-related problems do exist, but they are by no means the major cause. Some important facts have emerged with recent studies:

1 There is a gradual decline in testosterone levels and the effect this hormone can have on target organs such as the penis.

2 Erections take longer to develop and may require more tactile stimulation. Yes, the old Bentley may take longer to start than the new Porsche but it will give you a more comfortable ride. Might not run out of petrol so soon either.

3 Self-image and concerns over sexual activity tend to be problems in later life. Men are notoriously bad at confronting these problems and will often let age take the blame.

4 Physical illnesses take their toll on sexual activity, not least through the drugs which are commonly prescribed by way of treatment. We do tend to accumulate chronic conditions as we age.

5 Gaps in sexual activity can be important, if only because of the toll they can take on sexual confidence. Bereavement, illness of the partner or divorce are good examples.

6 Men are slow to admit depression to their doctors, older men even more so. Depression is a major factor for erectile dysfunction.

Common medicines and alcohol can be a factor

Some medicines are known to cause problems with erections:

1. Some antidepressants are paradoxically capable of making erectile dysfunction even worse. Talk to your doctor.
2. Some antihypertensive drugs for high blood pressure are common culprits. ACE inhibitors, alpha and beta blockers, and calcium channel blockers can all cause problems for certain individuals. You can change your medicine to help. See your GP.
3. Alcohol is a common cause. Obviously, binge drinking has an immediate effect but chronic alcohol abuse can lead to permanent problems with erectile dysfunction. Small amounts of alcohol in the blood (up to 25 mg per 100 ml or a couple of drinks in plain English) make erections easier. Any more can cause the dreaded 'droop'.

Common disease culprits

Diseases which affect the nerves or blood supply can also cause problems:

1. Multiple sclerosis is the commonest spinal cord disease causing erectile dysfunction. There can also be bladder problems.
2. Diabetes can cause a peripheral nerve problem which affects the ability to have an erection.

Injections of drugs straight into the spongy tissue of the penis can mimic the way the nerves work by restricting the blood flow out of the penis, thus producing an erection in men with these problems. It is surprisingly free of pain, although most men cross their legs just thinking about it.

Vascular problems account for around 25 per cent of erectile dysfunction in men. It usually has an insidious onset and is made worse by taking even small amounts of alcohol.

Treatment

Thankfully, there is now a wide range of treatments which don't all make your eyes water.

Viagra (sildenafil)

Perhaps the best-known drug other than aspirin, it was originally designed as a heart drug but was found to affect the penis more than the heart. The little blue tablets will work in most men but watch out if you are already taking nitrates for any heart condition as a mixture of the two drugs can lower your blood pressure too much. Generally speaking, it takes about 50 mg around one hour before sex to make the erection possible. Viagra is not an aphrodisiac and you will still need all the sexual stimulation beforehand, if you will excuse the expression. But it does work, very well and there are similar products on the way, including one which you spray up your nose – definitely not to be sniffed at.

Hormone injections

Some men will not get any response from Viagra so hormone injections straight into the penis may be a better option. Caverject and Viridal Duo are hormone injections which will produce an erection in virtually all men with or without sexual stimulation. The needle is so fine it is virtually painless but you need to inject into different places to stop any scarring.

When all else fails

Even when sex therapy, counselling, injections, three of sand and one of cement have failed, there is still a way of artificially producing a stiff penis for intercourse. Some men will laugh at these treatments but they should remember how important sex is not only to the average man but to their partners. Relationships can be under immense strain and men even commit suicide over the inability to perform sex.

Vacuum devices

These have been around for over seventy years. They work by drawing blood into the penis under a gentle vacuum produced by a sheath placed over the penis and evacuated with a small pump. By restricting the blood from leaving with a tight rubber band at the base of the penis, a respectable erection can be produced. It makes sense to remove the band after thirty minutes or so to avoid problems with blood clotting. They can be used in men with vascular problems. Your GP will be able to advise you on suppliers.

Penile implants

If there is no response to injections a penile prosthesis may be the answer. Before you go down this road both you and your partner need to understand fully what is involved. There is a certain sacrifice of dignity which both of you will need to come to terms with. Having said that, many sexual couples find the release of sexual frustration far outweighs the temporary embarrassment. There are three versions of implantable devices:

1. Semi-rigid rods, made of silicone and sometimes covered with stainless steel braiding, are inserted into the spongy tissue of the penis.
2. Two-cylinder self-contained pumps are inserted into the penis and filled by squeezing the reservoir in the base of the penis.
3. Inflatable penis prostheses consist of a pair of inflatable silicone cylinders implanted in the penis which can be filled by squeezing a pump implanted in the scrotum.

They all work. But as the old saying goes, 'It's not the size, it's what you do with it that counts.' Foreplay, sexual experimentation, avoidance of routine and being honest with each other is just as important as having a functional erection. Oh yes, and a healthy dollop of a sense of humour too. Sex, after all, is not only enjoyable, it can be good fun.

Fuel mixture valve problems – prostate

Men talk about their bodies as if they are machines. Hearts are referred to as 'pumps', food is considered 'fuel'. In a survey conducted by MORI for the Royal College of Nurses, most men did not know where their prostate was or what it did. Women scored much higher for knowledge about men's bodies as well as their own. There is no euphemism for prostates, but if there were it would probably be a 'fuel mixture valve for the rocket'. This is not a million miles away from the truth.

The prostate does act as a one-way valve preventing urine and sperm mixing and also produces a battery of nutrients to keep sperm alive and kicking. Letters of concern came from both men and women. Prostate cancer kills around ten thousand men in the UK every year yet because it is slow-growing most men will die with it rather than because of it. There is no effective screen. In a 1997 report from York University, doctors recommended that requests from patients for a prostate cancer test (prostate-specific antigen [PSA]) should be discouraged as the results are equivocal and surgery can be debilitating, affecting potency and sexual enjoyment. Fine when it isn't your prostate.

The root of the problem

If you have found that as time goes by you are unable to push the deodorant blocks down the channel in the urinal, relax, you are in good company. Obstruction of the flow of urine by an enlarged prostate is common, particularly as we get older. Sitting at the neck of the bladder, straddling the tube which carries urine and semen, the prostate is roughly the size of a walnut and has an important job of providing nutrients and protection for the sperm about to make the long journey to the womb. The vagina is a hostile place so far as sperm are concerned. Prostatic secretions help neutralise the acid environment found in the vagina. Sperm have little room for carrying fuel for energy. The prostate produces large amounts of fructose, an easily absorbed sugar, to keep the engines running. It has nothing to do with the sex drive, which is a shame as it enlarges with age. Should the prostate enlarge too much, it can obstruct and even completely halt the flow of urine from the bladder to the penis. When this is caused by simple enlargement with no involvement of cancer, it is referred to as Benign Prostatic Hypertrophy (BPH).

Common problem

Over 30 per cent of men will have some problem with

passing urine by the time they reach fifty years of age, yet only half of those suffering will consult their doctor. Most men put it down to ageing and consider it inevitable. Many men, as high a number as 20 per cent of forty-year-olds, will need some form of treatment before they die. We don't know why the prostate enlarges but there are certain triggers:

1. High levels of testosterone
2. An imbalance between oestrogen and testosterone
3. Possibly low-protein, high-carbohydrate diets
4. Western diets

Symptoms of an enlarged prostate

Sure signs of an enlarged prostate are:

1. Poor flow
2. Frequent trips to the toilet even during the night
3. A persistent feeling of 'not quite emptying the bladder' often associated with dribbling after passing urine
4. Sometimes traces of blood in the urine or sperm, which should always be reported to your doctor

Your doctor can perform a few simple tests to check the size of your prostate and make sure it is nothing nasty.

Detection

The way an enlarged prostate affects you is very important to your doctor. Just from your description alone a working diagnosis can often be made. By examining your rectum with a gloved finger your doctor can check whether your prostate is enlarged. Blood tests will also give some indication of why it is enlarged as some of the tests are fairly specific for cancer (prostate-specific antigen or acid phosphatase). Ultrasound is also used by passing a sensor into the rectum to visualise the prostate.

Treatment

Thankfully, we are not doomed to walking around with a street map showing all the public conveniences.

Drugs

A number of medications are available which relax the muscles that are making matters worse. Side effects of the more commonly used versions include a dry mouth and a slow response from the heart when standing up. This might result in a drop in blood pressure and cause dizziness.

Surgery

If drugs fail or the obstruction becomes complete, surgery is required. What was once a major operation is now simplicity itself. Transurethral prostatectomy (TURP) has revolutionised the treatment of enlarged prostates. There are now 40,000 prostatectomies of various types performed in the UK each year. By the use of laser, heat or microwaves, the prostate lobes are trimmed from the inside. It takes about an hour, depending on how much tissue has to be removed, and you will be in hospital for only a day or two. Revolutionary new methods use robots under computer control to guide the tool removing the prostate tissue but these are still under trial.

Rare complications

Some men report a period of impotence after the operation which is usually temporary and is probably psychological rather than a direct effect of surgery. Even so, for the men concerned it is a very real problem and your GP may help with expert counselling. Most effects will wear off within two days. In cases of complete impotence, implantable prostheses can be used. 'Retrograde ejaculation', where the sperm are directed into the bladder instead of the penis, often occurs because the one-way valve at the neck of the bladder has to be widened to carry out the operation. It will not cause any pain or harm but it obviously can affect the number of sperm leaving the penis during ejaculation. This complication should not affect your enjoyment of sex. Incidentally, it is the action of this one-way valve which also prevents urine passing down the penis during ejaculation. This explains why it is difficult to pass water with a strong erection.

Prevention

Not knowing the cause of these conditions makes it difficult to give any solid advice on prevention, but the advice given below on prostatic cancer makes good sense. Early detection is vital. With modern treatment, the outlook is often far from gloomy. Sadly, men tend to see their doctor late, making treatment difficult and less certain.

Prostate cancer

Remember, cancer of the prostate can sometimes cause the same symptoms and be completely painless but early prostate cancer is almost always symptomless. It kills over nine thousand men a year, which is four times the number of women killed by cervical cancer. It mainly affects men between sixty-five and seventy years, although men as young as fifty-five can also develop the cancer. Survival at the age of seventy years is 50 per cent. Unfortunately, we do not know what causes prostatic cancer, but you are more at risk of developing it if:

1. A close member of your family (brother, father) has developed the cancer
2. You have high levels of testosterone
3. You are Afro-Caribbean
4. You eat a diet rich in animal products, particularly animal fat
5. You are over seventy years of age

Prevention

It is interesting that men from Japan and China have the lowest rates of prostate cancer in the world and this may be a valuable clue, particularly as this protection disappears if these men move to areas with a Western diet. The role of dietary oestrogen and traces of the hormone picked up from pollution is still unclear. As in many other cancers, antioxidants could be useful in preventing the disease. Vitamins E and C and beta carotene mop up free radicals, which damage genetic material in the cells, leading to cancer. Zinc is used by the body to make an enzyme which acts like a switch for certain protective genes. Red meat is considered a major factor in stimulating the cancer while nuts and seeds act as barriers.

A sensible protective diet would involve the following:

1. Lose weight if you are overweight. Oestrogen levels may be elevated in obese men.
2. Limit animal fat intake, and reduce all fats anyway. It should represent about 25 to 30 per cent of your energy needs.
3. Eat chicken and fish instead of red meat.
4. Eat at least half a kilo of fresh fruit per day.
5. Take a tip from the Orientals, eat their food.
6. Eat nuts and seeds, rather than sweets.
7. Increase your intake of antioxidants by eating carrots and citrus fruits or supplement them in your diet.

Detection

Along with rectal examination, your doctor can perform a blood test for enzymes released by the tumour. The PSA test gives an indication of prostate cancer but is not 100 per cent reliable. Ultrasound is useful but cannot detect very early cancers of the prostate. No matter what method is used, early detection could be the key to successful treatment so if you are concerned, and particularly if you fall into the higher risk groups, you should think about seeing your doctor.

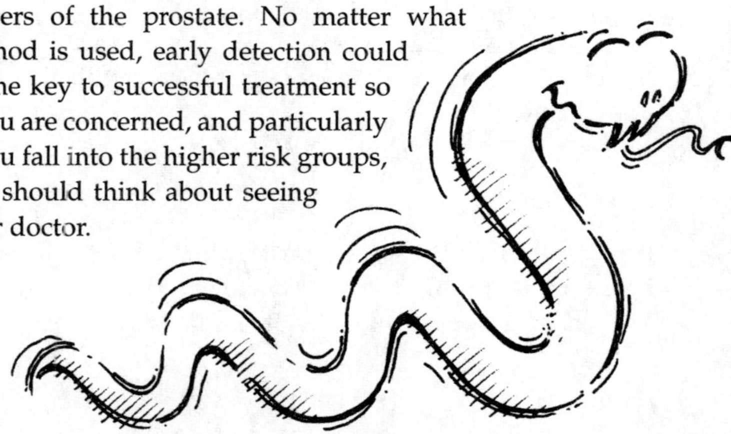

Treatment

Treatment can involve surgery and radiotherapy either to remove or reduce the bulk of the growth. Regular drug implants under the skin inhibit testosterone from stimulating the growth of the tumour. You will need to use these drugs for the rest of your life. Even if all of the tumour cannot be removed by surgery, this can slow it down quite dramatically, giving the man a relatively normal life for many years, and many men live to a ripe old age, dying from something other than their prostatic cancer.

Unwanted effects of treatment

Side effects depend upon the way the tumour is treated.

1. Radiotherapy is used for early cancers or when the tumour cannot be reduced by surgery. It is also very useful in reducing pain, particularly if the tumour has settled in bone. Temporary irritation of the bladder is common with a burning sensation when passing water. On the plus side, radiotherapy may not cause impotence.
2. Surgery can damage nerves which control the erection, resulting in impotence, but this is less common with improved techniques.
3. Hormone treatment can often result in impotence although it is possible to implant a penile prosthesis in some cases. There are also drugs available which cause an erection when injected correctly.

Prostate backfire

> I understand that following a prostatectomy a man can no longer ejaculate, the semen travelling backwards into the bladder. In spite of this happening, and assuming the man's erection is as good as ever, should he still be able to enjoy a satisfying orgasm?
>
> L.N.

Prostatectomy doesn't always lead to retrograde ejaculation

which you describe. In some cases, the valve which controls and directs the flow of urine and sperm can be damaged during surgery. There is no change in sexual enjoyment and you can still have children through the assistance of your fertility clinic.

The ball is in your court

Men have a staggering array of alternative names for testicles. I was once called out to a man whom I was informed was having trouble with his 'stones'. Convinced I was dealing with renal colic, I came prepared with a hypodermic full of pethidine. Unfortunately, he was referring to his testicles. Worse still, the young farmer had an advanced testicular tumour which he had ignored for nine months.

When men were asked to prioritise health areas that should receive more attention, testicular cancer came near the top. Smoking and cardiovascular disease were not far behind. Yet of the 1,600 cases per year of testicular cancer, only 150 men will die. Compare this to the 150 men *per day* who die from smoking-related diseases. Testicles are closer to a man's heart than his heart, it would appear.

Getting men to attend their doctor for any reason is difficult at the best of times. Men are particularly slow to attend their doctor with problems in their boxer shorts, which is a pity. Many would live a lot longer if they did, as 95 per cent of all testicular cancers are successfully treated if caught early.

Genuine concern

Letters mainly came from men, but the ones which came from women confirmed what the Health Education Authority has suspected for some time – it is often the man's partner who discovers problems with his testicles.

> I have noticed a small bump on my boyfriend's testicle which seems to be getting bigger. He says it isn't painful and it is perfectly normal. I've asked him to see the doctor but he says he hasn't got time. What can I do if he won't listen to me?
>
> S.K.

If the lump is only on one side you are correct to be concerned. There are many things it can be which are fortunately not serious. On the other hand, it could be something which he most definitely should get seen to. Testicular cancer is most common in young men but it is very treatable when caught early. Have a chat with your own doctor, who might be able to convince him that it is in his own best interests to be examined. Ideally, you should approach your boyfriend's doctor but remember that he may take great exception to 'interference'. Your own doctor will give you good advice as he may know your boyfriend's GP.

A whole new ball game

Loosely held in the scrotum, the testes have a number of functions such as secreting testosterone and developing sperm. After puberty the testes produce sperm at a fairly constant rate. If they are not ejaculated the sperm are reabsorbed. We don't really know why they hang outside the body, and most men could think of plenty of less vulnerable places. It might be that sperm production maximises at temperatures slightly lower than that of the body. On the plus side, having them in such a handy place makes self-examination much easier than if, for instance, they were between your shoulder blades. Few men will dispute the amount of pain which follows a judicious kick in the groin as testes are well served by nerve fibres. Unfortunately, serious conditions such as cancer can be quite painless, making examination all the more important.

Exploding testicles

> I have a most embarrassing problem. If I don't masturbate at least three times each day I feel as if my testicles are going to explode. I've tried to stop but then I just lie in bed worrying. I've even tried putting ice bags on them but it only seems to make it worse. What can I do?
>
> W.B.

Relax. 'Unused' sperm are simply reabsorbed. There is no danger from testicular shrapnel. In fact, at the rate you are performing the five-knuckle shuffle your semen will be on the low side when it comes to sperm count. This is why couples trying for children are advised to have sex once per week rather than at every possible opportunity. You are quite right about the ice bag. The testes are well supplied with nerves. Slapping a bag of ice around them just at the point of orgasm is supposed to blow your mind. Avoid reusing the ice unless you have a penchant for anchovy-flavoured orange juice.

Early death

Although it is relatively rare, representing only 1 per cent of all cancers in men, testicular cancer is the single biggest cause of cancer-related death in men aged between eighteen and thirty-five years. The number of cases has doubled in the last twenty years and is still rising. We don't know why this is so but with early recognition of the problem and prompt treatment, few men need to lose their lives.

Cause unknown

Unfortunately, we do not know the cause but undescended testes are implicated and young boys are routinely examined because, if untreated, this increases the risk of testicular cancer in later life by a factor of five times. Otherwise you have a 1 in 450 chance of getting testicular cancer in your lifetime. Even the food eaten by your mother during pregnancy could be a factor. Oestrogen may also have a role, which is why drinking milk may be a factor as it contains oestrogen. Certainly, the fact that obesity is on the increase may be related as fatty tissue produces oestrogen. The finger has even been pointed towards water supplies which contain trace amounts of oestrogen from the oral contraceptive pill passed in women's urine. Phthalates (pronounced 'phthalates') are also implicated as this plasticiser, found in most plastic food wrappings, can exert an oestrogen-like effect. The unborn male child may be affected by these substances without the mother even realising what is happening.

In the family

As with some other cancers, testicular cancer can run in families. If you have a brother who has had this cancer, there is a ten times greater chance of you also developing the condition. This doesn't mean you *will* develop cancer of the testes but you should pay close attention to any changes which may occur in their shape or feeling. Evidence from the USA shows that white men have a six times greater incidence of testicular cancer than black men. Similarly, Oriental men have a lower rate of the disease.

> I hope you can reassure me. I love my boyfriend very much but I recently discovered that he has only one testicle. He told me he had lost it in an accident when he was little. We are talking about getting married and I want to have children. Will he still be able to father babies or will I have to use donor sperm? I know this sounds awfully selfish but I really don't want to do this and I am badly torn about still seeing him. Please help as I do love him although I'm sure you think I'm terrible.
>
> B.M.

No. You are not terrible. You are simply confused and badly informed. Millions of sperm are produced by each testis and it takes only one to fertilise the egg. Obviously, the higher the sperm count the better the chance of a single sperm successfully making the long journey. Below a certain number, a man becomes subfertile but can still be a father although it may be necessary to give the sperm a 'helping hand' by placing them closer to where they are needed. Some men prefer to explain the absence of one testicle as being the result of an accident. Your boyfriend may simply have an undescended testicle. If so, he should make sure that the one which failed to arrive on time has been removed as there is a significantly increased chance of testicular cancer otherwise. Being honest with him about your concerns is the best policy. Your GP can help.

> I am twenty-four years old and I was brought up by very strict parents who were very religious. Masturbation was a real taboo for them. My boarding school was also very strict and it has all left me with a phobia about touching myself on the penis or testicles. I even tend to sit down rather than stand at the urinal. I have been reading about

self-examination of testicles, which sounds like sensible advice, but for me it would be almost impossible. Is there any other way of checking?

A.N.

Listen, forget about cancer for a minute. You are seriously missing out on fun here. First things first, you need to sort out the mental block imposed by your parents and school. Have a chat with your GP, who will refer you to a psychosexual counsellor. They really know what they are talking about and can help. Yes, it is possible to check for cancer without doing it yourself. Your partner can do it. More fun too. Unfortunately, I suspect you may have some problems here as well which your counsellor will help sort out. Once you are back to normal service, ask your GP for the leaflet called *A Whole New Ball Game*, which explains self-examination.

Self-examination, symptoms and being 'testes-aware'

Check your testes monthly in the following manner. Do it lying in a warm bath or while having a long shower, as this makes the skin of the scrotum softer and so makes it easier to feel the testes inside.

1. Cradle the scrotum in the palm of your hand. Feel the difference between the testes. You will almost definitely feel that one is larger and lying lower. This is completely normal. Ask any tailor.
2. Examine each one in turn, and then compare them with each other. Use both hands and gently roll each testicle between thumb and forefinger. Check for any lumps or swellings as they should both be smooth. Remember

that the duct carrying sperm to the penis, the epididymis, normally feels bumpy. It lies along the top and back of the testis.

If you feel anything out of the ordinary, let your GP check them for you. Remember, cancer is often painless, so don't delay. If there is a problem you will be referred to a specialist.

Hospital tests

1. You will be glad to hear that you will be physically examined once more. By this time most of the embarrassment has worn off anyway. This will exclude simple problems like cysts or infections.
2. Ultrasound is sometimes used to visualise the testes through the scrotum.
3. Blood tests will identify marker proteins such as human chorionic gonadotrophin which are present in much larger amounts in testicular cancer.
4. Any spread of the tumour can be located with a CT scan, a sophisticated form of X-ray examination.

Treatment will depend on what is found from these tests.

Treatment

You may need the affected testis removed. Even so, this will not necessarily mean that you cannot have children. The remaining testis will produce enough sperm to allow conception. If you had only one testis, or if chemotherapy or radiation is used, it is possible to store your frozen sperm.

You will not appear strange either. A special implant makes the scrotum look and feel as normal. A single testis is more than adequate to maintain testosterone levels. If both testes are damaged, either from disease or from treatment, hormone replacement will supplement your testosterone levels. Impotence is *not* an automatic result of treatment but it can occur in a small number of cases. Sex can still be enjoyed, and most reported problems are psychological rather than physical.

> I'm not really sure if you can help me. My GP has refused to see me any more even though I am really worried about my testicles. He makes me very angry because I'm doing his work for him yet he won't even examine me any more when I ask him to. I check my testicles every day and I have found a number of things wrong, including a lump which my GP says is just a hydrocele and is harmless. I'm still finding lumps and bumps but he ignores me. Should I complain? I'm not expecting you to stick up for me as you are a GP yourself.
>
> Anonymous

Yes, I am a GP as well but I can still give you objective advice. You are probably worrying far too much and examining yourself too often. As you know, the surface of the testes is naturally bumpy and this is not helped if you have a hydrocele which is just a small bag of fluid in the cord that passes from the testis into the body. Complaining is not as productive as explaining to your doctor just why you are so concerned. Perhaps a brother or friend suffered from testicular cancer? Write to him first. He may refer you for a second opinion to reassure you and put your mind at ease.

Sensible approach

Obsessive examination and fear can make life miserable. Keep it all in perspective. Even so, you may be glad you showed your doctor the boxer shorts you got as a Christmas present.

Bloody nuisance

> My normally active sex life ceased six months ago when I was diagnosed with haemospermia. Previously, I had occasionally ejaculated blood and sperm but assumed that it was due to my partner's tight vagina and squeezing of my penis during intercourse (it is a slimmish six inches). Hospital

tests yielded nothing and no reason for my condition was given. Sometimes I have a 'wet dream' and also masturbate but any ejaculation causes discomfort for a few days. Understandably, women are put off. Can you please help?

T.Y.

Blood in your sperm – haemospermia – is fairly rare. It should always be investigated as it can be caused by problems with the prostate, bladder or testes. It can also be brought on by trauma. A good kick in the nether regions is a classic cause. Standing with both feet on the top of a slippery pole three foot high when your inside leg measurement is two foot eleven inches is another. Bicycles with crossbars will also introduce you to the condition if your feet slip out of the pedals while you're going up a steep hill. So long as nothing has been found, you should still be able to enjoy sex. Condoms are essential for safer sex anyway so simply wear one when making love, even during oral sex. Blood coming into contact with your testes can lead to infertility so you need to know where it is coming from.

Not a patch on the real thing – TRT

Despite controversy, HRT for women has a lot going for it. Although early claims proved to be too optimistic, it does have a place in the prevention of osteoporosis – thinning of the bones. In the USA a patch has been developed which gradually releases testosterone, the male sex hormone. It is now available in the UK. There have been enthusiastic reports in the media about the effects this can have on libido, muscle development and general well-being.

Unfortunately, most of the information comes from an ill-informed press. When things are not going quite right in the sex department, at work or within the family, it is tempting to look for a simple reason. Lack of testosterone is an easy target. Hormone Replacement Therapy (HRT), or more accurately Testosterone Replacement Therapy (TRT) for men, has become a real possibility.

Something missing

> I read in the paper that men can now get hormone replacement therapy just like us women. Is this true and what effect does it have on his sex? I thought only women could use it as it kept your breasts in shape.
>
> R.T.

Fortunately, the hormone in this case is the male hormone testosterone and not the female hormone oestrogen. Getting the two mixed up could definitely have some effect on your partner's sexual activity, but not in the way you would appreciate. Testosterone patches certainly help men who have a proven lack of their own natural hormone but the jury is still out over its use for the so-called 'male menopause', if it even exists.

Role of testosterone

Testosterone is released from the testes under direct control of a small gland in the brain called the pituitary. This gland secretes FSH (follicle-stimulating hormone), which stimulates the production of sperm, and LH (luteinising hormone), which stimulates the testes to produce testosterone. It is partly responsible for secondary male characteristics such as facial hair. It also has a role in maintaining muscle power and keeps your tackle in good order. Blood levels of testosterone remain fairly steady with a gradual fall over the years. For some unknown reason, testosterone exerts a diminishing effect as we get older but big drops in blood levels occur only with damage or disease of either the pituitary or the testes. Men with hypogonadism have a reduction in the amount of testosterone in their blood. Hormone replacement for these men is essential to maintain normal body functions. This is the main reason for the manufacture of testosterone hormone replacement.

Worrying confusion

> I've heard about these patches for men to help with impotence. My doctor already gives me hormone replacement. Unfortunately my husband has to pay for his prescriptions. Can he use my patches instead and save the money? Is there any chance it might help him as he has problems sometimes getting an erection?
>
> W.W.

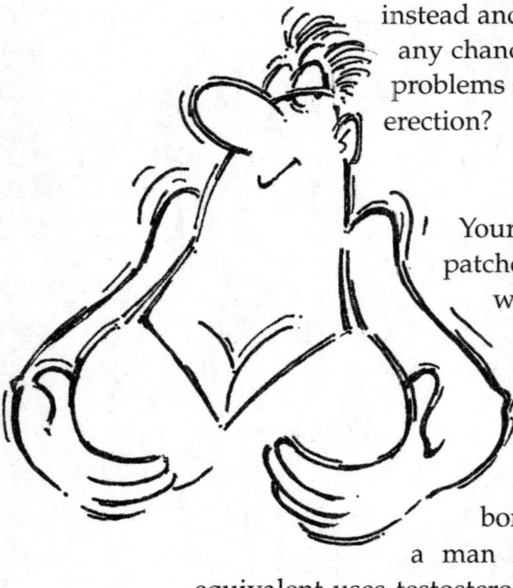

Your husband can certainly use your patches. He may find, however, that he will also have to use your Wonderbra. Hormone replacement for women involves the use of the female sex hormone oestrogen. While it most definitely is useful in preventing thin bones in women, it does nothing for a man in a wet sweatshirt. The male equivalent uses testosterone, the male sex hormone. It can help with impotence but only if the problem is caused by a lack of the hormone in the first place. Check with your GP.

Penile erectile dysfunction

Most men who request hormone replacement therapy do so in the hope of correcting their penile erectile dysfunction, or impotence. Such problems are common, but except for recognised medical conditions such as advanced diabetes, there is often no organic reason. Levels of testosterone are usually normal in men with erectile dysfunction. Sexual problems, stress, tiredness or marital disharmony are more commonly the main culprits.

Building hormone

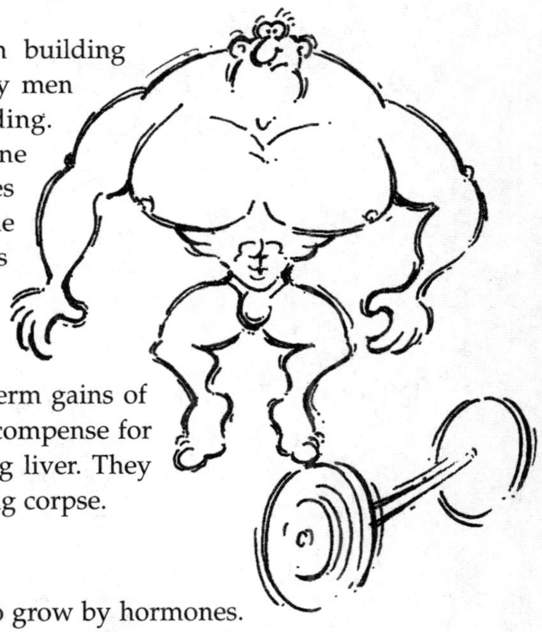

Testosterone's involvement in building muscles has been exploited by men obsessed with body-building. Earlier forms of testosterone were dangerous in high doses and have been withdrawn in the UK. Even so, although injections of high doses of testosterone increase muscle mass they can still have serious side effects on the heart and liver. Short-term gains of bulging muscles are a poor recompense for a weakened heart and a failing liver. They just make you a healthy-looking corpse.

Danger

Some cancers are stimulated to grow by hormones. Prostate cancer, which kills around ten thousand men in the UK each year, thrives on testosterone. In fact, stopping the body producing testosterone often slows down the tumour's growth. Obviously, giving high doses of testosterone to a man with undiagnosed prostate cancer could be disastrous so they must first be carefully checked. Rectal examination with a gloved finger by your doctor gives some indication of any problems but blood tests are more accurate. Prostate-specific antigen, for instance, is a useful marker of prostate cancer. Unfortunately, its value decreases as you get older as the levels rise even without the presence of any tumour. Ultrasound can also be useful although most doctors will require blood tests before giving any additional testosterone.

The male menopause

> My husband reckons he is going through the male menopause. I told him that only women can have a menopause but he is adamant and says he is suffering all the things that I went through when my periods stopped. I don't want to hurt his feelings by not believing him but it's the first time I have ever heard that men can have a menopause as well as women. Is he telling the truth?
>
> S.W.

At a certain stage in a man's life, usually around the ages of forty-five to fifty-five, a so-called 'mid-life crisis' can occur. It has been labelled the male menopause or the 'viropause' although there is little comparison to the female version. Unlike in women, there is no evidence of a dramatic drop in sex hormone levels. Even so, some workers in the area have suggested that we should measure not testosterone but FSH (follicle-stimulating hormone), which stimulates sperm production, and LH (luteinising hormone), which stimulates the production of testosterone. Similarly, testosterone circulates in the blood attached to a protein, sex hormone binding globulin (SHBG). This can inactivate the hormone until released. The levels of bound testosterone gradually rise with age, thus reducing the effects of testosterone on the target organs. Perhaps the reason we don't have any evidence of hormonal variation is that we are looking at the wrong hormones.

We do know that it is at this time of life that uncertainty, under-confidence and inability to fit the media image of a sexually powerful, competitive macho male can affect a man's self-image. It is tempting to put this down to a lack of sex hormone. Compounding all this is the fear of ageing. Some of the claims for testosterone therapy go beyond simply replacing what is missing and this can be eagerly accepted by men with no organic problems.

Check it out

Many things have an effect on testosterone levels. Chronic alcohol abuse, for instance, reduces the ability of the testes to produce testosterone. If you think you would benefit from TRT, get it clear in your mind *why* you would like it and then sit down with your doctor. Most of the problems people hope will be 'cured' by TRT can be solved without any hormone treatment.

Check out the basics first

1. Sort out problems with your partner, counselling can help.
2. Take a close look at your lifestyle. If you are smoking, drinking or avoiding exercise, this will contribute to the vicious circle of feel-bad factors.
3. Ditch that beer gut. Only people like Oscar Wilde got away with it anyway.
4. Relax, rather than collapse. You can be active and yet relax. Kids are a marvellous source of cheap entertainment and relaxation, if you are prepared to be the horse/elephant/train.
5. Get rid of the kids. You don't have to sell them to the local white-slaver but sex and intimacy can improve when the children are with someone else for the night. A romantic break can be as simple as telling the kids to entertain themselves for a couple of hours while you have a cuddle. Better still, take a night away once in a while and let the in-laws benefit from all the exercise of being a horse/elephant/train for a change.

A clinical deficiency of testosterone, hypogonadism, is relatively rare.

Menopause is a strictly female phenomenon as men do not have a menses (period). Viropause and andropause are the so-called equivalents for men but their existence is hotly disputed by leading endocrinologists (doctors dealing with hormones).

Cancer of the pituitary, a small gland in the brain, can mimic a problem with the testes by failing to stimulate them to produce testosterone. This needs to be checked before any therapy.

Testosterone is thought to stimulate the growth of an established prostate cancer. So you should be checked every six months while on TRT. You don't need to stick the patches where you think they will do the most good. This could also raise your voice an octave or two on removal.

No hiding place – vaginas

While men write about the size of their penis, letters from women complain about the size of their vaginas *and* the size of penises. It is not PC these days to say that the size of a man's penis is everything, but to some women it most definitely is. These next letters are only two of many to prove this point.

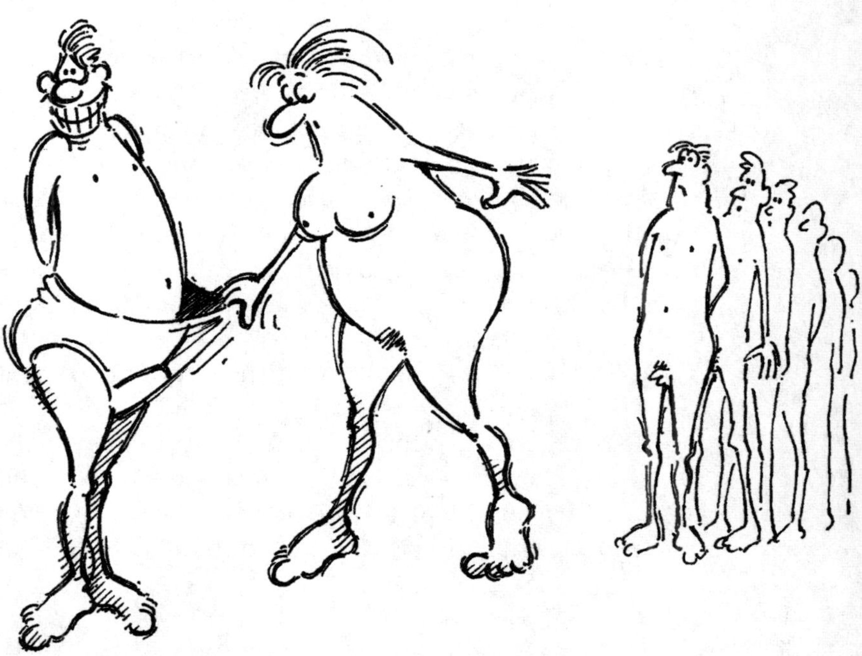

Big and boring

> I am a 27-year-old woman, who happens to believe (totally) that the size of a man's penis is everything. Since the birth of my child five years ago I feel as though my vagina is twice as wide as before. Sex with my partner became really boring as I couldn't even feel him inside me, whereas before it was wonderful. We have since split up and I have become involved with several men since, but when we have sex the size of their penis always puts me off them. I regularly do my pelvic floor exercises but my sex life hasn't improved. I can and do enjoy sex in various ways but I think that penetration is the ultimate ingredient within a full and happy sexual relationship. Please help me. It's hard enough to find a decent man, let alone find one with all the matching vital statistics.
>
> D.E.

All over the world, men are now reading this and muttering, 'typical woman'. Bill Shankly once declared, 'Some people think football is a matter of life and death . . . I can assure them it is much more serious than that.' Penises are just about the same to men. We are educated from puberty to believe that it's not what you've got that matters, it's what you do with it. This letter blows that myth to pieces. In actual fact, many if not most women do think that penis size is important. In your case, you are finding fault with the whole of mankind when you have already given the explanation for your poor sexual stimulation. If the average guy in the street had to pass a concrete rugby ball through his anus he would not be surprised if it was a little wider from that point on. Babies' heads are a little unforgiving on vaginas. If a tear occurs or an episiotomy is performed, the tightness of your vagina will depend to some extent on how well they were repaired by stitching. Pelvic floor exercises will help but if the increase in size is considerable you need to practise different positions. The 'cat' position, where the man lies higher up while face to face, helps press the penis against the clitoris. If all else fails, you would probably be better seeking advice from a plastic surgeon or obstetrician than wearing out and demoralising half of the male population.

Loose around the edges

> Whenever my boyfriend and I have sex, my vagina becomes loose after a couple of minutes. This makes it difficult for both my boyfriend and me to achieve orgasm as it feels as if there is no contact. Is there anything I can do to prevent this happening? Please help as it's ruining our sex life.
>
> P.P.

The vagina is essentially a blind-ending tube. With vigorous lovemaking air is forced in, which causes it to balloon somewhat. This is more common if the muscles which surround the vagina are lax, say after childbirth. Pelvic floor exercises to strengthen the pubococcygeal muscles can help. Imagine you are about to pass water. Bear down while at the same time using your pelvic muscles to stop yourself actually wetting yourself. You can do these exercises anywhere, any time, but you do tend to attract unwanted attention while at the bus stop.

Vaginal myth

There are some beautiful stories going around about men and women who become locked in place during intercourse. Most of these come from the same stable as the ones about women having teeth in their vagina. Even so, spasm of the vaginal muscles can cause problems, as can the terminology.

Vice-like grip

> I am a 21-year-old woman who is very confused. I have a really embarrassing thing wrong with me which might not be as serious as I think. When I

have sex with my partner I suffer a lot of pain. A doctor told me I have vaginism. What exactly is this?

A.A.

Vaginismus is common. It is not caused by any physical disorder. Anxiety, dryness or lack of foreplay can result in a spasm of the muscles which surround the vagina. Stories about men being trapped in women's vaginas because of this spasm make great reading in the tabloids but have little basis in truth. What vaginismus does cause is pain on intercourse which can create a vicious circle of anxiety, dryness then muscle spasm. Each time it happens it serves only to reinforce the expectation that it will always happen. Forget about penetrative sex for a while. Use mutual masturbation and other forms of sexual play instead. Once penetrative sex comes back on the scene use plenty of foreplay and lubrication.

Doing the sand dance

Have you ever watched a romantic film where two lovers are lying on the beach? At just the right moment great crashing waves substitute for what the film censors saw but thought was unfit for everyone else to see. What we also don't see are two people walking like John Wayne afterwards as sand can get in the most sensitive places. Load-bearing surfaces become worn and rough, ask any mechanic. Nature has its own way of ensuring a smooth ride, as it were. Unfortunately, there are plenty of things which will throw sand into the works. On the other hand, there also plenty of ways of getting it out again.

Sex like sandpaper

> Please could you help me. I am forty-seven and have a very dry vagina and I now don't get aroused when I have sex with my husband. We used to be able to do it any time and anywhere. I have been put on HRT as the doctor thinks I've started the menopause. I have tried using jellies but my husband says I still freeze when he tries to penetrate me. How long will the dryness last as sex is so painful?
>
> C.E.

You may have a combination of two conditions: dry vagina and vaginismus. They often coincide. Your doctor can tell from a blood test whether you are likely to be going through the menopause. There is a significant drop in oestrogen levels with a big rise in follicle-stimulating hormone (FSH). This shows that your ovaries are no longer releasing any eggs. Vaginal dryness is common during this phase as the lining is maintained to some extent by oestrogen stimulation. Hormone replacement therapy may relieve this. If one form of treatment fails, you should consider others before abandoning HRT completely as there are different combinations of hormones. The 'freezing' your husband talks of may well be spasm of the muscles surrounding the vagina, vaginismus. Anticipation of pain during intercourse because of the dryness will provoke this response. Once this happens it becomes a self-fulfilling prophecy with even more dryness and muscle spasm as a result. Break the vicious circle by introducing more non-penetrative sex, longer foreplay and the use of lubricating creams (you can get these from your pharmacist).

Hairy suits

Hair is funny stuff. We are constantly bemoaning its loss, change in colour or growth in the 'wrong' place. Despite being perfectly natural, dark hair on a woman's upper lip is considered unsightly in some cultures. On the other hand, lack of hair either on her head or around the vagina is considered equally unacceptable in others. It is impossible to satisfy all the different perceptions of what is beautiful or normal. Thankfully, what turns one person right off is a green light for sex to others. This letter gives you some idea of just how mixed up we are when it comes to hair.

A close shave

I have just started seeing a new woman, we've been getting on really well and I thought everything was going fine. Our sexual chemistry was really running

> high and neither of us could wait until we first had sex. But when it came to the crunch and we were undressing, I found out that she had shaved her pubic hair. I thought she was a really nice girl and I really fancy her a lot but surely this is a bit weird? I don't really go for it at all as I think it's a bit strange. I do want to try and understand because I like her a lot, but I couldn't ask her in case she gets offended. What should I do?
>
> D.E.

Many women shave their pubic hair, or at least the bits which show around a bikini bottom. Some women think shaving their pubic hair makes them appear younger, and sexier. This is in contrast to the concern over childbirth where women were routinely shaved before the onset of labour. Hair is difficult to sterilise and surgeons were keen to remove it to prevent infection should any surgery be required. As it happens, shaving itself probably causes as much infection and is best avoided. Simply telling your girlfriend that you prefer her au naturel will save her all that work in the bath. She may be relieved to hear it.

Adolescent fears

People can be so hurtful, often without any realisation of the pain they have just caused with a throwaway remark. Women are every bit as conscious of their vaginas during their development as men are of their penises. Nature can also be cruel and different rates of growth, along with the natural variation in sizes, can make a young woman's imagination and confidence go into a downward spiral. Of all the letters from young women, this one is typical.

Big is beautiful, handy too

> The problem is that I think my clitoris is too big, as my schoolfriend showed me hers and I could hardly see it. Normally, it is about an inch long but when I

> get aroused it becomes quite hard and sticks out. My boyfriend thinks I am deformed and says that I have a penis. Am I deformed? Will I have to have an operation?
>
> S.A.

The clitoris is anatomically the equivalent of the male penis, so your boyfriend is correct. All women have a penis, just as all men have nipples. During development the foetus decides which sex it is going to be rather late in development and so both sets of organs develop. Once it has made up its mind which colour booties it will be wearing once born, the foetus suppresses the opposite set of sex organs. They are still there, however, if only in a rudimentary form. It is possible for a person to have both sets of sexual organs but, although seen more often, this remains rare. The clitoris is an erectile organ so should get bigger on arousal. Like other sex organs it only really fully develops at puberty, so your friend may not yet have her full complement of sex hormones in circulation. There is no 'normal' size for a clitoris and large ones are considered highly attractive to most men. If you really cannot stand its appearance, plastic surgery may help but would be expensive and most surgeons would be reluctant to perform the operation, particularly on a young woman. Your boyfriend needs to be your ex-boyfriend as soon as possible but before he goes you should just whisper in his ear that his penis reminds you of an average-sized clitoris.

Sweet sounds of love

Sex is noisy. Doing it quietly is something younger people try to master but invariably fail at when their parents walk into the front room. Parents are more adept at it, knowing that the slightest indication of being awake will lead to a passion-crushing avalanche of children wanting milkshakes for breakfast. Spare a thought then for this poor woman, whom I suspect is going to be preparing milkshakes every morning for the rest of her life.

Blowing round the horn

> I am just screaming with embarrassment, but I don't know where to turn. My new man and I are about to make love for the first time but I am so scared about it, because – to put it bluntly – I break wind all the time during sex. From the front! I know what you'll say, just laugh it all off and it will be fine but you don't understand. It happens so often. I wrap my legs around my boyfriend's neck as he prepares to enter me and . . . then it happens. I think I will die of shame. Please, please, please help me.
>
> P.P.

I once knew a student who could do a passable rendition of 'The Blaydon Races' in just the same way. It was her party piece, which made her very popular. I never actually took her home to meet Mum and Dad as they were both tone-deaf. Air trapped in the vagina has only one way out. During intercourse, air is pushed in only to be released just when you could do without the noise. I am reliably informed that non-circumcised men tend to cause this more often as the foreskin acts like a piston ring. Yes, I thought this was a load of rubbish too. Sex is noisy. A sense of humour is essential for love play. You are anxiously waiting for it to occur, which makes you tense and more likely to retain air. Light-heartedly mention it to your boyfriend and if he is any kind of decent guy he will laugh.

Smear campaign – cervix

Not surprisingly, a large number of letters came from women about their cervix. While women generally know where their cervix is and what it does, men display little insight other than knowing it can develop cancer.

It is the bottom part of the womb (uterus), often called the 'neck of the womb'. You can feel it by placing a finger as far back into your vagina as you can reach. Thankfully, cancer of the cervix normally takes several years to develop. This gives doctors a chance to diagnose it from the cells in the area which start to change in their appearance. Obviously, this works only if you attend your doctor for screening tests. The medical term for the changes is cervical intra-epithelial neoplasia, CIN. The seriousness of the changes is graded from CIN 1 – mild change – to CIN 3 – severe changes. This terminology can lead to confusion, as this letter shows.

Without sin

> Please help me. I went to my doctor because my boyfriend found blood on his penis after making love. My doctor did a test which showed I had been very bad. He told me my cervix was full of sin. I'm so upset. He has sent me for more tests in the hospital but I don't want to go because they will all talk about me. What can I do?
>
> S.W.

First, stop worrying. Your doctor is not judging you. He is talking about the way doctors can tell if there is something wrong with your cervix. It's called CIN, not sin. Don't worry about what it actually means, but you must attend your appointment with the hospital or it could get much worse. Changes in the cervix called CIN are very common and may not need immediate treatment. Leaving it without getting an expert opinion is really asking for trouble later in life.

Hidden problems

Most cases of cervical cancer are symptomless, which makes it vitally important to have regular smear tests to detect any changes. Symptoms such as bleeds between periods, especially after intercourse, or bleeding after you have reached the menopause should be checked by your doctor. More than two thousand women in Britain die from cervical cancer each year and many of these deaths could be prevented through detecting and treating early changes in the cervix. Of the two thousand women who die, over sixteen hundred never had a smear test.

Youth is no barrier

Although the overall rates of cervical cancer are falling, the incidence and death rates in younger women are increasing. Afro-Caribbean women have the highest mortality and there is a high incidence in some Asian countries, including India. We are not sure if this is true of Asian women living in the UK.

Risk factors

Certain things increase your risk. Fortunately, some of them can be avoided. Obviously, it doesn't mean you will develop cervical cancer just because you have some or even all of the risk factors.

1. Having first sexual intercourse at a young age.
2. Being or having been heterosexually active. Cervical cancer is very rare in virgins.
3. Smoking. This may double your chances of developing the cancer. Living with a partner who smokes may also increase your risk to a small extent.
4. Use of the contraceptive pill. We don't know why this increases the risk. It is especially true with prolonged use (four years or more). On the other hand, the use of condoms and the cap reduces your risk.
5. Work involving contact with substances like dust, metal, chemicals or textiles. This can increase your risk, even if only your partner works in these conditions.
6. You or your partner having had several sexual partners in the past.
7. Genital warts (virus HPV) are thought to be linked. Check both yourself and your partner.

Smear test

Make sure you have a smear test once every three years. If you are at particular risk you should ask your doctor about more frequent tests. If you have never had a smear test or have not had one in the last five years you should check with your doctor for an appointment. Even if you have reached the menopause, you still need to be tested. Negative tests up to the age of sixty-five years generally mean you don't need any more performed. It's an ill wind that blows nobody any good, eh?

How is it done?

Some letters demonstrate irrational fear, not just about the possible outcome but about the procedure itself. Unfortunately, the moral crusade has a lot to answer for when it comes to putting women off going to their doctor for a smear test.

> I'm not really sure why I'm writing as I know you will think I am stupid. I don't want to have a smear done because they can tell if I have been unfaithful, which I have. I read in a magazine that more than one partner can cause cancer of the cervix. Is there any way I can have the test done without my husband knowing?
>
> H.S.

Your own doctor will perform this test in total confidence. There is no reason why your husband should be told the result or even that you have had the test in the first place. There is no way anyone can tell whether you have been unfaithful or how many sexual partners you have had. It is sometimes possible to have the smear performed in family planning clinics and even at your workplace.

Not quite a fate worse than death

Doctors and increasingly practice nurses carry out the test,

which takes just five minutes. An instrument called a speculum will be gently inserted into your vagina to view the cervix. Ask for a plastic version, they are not so cold. Then a smooth wooden or plastic spatula, which looks suspiciously like an ice lolly stick, will be lightly wiped over your cervix. The cells collected are put on a slide, and sent away to a laboratory for examination.

Not always bad news

As they say in the B-films, 'The waiting is always the worst.' It takes about three weeks to get a result. You may be asked to have another smear in six months or a year. This is generally because there were not enough cells collected to know what is going on. If you have an abnormal smear test, you will be asked back to see your doctor or referred directly to a hospital specialist for colposcopy. This is a painless examination of the cervix through a high-powered microscope placed at the entrance to your vagina. Depending upon what is seen, you may need only to have the abnormal cells removed, which almost always gives a permanent cure. If the number of abnormal cells is small, laser treatment may be recommended. A high-energy beam is trained directly on to the abnormal cells and destroys them; again it is painless.

When larger numbers of cells are affected, you may need the removal of a cone-shaped portion of the cervix under a general anaesthetic. Only the tip of the cervix is removed, and it will not affect your ability to have children or enjoy sex.

More extensive spread will require radiotherapy, surgery or both. The name of the game is not to allow this to happen in the first place by having regular cervical smears done.

The breast things in life

In the book *The Houseman's Tale* a young doctor was horrified by the way a surgeon examined a woman's breasts. Basically, the surgeon felt she would be better off having them removed as there was then no chance of breast cancer. This is one end of a spectrum, the other end being advertisements for brassieres.

Breasts are a supremely important part of female personal identity. This is not helped by the fashion world's obsession with them, which wouldn't be quite so bad if only it could make up its mind over what is their most desirable shape. Trends have swung from Elizabethan times, where breasts were compressed out of existence, to Georgian days, where they were pushed somewhere round your ears. The twentieth century hasn't been any better with fashionable breasts rising and falling, expanding and deflating with speeds that defy Darwinian evolution. It is little wonder that so many women send in letters about worries over their breasts. Instead of conventional implants, somebody is going to become very rich by inventing inflatable versions which allow for rapid changes in fashion.

To B cup or not to B cup – that is the question

> I have decided to have a breast enlargement but since my consultations I have been very confused. One doctor says that oil implants are better than silicone but another doctor I consulted said that silicone implants guarantee a much better result. In America, he told me, women who have the oil ones have to sign a form saying that they cannot sue if things go wrong because oil implants are not approved by the government. Please help me to understand which is better – oil or silicone. Which doctor shall I trust?
>
> C.S.

For many women all their problems would be solved if only they had bigger breasts. At the same time an equal number of women wish they had smaller breasts. Media pressure through fashion has a lot to answer for. The 'ideal' breasts have gone from voluptuous (Marilyn Monroe) to non-existent (Twiggy) and back again (Pamela Anderson). Before contemplating any surgery you should be counselled. This comes before any treatment by reputable plastic surgeons. Sadly, some women have breast surgery only to find they are just as unhappy afterwards. Silicone implants have received a bad press because of leakage. Manufacturers are being taken to court by women who claim to be ill or in some way damaged because of the silicone. It is a rubbery, semi-liquid substance which was thought to be inert. Unfortunately, some women have had quite serious reactions to the material, which is difficult to remove once it has moved throughout the body. Soya oil is used for some implants. It works well but can be disastrous in women allergic to soya. Water is also used although some women complain of a swishing noise when they move. Air balloons are not used. Not only would they expand in aircraft, which pressurise lower than sea level pressure, but a leak could be lethal, causing a potentially fatal air embolus.

When things go wrong

Breast cancer is common. The breast is made up of fatty tissue, milk ducts and milk-producing sacs. The lymph system, which protects the body from infection, drains the breast into lymph nodes in the armpit and under the breastbone. Cancer cells may start to grow in the milk ducts or sacs and then spread into the lymphatic system. While the tumour is only within the breast, it is fairly easily removed. Once it spreads to the armpit and more widely round the body, it becomes more difficult to treat, so early detection is vital.

Breast cancer is by far the most common type of cancer in women. One woman in twelve in the UK develops breast cancer. England and Wales together have one of the highest rates in the world. It is the second commonest cause of death among women under the age of sixty-five, after circulatory disease, although death rates seem to be falling. The likelihood of developing breast cancer increases with age, and it is very rare in women under thirty years. One-third of women are in their seventies when they develop breast cancer. Afro-Caribbean and Asian women have a lower incidence. Breastfeeding seems to protect against developing breast cancer.

A number of factors affect your chance of developing breast cancer. Take note: just because some of these may apply to you does not mean you will get breast cancer.

1. Never having children, or having your first child after the age of thirty; this increases your risk.
2. Starting your periods early (before twelve) or finishing them late (after fifty): this gives you a slightly higher risk.
3. A high-fat diet may be linked to breast cancer. In countries such as Japan with low fat intakes, the incidence is low, but it rises dramatically for Japanese women who move elsewhere and have a Western diet.
4. Your mother or sister having had breast cancer: this doubles your risk.
5. Being overweight: this increases your risk.
6. Age: the older you are, the greater your chance of developing breast cancer.

How can you protect yourself?

Breast screening, or mammography, is an X-ray examination of the breasts. It can help to find small changes in the breast before there are any other signs or symptoms of cancer. If these changes are found at an early stage, there is a good chance of a successful recovery. With early detection and effective treatment, around 80 per cent of women with breast cancer will recover.

Be breast-aware

While it is important to recognise the normal look and feel of your breasts, it is not necessary to perform a ritual breast examination at a certain time in your cycle each month. What is more helpful is to be aware of your breasts at all times, to look out for any unusual signs. More to the point, once you find something different, report it to your doctor straight away. Of particular concern is any unusual change in the outline, shape or size of the breast, puckering or dimpling skin, discharge from the nipple or any unusual pain or discomfort. A change in position of the nipple, for instance pulled in or pointing upward, is not always a sign of something wrong but should be checked by your doctor. Stand next to a mirror, and watch for any changes when you raise your arms. Before you reach the menopause, you may notice that your breasts feel different at different times in your cycle. In the days leading up to a period, the milk-producing tissue becomes active, and your breasts may feel tender or lumpy, especially near the armpits. After the menopause, your breasts may feel soft, less firm and not lumpy. If you have had a hysterectomy, you may notice the same changes in your breasts during each month until you reach the time when your periods would have ceased.

Letters still come in about these concerns when really the person should go to see their own doctor. This is a typical letter which shows someone worrying about more than just their breasts.

Points the wrong way

> I am a 21-year-old woman who is very confused. I have got a couple of really embarrassing things wrong with me which might not be as serious as I think. I have got an inverted nipple, plus, I also have a really stringy piece of skin on my vaginal lip. I have one child and sometimes try and blame it on having a baby as they stitched me up after I gave birth. But I also say it had something to do with the way my ex-partner liked to really push his penis inside me. Please help and tell me what you know about the two problems I have.
>
> N.I.

Inverted nipples are common. If they have been that way for a long time there is unlikely to be any problem. If it has happened only over the past year or so you should see your doctor, particularly if there are any lumps or discharges. Breast cancer can show itself in this way. It is possible to bring the nipple back out into the correct position using plastic surgery. This may be available through the NHS. Ask your friendly family doctor – remember it is your right to see a female doctor. Most of us are actually unaware of how our vital bits look and what is normal. The vagina has a number of labia which can be mistaken for abnormal 'flaps'. As vaginas were designed for penises it is unlikely that your partner caused this flap through intercourse, unless he was extremely violent. It may also be the result of childbirth although such irregularities generally resolve themselves with time. Episiotomy repairs were once carried out by junior staff. They considered it part of their practice in learning how to stitch wounds. Times change and now only senior staff or those under direct supervision perform this most delicate task. It is possible that the flap on your vagina may have resulted from poor technique. It's also possible that it came from tearing of the vagina during childbirth. Either way it can be corrected by simple surgery. Ask your GP for an appointment with the consultant who was in charge of your pregnancy and delivery.

Home delivery

Men are probably more fascinated by breasts than are women. Some men are unable to have an orgasm unless there is physical stimulation from breasts. Sometimes the desire to please and be pleased goes further than the milk of human kindness, as this letter shows.

The milk of happiness

> I have been seeing my boyfriend for ten years, we are very much in love and have done most things together. We fancy each other like mad and love experimenting with sex and different positions, but there is one thing that it would really turn us both on to do and we don't know if it's possible. This is

for my boyfriend to drink milk from my breasts without me being pregnant. Can you please tell me – is there something I can take or a way of stimulating milk? I know it may seem odd but we really want to do this. Can we, or is it only mothers who can produce milk?

L.A.

It's not quite so strange as you may think. Many men find the idea exciting and have admitted to pinching the milk off the step before their baby opens the door. At the same time some men are really turned off by their partners producing milk and dislike the appearance of her breasts engorged with milk. Lactation, milk coming from the nipple, can turn some men into sexually deranged milkmen while others would sooner be TT-tested rather than have a nibble. Unless you are pregnant or have just had a baby, your breasts should not produce any milk as prolactin is not in circulation. Changes in hormones can trick the body into thinking it is pregnant and thus prepare the breasts to produce milk. Once the breasts get started they will continue to lactate until stimulation from suckling ceases. This was the basis of the 'wet-nurse' who fed babies of mothers either unable or unwilling to breast feed themselves. Bromocriptine is used to switch off milk production in those women who choose to bottle-feed. Some women find that having their breasts suckled will stimulate lactation. Even if this doesn't work it's great fun and a brilliant excuse to get your partner's attention. It beats the hell out of the usual routine where the baby gets the milk and Dad gets to play with the empties.

Planning for the future – contraception

In one way the oral contraceptive pill may have freed women but it also enslaved them. Research into the male version slowed down and it became the woman's job to provide protection. This is still seen among some couples when it comes to sterilisation. Despite the procedure being more complicated and potentially hazardous for women, they frequently are volunteered. Exciting new developments may change all this in the future.

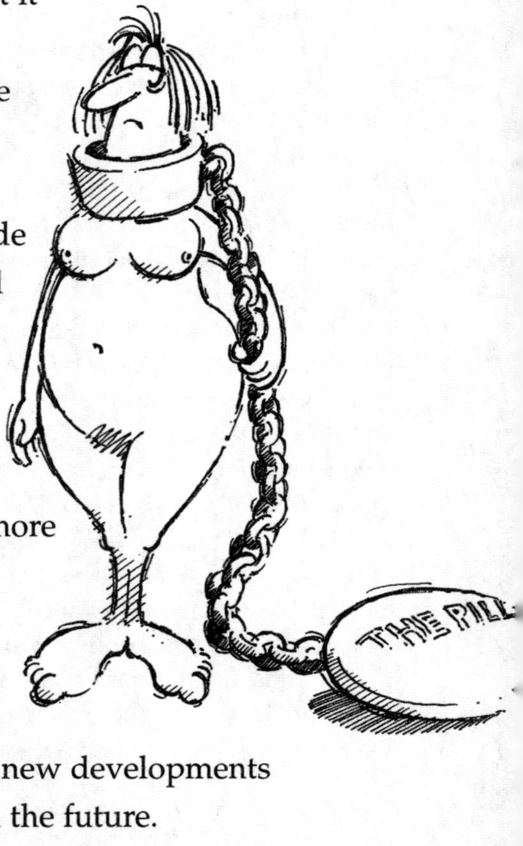

New horizons

For him

Nofertil, a male contraceptive pill, was launched in 1997. It prevents the normal maturation of sperm. Taken each day like the female version, it has the backing of the World Health Organization. So far no serious side effects have been identified and normal fertility returns within six weeks of stopping the pill.

Topaz is a condom which comes complete with its own applicator ring.

Drug-induced 'dry orgasms' may be possible by using the accidentally discovered side effects of two classes of anti-hypertensive and psychoactive drugs.

For her

A protein which coats sperm allowing them to bind to the ovum has been discovered. Research workers are already trying to find a vaginal cream which will destroy this protein, thus rendering the sperm incapable of fertilisation.

B-Oval is a new development which uses melatonin, a brain transmitter, instead of oestrogen. It is hoped it will avoid all the possible side effects of oestrogen, particularly in women who are very sensitive to the hormone.

The condom

Condoms go back a long way. As the pyramids were being built, Egyptians were using condoms to protect themselves from sexual nasties and animal bites. A plague of locusts can do wonders for condom sales. In the sixteenth century the man who gave his name to the tube which takes the egg from the ovary to the uterus, Gabriel Fallopius, reckoned he had linen condoms which protected from sexually transmitted diseases. At the time, this meant syphilis, a real killer. Japanese men were wearing leather versions centuries ago. This may explain their inscrutable expression. Linen and silk handkerchiefs were in common use in Britain two hundred years ago, but only among the gentry and only for protection from infection. The first real mass production of condoms came in 1932. Durex had arrived. The name became synonymous with condoms, a bit like Hoovering the carpet. Most people think that female condoms are a very recent invention. In fact they appeared very soon after male condoms in 1934.

Although vending machines appeared in pubs in 1968, it wasn't until 1992 that condom vending machines joined cola vending machines on the street. Only one of these two machines might save your life rather than quench your thirst. It's all very well saying you are safe but condoms need to be very safe. It takes only one sperm to fertilise the egg and a single ejaculation contains over five hundred million sperm. A single drop of body fluid can transmit hepatitis B or HIV. The modern condom can stretch to over five feet without breaking – more than enough for the most well-endowed man. The protection value is checked by passing an electrical current through the latex. Any holes, no matter how small, will show up as an increase in current. Society is accepting the condom more and more as one of the normal requirements of modern life. This has led to a wider availability – in supermarkets, from garages, through vending machines, as well as in pharmacies.

Television is no longer a no-go area for advertisements. I returned home one evening to find my wife fielding questions from our four children about a condom advertisement. She was doing an admirable job so I didn't interfere, sitting at the far end of the room. With all the authority of someone who knows when they are well out of it, I nodded sagely. As each question inevitably led closer to infectious diseases, my head soon resembled one of those ruby-eyed dogs seen on the back shelf of every Ford Anglia. With the slowness of time often described by victims of head-on car crashes, my eldest daughter turned to me. 'But why, Daddy,' she asked with eyes eager for clarification, 'do they make them in different flavours?'

Even within a stable heterosexual relationship, the protection provided by condoms can be valuable as herpes, thrush and genital warts can be difficult to get rid of completely. Anal sex is widely practised irrespective of sexual persuasion and is legal between consenting adults of either sex. Condoms provide simple protection from HIV, hepatitis B and bacteria which normally live in the bowel. E coli is a common bug and causes misery for women in the form of cystitis. Look on the packet for the Kitemark of the British Standards Institution when you buy condoms. Various brands are coated with the spermicide nonoxyl-9, which has been linked by some researchers to a very small increased risk of birth defects. On the plus side it also gives added protection against HIV.

Use of condoms

Putting a condom on in the correct manner is important. Air should be squeezed out from the tip from the end of the condom as it can cause it to burst or slip off during sex. Rings, jewellery, fingernails and sharp teeth take their toll.

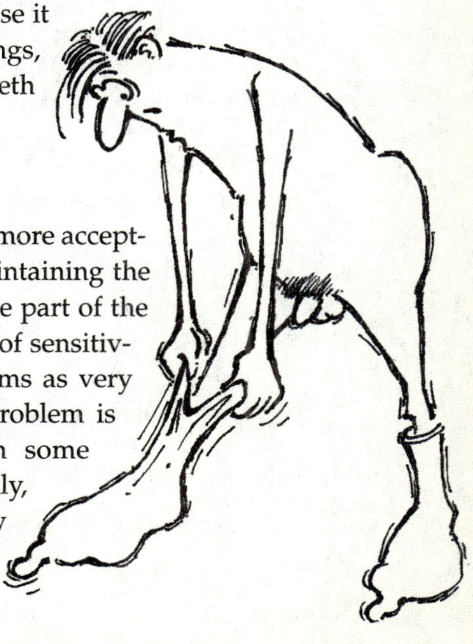

Spontaneity

As the use of condoms has become more acceptable, new and exciting ways of maintaining the spontaneity of sex have also become part of the sexual experience without any loss of sensitivity. Many men still think of condoms as very thin wellies. A great deal of the problem is with the psychological inhibition some men have about their use. Thankfully, there is no shortage of books on how to improve sex, and there is less embarrassment about buying them as they can be found in most popular book and magazine shops.

> [The] funny thing was, just because we couldn't have penetrative sex we had much more fun in other ways. We still do. I don't consider penetrative sex as the end point, if you will excuse the expression, of sex any more. I will teach this to my kids when they are old enough to understand. It could save their lives nowadays.
> (Father of child born by Caesarean section because of placenta praevia, where the placenta covers the opening to the womb)

The female condom

The condom for women is already very popular in the USA. It's not just women who appear to favour them, many men also prefer them to the male condom. The female version is much larger in diameter than the male and has two flexible rings at each end. The smaller ring fits inside the vagina while the outer, much larger ring remains on the outside of the vagina. After ejaculation this outer ring should be twisted to prevent escape of the sperm and gently withdrawn. Make sure your partner has withdrawn first unless you go in for that sort of sex play.

> When [my partner] reached thirty-five years and our family was complete, we decided that she should stop taking the pill because she had once had a clot in her leg. I hated the thought of using condoms but once we had got used to them it was a bit like wearing a safety belt in a car – you don't enjoy driving without one on.
> (Father aged forty-two years)

The oral contraceptive

In 1995 the Chief Medical Officer warned about a possible

link between the combined oral contraceptive pill and thrombosis. Later on the Imperial Cancer Foundation advised of a possible link between the combined pill and breast cancer, though the cancer to which it was linked is less aggressive and more treatable than the others. In a poll conducted in September 1996, around one million women were found to be risking unprotected sex on a regular basis. In the UK there were three thousand extra abortions that year. Mixed hormonal contraceptive pills mimic pregnancy, thus inhibiting the release of hormones which stimulate the final development and release of ova (eggs) from the ovary. This partly explains why some women suffer the milder symptoms of pregnancy during their use.

While the combined contraceptive pill is convenient and relatively efficient, there are definite health risks if a woman is over the age of thirty-five years, smokes, is overweight, has a family or personal history of heart disease, high blood pressure, liver disease or elevated cholesterol levels. You need to balance this against the possibility of an unwanted pregnancy and all the health problems this can cause to a woman in her late reproductive years. The 1995 scare has driven research into alternative methods which do not rely on artificial hormones.

Progestogen-only pill ('mini-pill')

The progestogen-only pill discourages sperm from getting anywhere near the womb by maintaining the natural plug in the neck of the cervix which will not allow the passage of sperm while the levels of progesterone are high. It is around 96 to 99 per cent effective. This pill has many of the advantages of the mixed pill without the pseudo-pregnancy. It must, however, be taken regularly at the same time each day. Being even an hour out can reduce its effectiveness quite dramatically, so it is to be avoided if you have a poor memory. On the plus side there is no evidence of an increased risk of thrombosis. If you smoke, are on the wrong side of thirty and intend breastfeeding, this is the pill for you.

Nature knows best

The personal fertility monitor is a natural contraceptive that looks like a case for glasses. On month one you programme the monitor with sixteen urine samples. After this you need to do only eight tests each month. The machine flashes a red light on fertile, no-go days and a green light when your fertility is at its lowest. A yellow light tells you to test your urine first before unprotected sex. It is said to be 95 per cent reliable, which is less than the pill. Obviously, there are no side effects except nail-biting while waiting for the results. It is expensive at around £50 for the first month's kit and then £10 for each month's subsequent kit. It will not protect you from STDs and is best suited for long-term stable relationships. Trying to wear the machine on your nose is a dead give away.

Intrauterine contraceptive device (IUCD)

These small plastic devices, inserted by GPs or doctors at family planning clinics, cause a mild inflammation within the womb which renders the lining of the womb unsuitable for implantation by the fertilised egg. They can be left in the uterus (womb) for up to five years, although some of the newer versions, which release a measured amount of progesterone (see 'Progestogen-only pill', p. 171), need to be replaced yearly. Most doctors recommend them to be used only after the first pregnancy, and as there is a small risk of infection which can lead to infertility, some doctors feel they should be used only once a woman has completed her family. The Dalcon Shield gave IUCDs a bad press in the 1980s. They made women particularly susceptible to infection, leading to personal tragedy and not a few lawsuits. Newer versions are safer and are around 98 to 100 per cent effective. Stable faithful relationships reduce the risk of infection even

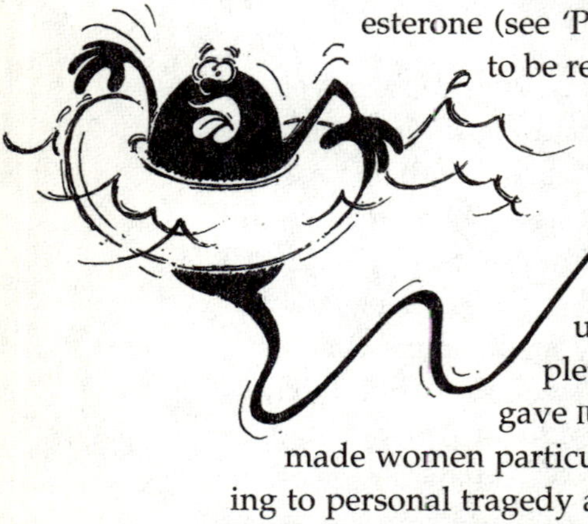

further. They are removed very easily by a doctor and have no effect upon sensation during intercourse. Bungee jumping? No problem.

Diaphragms and caps

Both are made of rubber and cover the cervix (the diaphragm covers the whole cervix while the cap covers only the cervical opening). It can be put in before sex and left in for at least six hours afterwards. It must be used with spermicide for maximum protection. If it is used according to instructions it is around 92 to 96 per cent effective. The good news is it can be put in just before sex. If you have inserted it more than three hours before sex, you need to use extra spermicide. There is some evidence that it can help protect against cervical cancer and that the spermicide can protect against some sexually transmitted diseases. As there are no hormones involved, it is a perfectly natural method. It can also be used during a period as the cap holds back blood until taken out.

The major disadvantage is that it can interrupt sex and you have got to be confident and intimate about touching your own body. Some women find that they suffer from cystitis more often when using a diaphragm. Changing to a smaller or softer-rim device may help. You need to have the fit of the diaphragm checked each year, although if you lose or gain weight you should see your doctor or family planning clinic to check that the diaphragm still fits well.

Vasectomy

As a form of contraception, vasectomy has maintained its position as a popular, almost 100 per cent, means of preventing unwanted pregnancies. It is, along with the condom, one of the very few ways where a man really does have control over conception. For most men, its single biggest attraction is its lack of intrusion on the actual enjoyment of sexual intercourse, while providing as near absolute contraception as can be achieved.

Risks

There have been reports of an increase in the possibility of testicular cancer in men with a vasectomy, but the risks, if present, are extremely small. A similar risk is involved for impotence, which has also received attention in the press. All these reports must be put in perspective. Your decision will depend upon your age, how many children you already have and the impact any further children may have on your family. Doctors are obviously not keen to perform a vasectomy on men who do not have any children. Similarly, while divorce may be the last thing on your mind, you may want to have more children should this ever occur.

The operation

The operation is relatively simple, and although in the majority of cases it is carried out in hospitals, it is performed in an increasing number of GP surgeries. One American urologist performed his own vasectomy with a mirror. He is the only known sufferer of a painful neck as a complication from vasectomy. It is effective: only one vasectomy in 2,500 will spontaneously reverse. Even so, it is never guaranteed 100 per cent.

Basically, the vas deferens, which conducts sperm from the testes to the penis, is cut and tied off, or clipped at both cut ends. This effectively prevents any further sperm from reaching the penis. A small cut is made through the skin of the scrotum, under either a local or a general anaesthetic. Once identified, each vas is cut, a small piece removed, and the cut ends tied off. Each of the segments which have been cut away is sent off to the laboratory to ensure that the correct tubes have been treated and that there is no sign of any serious medical conditions which need attention. Using a couple of stitches or staples, the wound is closed. It takes no more than about fifteen minutes and is extremely safe. Testes do not swell from sperm building up within them.

One hundred per cent?

Nature can determine when a normal body function has been interfered with. There are a number of cases, thankfully very few, where a successful operation has been confirmed with a definite removal of the vas tissue and yet a few years later the men concerned have fathered a child. It appears that the body is capable of overcoming the surgical intervention by creating fresh canals for the sperm to travel to the penis. It has to be said that the risk is extremely small, but it explains why the form you sign consenting for the operation will not guarantee 100 per cent success.

> I have to admit I was absolutely terrified of not only the operation but also the effect it could have on my sex life and how I felt about myself. I had to go through with it as I had promised [my partner] after our last baby was born. As it turned out all the horror stories my mates told me about were not true and if anything it has improved our sex life. We are more relaxed now that we don't have to worry about the pill or [my partner] getting pregnant. (Father of thirty-seven, with three children).

Reversal

Many men may have been in perfectly stable relationships when they had their vasectomy performed only to find themselves in a new relationship a few years later. Some of them will want to start a new family. All doctors explain that a vasectomy is very difficult to reverse. The procedure is usually performed under a general anaesthetic, which will require an overnight stay, although some surgeons will work under a local anaesthetic. Results are variable. Success rates over 40 per cent are considered exceptional. There are a number of reasons for this. Antibodies to the sperm are produced after vasectomy which reduce their motility once the vas deferens has been rejoined. Fibrous thickening can also inhibit the passage of sperm. Both of these causes increase with the time interval between vasectomy and reversal. One in thirty-three vasectomised men will seek a reversal. They are usually men in their forties who have remarried a childless younger woman. It is possible to have the reversal performed on the NHS but waiting lists tend to be long as it is a common operation. It will cost you around £1,200 to have your privates treated privately.

> Never in my wildest dreams did I think I would ever split up from my former wife. I paid to have a vasectomy done privately. After we split up my new partner wanted desperately to have children as she had none in her previous marriage. I paid again to have the vasectomy reversed. It was the best money I ever spent. Our relationship seemed to blossom with [our child]. I haven't even asked whether it is possible to have a vasectomy twice.
> (Father of three children. It is possible to have repeat vasectomies but rarely under the NHS.)

Female sterilisation

> Recently, my husband and I made the decision that I would be sterilised. I was told to abstain from sex for seven weeks after the operation. Unfortunately, I only lasted for five days after the operation and now, every time we make love, I suffer muscle spasms which really hurt. Have I damaged myself internally by having sex too soon?
>
> S.B.

Female sterilisation is more complicated than the 'snip' for men, but even so, complications are rare. Before any such operation you should be counselled to make sure you are sure of what you are doing. Few obstetricians will perform a sterilisation in a young woman without a very good reason. Unlike vasectomy in men, the operation is now usually done under general anaesthetic. A small opening is made just near the navel so the scar is less noticeable. After inflating the abdomen with carbon dioxide, to give some elbow room as it were, a small telescope is used to guide the surgeon to the Fallopian tubes. These are cut and clipped off at each end. The small piece of cut end is checked in the laboratories to confirm that it really was the Fallopian tubes that were cut and not a piece of garden hose which just happened to be lying around at the time. Many women experience discomfort immediately after the operation but this soon disappears. A fair proportion of women also complain of pain at the right shoulder tip. The diaphragm, which separates the chest from the abdomen, is served by the same nerve that serves the shoulder tip. It may be that the carbon dioxide pumped in to inflate the abdomen irritates the diaphragm, which is interpreted as shoulder pain. Either that or a cynical surgeon was misheard when he said, 'Give the boulder a tap to help it deflate.' You are advised to abstain from sex for a further four weeks or so after the operation because there may still be an egg sitting in the Fallopian tubes or womb which could be fertilised by sperm even though the tubes have been cut and sealed off. There is little if any danger of harming yourself inside by jumping the gun. It is more likely that you are simply anxious and this has set up a vicious circle of expecting pain during intercourse. Try some more foreplay and relaxation.

Emergency contraception

Emergency contraception, in the form of the so-called morning-after pill, is actually two pills, which must be used within seventy-two hours of unprotected intercourse. Similarly, the unplanned insertion of a coil should only ever be used in an emergency, for instance if a condom tears. The risks involved, although small, make them unsuitable for regular use. They are also not as reliable as the contraceptive pill taken regularly.

Natural methods

Theoretically, it is only possible for your partner to conceive within seven days of an egg leaving her ovary to pass down her Fallopian tubes, or twenty-four hours afterwards. The woman can estimate the time the egg is released (ovulation). By using a thermometer and a chart it is possible to detect the sudden rise in temperature of around 0.5 degrees Celsius which occurs at ovulation. Readings must be taken first thing in the morning, before any exercise, food, drink or even smoking. Obviously, this can be confused by increases in temperature from a cold or flu. The 'safe' phase begins on the morning of the third day of increased temperature. This can be made more accurate by testing the cervical mucus, which becomes thicker and less sticky, tending to resist being drawn out between the fingers, just after ovulation. Compared to the other methods described, the 'natural' method is not very safe and requires a degree of self-control which may not be present in every man or woman.

Once per night religiously

Please can you help. The problem concerns my husband of seven months. When we met three years ago we both agreed to abstain from sex before we married as we are both Christians. However, since we have wed I find my husband's demands rather odd. He gets me to wind string around his penis and then – for want of a better word – he sodomises me because he says we can't have a baby yet. I was naive about sex until I read a bit recently. I secretly watch sex programmes on a mini-TV whilst my husband sleeps. We are not allowed television and most evenings are spent at Bible study. My husband says his behaviour is normal between husband and wife and only abnormal between men. Is this true?

M.K.

I suspect that all is not well with your relationship. Anal sex is accepted by many cultures as a means of birth control. Opinion varies as to whether anal sex between men is abnormal. The old worn-out arguments are starting to give way to reality. You have every right to expect enjoyable sex between you and your husband. It appears at the moment that you and your husband have a very one-sided relationship. A great deal depends upon what you want from your relationship and whether you are happy with the way that things are – if so, then fine. But if you feel that you are not enjoying the way your relationship is going then you need to talk about it to your husband.

Out for the count

Long, long ago a man containing a large amount of falling-down water came into casualty at 3 a.m. demanding a sperm count. A young, tired but good-looking casualty officer gave him a milk bottle and told him to come back when it was full.

A report in the *British Medical Journal* (BMJ) highlighted the decline in quality and quantity of sperm throughout Europe. Men born after around 1970 have a disturbingly high number of abnormal sperm. Basically, sperm are tiny torpedoes with a warhead full of genetic material (DNA), an engine and a propeller in the form of a tail. Although millions of sperm are released with each ejaculation, relatively few ever reach the egg. Only one will actually fertilise it. Abnormal sperm can be seen down the microscope as having two heads, two tails, or neither. Despite looking perfectly normal, some sperm appear unable to swim at all. As the number of normal sperm falls, so the chances of successful conception are reduced. While there are enormous numbers being produced it doesn't really matter, but below a certain point the man is said to have impaired fertility.

Worryingly, the article pointed out a 2 per cent decline each year in the number of sperm men produce. Predictions are that men in the new millennium may be unable to produce any normal sperm, with obvious consequences for the human race. The blame is being placed on plastics, pollution and oestrogen in recycled water coming from women taking the oral contraceptive pill. Amazingly, many plastics used for food wrapping contain substances which mimic the action of oestrogen. This may be affecting the unborn male child and could explain the dramatic twofold increase in undescended testes and testicular cancer in the UK over the past twenty years. Worse still, there may be a link with the increasing numbers of babies born with both male and female genitalia. Tight trousers and driving for too long are both also possible causes of the decline in the production of sperm. This is probably due to constant warming of the testes, which prefer a cooler than body temperature for maximal sperm production.

It can be very distressing for a man to be told he has abnormal and reduced numbers of sperm. Some feel they are 'less of a man' and their workmates can be cruel without realising it. Unfortunately, there is no cure for this problem but it doesn't always mean that having children is impossible. Healthy sperm can be separated out and given a short cut by being placed directly into the cervix. In vitro fertilisation (IVF) is now almost routine. Sperm and egg are brought together in the laboratory before being returned to the womb.

Even so, the trend is very worrying. It is just our luck – not only do we suffer more from every medical condition common to both sexes but we are being attacked where it hurts most. It is going to take a serious high-level degree of action from the government to address and reverse this problem. After all this, you won't be surprised to hear that the man who was given the milk bottle at 3 a.m. never came back.

Hangers-on – STDs

Not surprisingly, letters were not thin on the ground when it came to sexually transmitted diseases. Catching something down in the nether regions carries a double whammy. Not only is it a nuisance or even life-threatening, it's your 'own fault'. Society has little sympathy with people who contract such infections yet does not adopt the same attitude to lung cancer, which is almost invariably connected to cigarette smoking.

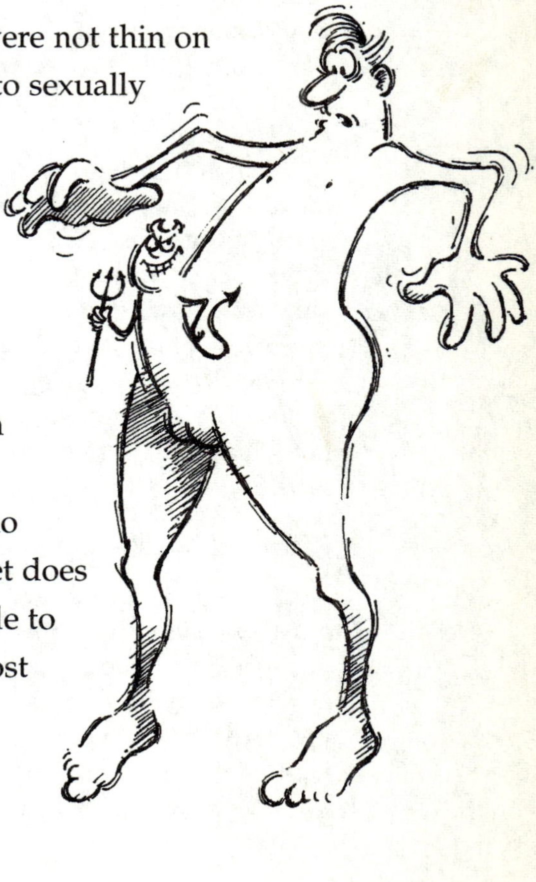

When the state of Oregon in the USA decided to set up a prioritised health service it asked the populace to list the order in which diseases should be treated. Premature babies came very high on the list. 'Self-inflicted' diseases such as HIV came at the bottom. Sports injuries, every bit as 'self-inflicted', were not given the same low status.

Terminology moves on, often leaving confusion in its wake. Diseases you caught during sex used to be called venereal diseases or VD. This actually referred only to syphilis and gonorrhoea. Progress in the area now means you can catch much more than just these two so the term has been replaced by *sexually transmitted diseases*, which covers everything. The abbreviation STD has stuck and is now the accepted term.

As usual, men come top of the class for catching STDs. Worse still, in the UK four times as many men are contracting sexually transmitted diseases now as were in 1975. A rough estimate puts the figure each year in the UK at around 35,000 men. This figure of attendance at genito-urinary clinics in England and Scotland does not include those men who only attended their GPs. Like an iceberg, the true figure may be even greater because some men do not realise they are infected as they have no symptoms. Luckily, not all the infections are dangerous but some will most definitely kill. Despite all the advertising, the use of condoms, which gives almost 100 per cent safety from the real killers, is still not widespread enough to prevent the figures rising even further.

Misconceptions

Nothing is guaranteed to cause more mistrust and friction in a steady relationship than the sudden appearance of an STD. It can be difficult to convince either partner that you do not have to be unfaithful to get a dose. Thrush is a good example. It can be considered a sexually transmitted disease as you can be infected during sexual intercourse. It also, however, can appear spontaneously, often after prolonged use of antibiotics. Both partners need to be treated to eradicate the infection. Many other STDs can lie dormant and reappear years after they first developed.

In confidence

The world is a funny place. Some diseases are acceptable while others are not. STDs come into the *not* category for most people. The irony is that STDs are so common. Most people who have sex at some point will have had a form of sexually transmitted bug despite not realising it at the time. Even so, people demand, and rightly so as with any other disease, absolute confidentiality. Your GP fully understands this but if you want to be totally sure you can attend your local genito-urinary clinic and use a false name or a number or even no identification at all. This is considered quite acceptable. The clinic is not allowed to tell anyone you attended – your own GP, insurance companies, employers or the police – *even if you are under the age of consent*. It will ask you to take part in confidential partner notification to help stop the spread of the particular STD from which you are suffering.

Of one thing you can be assured. No one in a GU clinic is going to judge you, laugh at you or make you feel dirty. These nurses and doctors are specially trained in the area but much more importantly, they are sympathetic and understanding. You will be treated as if you had just broken your finger – it is less painful too. If you want to use a false name fine, but avoid Smith or Jones. When it comes to working out which people catch sexually transmitted diseases, people with the surname Smith or Jones come right at the very top. It also raises the dilemma of what you want to call yourself if your name really is Smith or Jones – a case of alas rather than alias.

HIV and AIDS

Never has a single disease captured the imagination and exposed the thinly disguised prejudice endemic in our society as has acquired immune deficiency syndrome (AIDS). Following infection with the human immunodeficiency virus (HIV) the white blood cells called CD4 are depleted, thus lowering the body's resistance to infection. At least thirteen million people in the world are HIV-positive. Despite controversy in the popular press, designed more to sell newspapers than to present the facts, HIV is not confined to gay men. It is on the increase among heterosexuals and intravenous drug abusers.

Symptoms like the tip of an iceberg

Early stages of infection generally go unnoticed and it needs an antibody test from a blood or saliva sample to confirm the presence of the virus. The appearance of the antibodies can take months and is known as seroconversion. A vague non-specific illness similar to flu or glandular fever sometimes follows the infection at around six to seven weeks later. A considerable period of time, years even, can then pass completely symptom-free. The occurrence of oral thrush, persistent herpes (cold sores) or strange chest infections which clear only slowly with treatment are ominous signs of the body's declining ability to fight off other infections.

How to catch it

Body fluids are often cited as the carrier of the virus. Actually, this can be narrowed down to blood, semen and saliva. Although the risk of infection from saliva is extremely small, it makes sense to avoid obvious risks such as oral sex without adequate protection. Similarly, there are only two known cases of medical workers passing on the virus to their patient, although a number of doctors suffer from infection in the opposite direction. The main routes of infection are:

- Sexual transmission via blood from small cuts in the mouth (oral sex), vagina, anus or penis. Both gay and straight people are at risk. Lesbian women are at the least risk.
- Blood transfusion in countries with poor medical resources. This is still a risk and you can buy a travel kit from your GP.
- Sharing dirty needles or even razor blades.

According to the World Health Organization (WHO) up to 90 per cent of those people infected in the world contracted HIV through heterosexual sex of whatever form. Dental dams (oral condoms preventing contamination during oral sex) and male and female condoms provide a high degree of protection, particularly those condoms containing the spermicide nonoxyl-9. There is a question mark at present over nonoxyl-9 and its possible effects on foetal development. Use stronger condoms such as Durex Extra Safe, Mates Extra Strong, HT Specials or Gay Safe.

If extra lubrication is required, do not use an oil-based lubricant such as Vaseline, baby oil, margarine or butter, as these will damage the condom. There are water-based lubricants available such as KY Jelly or Foreplay. If you need advice, ask the chemist.

HIV test

The decision to have a test for HIV infection is a difficult one. You cannot tell who is HIV-positive simply from appearances, the way they dress, act or speak. More importantly, every time you have unsafe sex you put yourself at risk. In the past, many people did not ask for a test. They were afraid of insurance companies, building societies and employers discriminating against them. To a very large extent this has changed.

If you are aware of your HIV status you can adopt a lifestyle which will help keep you healthy. This includes avoiding unnecessary risks to your health and provides your doctor with the insight to recognise more quickly early warning signs of potential medical problems and deal with them more effectively.

Even so, it is still a difficult decision and you should discuss it with your friends, partner and doctor. Most centres have good counselling for before and after testing. It is important to remember that you may remain 'HIV-negative' according to the test for up to three months after you have actually become infected. You can still pass on the virus to your partner during this time.

Living with HIV

Human immunodeficiency virus is a relative newcomer, having been discovered only in 1981. Although we know a great deal about how it infects and what it does to a person, we have yet to produce a vaccine or a cure so prevention is the name of the game. People tend to use the term HIV-positive and AIDS interchangeably. This is incorrect. Only when the immune system of an HIV-positive person has broken down can they be said to have the acquired immune deficiency associated with HIV. Once the body is unable to fight off infections, the person is prone to attack from bugs not normally considered a risk to life. This state of affairs has a variable onset but averages out at about twelve years after becoming HIV-positive. Survival after developing AIDS is also variable but generally you have a 50 per cent chance of living for three years. It sounds bad, but things are improving and new vaccines and treatments are just round the corner.

So if you are HIV-positive do you just give up? Not quite. By watching what you eat and drink your survival time can be increased significantly. Most health advice also applies to people with HIV. Avoiding smoking and excess alcohol, for instance, makes good sense. There are some specific points which should be considered.

Diet

Healthy diets are not quite the same when you are HIV-positive. Reducing cholesterol and fat intake will reduce your chances of having an early heart attack at say sixty years. Common sense will prevail as regards how useful this diet will be to an HIV-infected person, depending upon their age on infection. In fact, full-fat milk, cheeses, creamy yoghurt, butter and ice cream are all preferable to their low-fat alternatives. Fat supplies not only a valuable energy source but vitamins which are found only in fatty products.

The ideal body weight for a man with HIV is about 5 kg (11 lb) heavier than for other people of the same height. It is better to be a little 'over weight' than under although frank obesity should be avoided.

Salads are potentially hazardous. All vegetables should be thoroughly washed and salads should be avoided outside of your own home or when you cannot be sure they have been suitably prepared. Chicken, eggs and seafood must be fresh, hygienically stored and thoroughly cooked. Similarly, water, whether from taps or bottled, can contain organisms which are potentially dangerous to people with HIV. Drink only water that has been boiled then stored in the fridge.

Keeping fit makes good sense for anyone, but an HIV-positive person should avoid overexertion. Vaccinations are important, although your GP will advise you on ones which should be omitted. Flu jabs are very important and you should visit your GP each year before the winter.

Doom and gloom

It is easy to see all this as restrictive. But remember, you have as much right to happiness as the next person. There is no reason why you should not be sexually active, once you take the precautions of safer sex. You have a right to be loved and to love. The person you loved before they had the infection is still the same person after the diagnosis, only more precious. Count the 'do's' as well as the 'don'ts', they usually outnumber them and are more fun anyway.

The aim is to be as healthy and as happy as possible for as long as possible. So what's new, HIV or no HIV?

Hepatitis B

Fortunately, one of the more deadly sexually transmitted diseases, hepatitis B, now has a protective vaccine. The number of infected men is rising steadily and stands at roughly seven hundred each year. Women are not quite so badly affected although cases are on the increase. It can cause from as little as a flu-like illness to total destruction of the liver. Typically, it will cause varying degrees of jaundice, or yellowing of the skin and the whites of the eyes. This is the result of a build-up of a pigment which is normally broken down by the liver.

Obviously, most people will not require immunisation but depending upon your lifestyle it may be wise to consult your GP. It is transmitted in the same way as HIV, i.e. via the bodily fluids. There is evidence which suggests it is easier to become infected by the hepatitis B virus than by that causing AIDS. Indeed, it requires only a tiny fraction of a drop of blood to transmit the disease. For this reason it can be caught from sharing a toothbrush or kissing when there is bleeding from the gums. Worse still, the virus can survive a week or more in the dried state so can be picked up from, for instance, a razor. Like HIV infections, there is no way of knowing if the person with whom you are sleeping harbours the infection. The incubation period, i.e. how long it takes before the illness manifests itself, is six months from infection. Some people can 'carry' the virus and yet not exhibit the condition. There is no way of knowing if a person is a carrier simply from their appearance and it requires a blood test to be certain.

Genital herpes

This is the third most common STD in the UK. It is on the slow increase with around twelve thousand men infected in 1994. Slightly fewer women are affected. Doom and gloom once pervaded the scene when herpes was discussed. In fact, roughly 50 per cent of people who have had one attack never have another. Unfortunately, it is impossible to get rid of the virus completely. Herpes Simplex Virus (HSV) comes in two forms, HSV I and HSV II. Both will infect the same places and have a predilection for parts of the body where two types of skin meet. The corners of the mouth, the outer parts of the genital areas and even the anus can be infected by both forms. Type II herpes is more dangerous as it can affect the brain, causing a form of meningitis. Fortunately, this is a rare complication.

Both cause crusted blisters and then ulcers which weep a thin watery material. This is highly infectious as it contains the virus which causes the condition. Genital herpes comes in attacks which can last for months and then disappear for years or even for ever. You are definitely infectious during the presence of the sores. Even when sores are not present, it might be possible to pass on the infection. Stress and coincidental illness can bring on these attacks. For some people the condition will pass unnoticed with only tiny ulcers on the penis or vulva to show its presence.

Treatment

Acyclovir is a drug which can be applied directly to the affected skin or taken orally. It is most effective when the sores have yet to break out and are heralded by a tingling, itchy, painful sensation in the affected area. While controlling the condition, acyclovir will not provide a cure and will be needed once more for any subsequent attacks. Condoms with a spermicide appear to offer greater protection than those without. You need to arrange your sex life around the condition if you are having symptoms as these mean you are highly infective. Otherwise the use of condoms gives maximum protection for your partner.

Genital warts

Papilloma viruses, which cause warts, will affect any part of the skin. The virus can be transmitted by physical contact, including sexual intercourse. Like the warts commonly seen on people's hands, they can vary in size when on the penis from tiny skin tags to large fungating masses like cauliflowers. While the latter are hard to miss, the less obvious form can be prevented from causing infection only by covering the area completely. One in eight people attending GU clinics will have genital warts. Around one hundred thousand men and women are treated for these warts each year in the UK; many more may simply put up with them. It is still not certain if they are a factor in causing cervical cancer in women and rectal cancer in gay men.

Treatment

Thankfully, there are drugs which can be applied directly to warts which will cause them to disappear. Liquid nitrogen is now used less often as it can leave a painful 'burn' in such sensitive areas. The warts usually cause little discomfort although they are often itchy and may bleed with scratching. Use a condom to prevent catching them in the first place.

Syphilis

As the English used to refer to this disease as the 'French Pox', it seems only reasonable that the French referred to it as the 'English Pox'. It takes, as they say, two to tango. Although a potentially serious condition, syphilis is now rare in the UK with around seventeen hundred people infected each year. It is caused by a spirochaete, a microscopic parasite, which is highly infectious. Most people are unaware of the infection. Men complain of a painless ulcer on the penis around two weeks after intercourse. It is made worse when the ulcer disappears and the only sign of infection can be a fine rash over the body. If not treated this can develop over a number of years into a condition which can affect the brain. Women show few signs of the infection in the early stages except for small ulcers around the vagina so it can be missed by the man on intercourse. The parasite cannot pass through a condom, which will give almost 100 per cent protection.

Treatment

There are numerous horror stories about men having injections of penicillin directly into their penis. Thankfully, the penicillin (if the patient is not allergic to it) is given as a single large dose, which can be given by injection to any part of the body and will invariably cure the condition if caught in the early stages.

Chlamydia

Non-specific urethritis, which simply means an inflammation or infection of the urethra, is an all-embracing term which includes infection by chlamydia. People suffering from this infection complain of an intense burning sensation when passing water. Men may also have a white discharge from the penis. It actually causes few problems for men other than this discomfort but can be disastrous if it is passed on to women. For women, there can be intense pain along with a green discharge from the vagina. It is not only the single biggest cause of infection of the Fallopian tubes (pelvic inflammatory disease) leading to infertility and ectopic pregnancy (a potentially lethal condition where the baby attaches to the wall of the Fallopian tube instead of the wall of the womb), but can cause blindness and pneumonia in the child born to an infected woman. Thankfully rare in the UK, this is one of the major causes of childhood blindness in the world. Condoms provide almost perfect protection.

Treatment

Symptoms of severe burning on passing water should be investigated by your doctor as it is eminently treatable with antibiotics.

Trichomoniasis

Causing a yellow/green discharge from the penis or vagina,

this microscopic parasite lives in the urinary tract and usually causes pain when passing water but can be completely symptomless. When it has no effect on the male partner, but the female partner complains of a smelly green discharge from the vagina, tests may show its presence in the man.

Treatment

The parasite is sensitive to the antibiotic metronidazole (Flagyl), which is distinguished by its interaction with any alcohol consumed while taking this medicine. As it is related to a drug once used to treat alcoholics by making them violently sick should they revert to drinking, it is no surprise that the same can occur with metronidazole. Alcohol should not be taken with any antibiotic and can actually be dangerous with Flagyl.

Gonorrhoea

Caused by a bacterium, this disease is commonly misdiagnosed as it can often give only minimum symptoms. It is commonly known as 'the clap' from the Old French *clapoir* meaning 'venereal sore'. Gonorrhoea is not rare, as the fourteen thousand people who are infected each year in the UK will testify. It can cause a yellow/white discharge from the penis or vagina along with pain on passing water. When it infects the anus there can be a similar discharge. Most of the symptoms will start within five days of infection and include a vague polymyalgia, an ache of the joints and muscles. Although these can disappear after a further ten or so days, the person remains infectious. It can cause reduced fertility in both men and women if not treated.

Treatment

Antibiotics are usually effective. Condoms provide almost 100 per cent protection from infection.

Thrush

Contrary to popular belief, this common condition caused

by a yeast *Candida albicans* also infects men. It has the honorary title of being a sexually transmitted disease and is common among couples where there is no other sexual partner involved. Frequently, the female partner will develop the symptoms, be treated by her doctor only to find them back again. While women usually experience a creamy discharge and intense irritation, men may often have no idea that they are infected. Thus the infection is passed on again after 'successful' treatment. When it does occur in men, thrush causes a white discharge under the foreskin (if present) and a mild irritation over the head of the penis which may be worse when passing water. Occasionally, the head of the penis can appear mottled with a red blotch. Women generally fare much worse. An intense itch or pain while passing water is common.

Treatment

Thrush responds well to antifungals which can be applied topically or taken orally. It is prone to reappear, particularly if you are taking numerous courses of antibiotics; these tend to upset the natural balance of the body's commensal organisms, which keep the bad guy bacteria at bay.

Pubic lice (crabs)

As you read this section you will begin to scratch. Ten thousand people each year will be scratching for the right reason. So called because of their resemblance to crabs, these tiny yellow/grey parasites attach themselves to the pubic hairs and live on blood sucked from the skin cut by their claws. It is for this reason that they are intensely itchy. They live only for about ten days but before the female dies she will lay three to four eggs (nits) on the pubic hairs which then go on to increase the population. They are closely related to the louse which infests the hair of the face and head and can be treated in exactly the same way. Close body contact such as intercourse will provide the bridge for them to cross but soiled sheets or towels will also transport them to your body. Although it evokes shudders in most people just to think about them, they are actually relatively harmless unless they provide a route for the infection of more serious organisms, such as bacteria that cause abscesses.

Treatment

Both partners, and the immediate family, should be treated with a special lotion or shampoo. All bedding and clothes should be carefully washed and if necessary the mattresses should also be treated as it requires only a small number to survive to cause reinfestation. You do not have to shave your pubic hair. Check with your GP which lotion to use.

Your choice for treatment

You can attend either your own doctor or the local genito-urinary clinic at one of the major hospitals in your area. Confidentiality is all-important at these clinics, otherwise people would lose confidence and refuse to attend, defeating the whole object of their existence.

You will need to be honest with the doctor who asks you questions as it can be impossible to work out what is wrong without the correct information. There is no reason why you should not give a false name if you feel more comfortable although there is no chance of the fact of your attendance going any further, let alone any diagnosis that may be made.

Certain tests may be needed to make an accurate diagnosis although it may be fairly obvious on your first visit and the treatment may be started immediately with no return needed. It is worth remembering that the doctors and nurses who staff these clinics are professionals who see you as simply a person who, like any other patient, needs treatment. You may well feel embarrassed, but infections have no respect for people's sensitivity over just where they might be affected. Thankfully, the medical and nursing staff will be more considerate.

Thrush in the bush

> As a teenager, I had four or five bouts of thrush, never to be seen again – that was, until June 1995. Every time my boyfriend and I made love, the thrush would appear. We would both be treated, then we would make love, and the thrush would reappear. I am now at my wits' end, and I have got to the point where I don't want to make love any more. In fact, it has caused us to split up. I have itched so much that my doctor has informed me I have an extra layer of skin on my vulva. I am now in a new sexual relationship and I have had to explain about the thrush. He is very understanding, but it's starting to get me down again as the problem is still there. A friend of mine who has had the same problem for thirty years has suggested that I add salt or vinegar to my baths and still this doesn't work. I am twenty-five years old, so please don't tell me that I have another twenty-five years of this hell.
>
> P.A.

Candida albicans has a lot to answer for. As a yeast it likes warm wet environments with low acidity. You can develop a thrush growth anywhere on the body but most places are either too dry, acid or protected by the body's immune system. The body is protected by good guy bacteria which stops yeasts like *Candida* taking hold. Long courses of antibiotics destroy this cover and leave you open to infection. I'm not so sure about salt and vinegar baths. I suspect eating the potato crisp variety would do more good. Instead slap some live yoghurt on both of you. Use an antifungal cream like Canesten, but make sure he gets a dollop too. Better still, both take Fluconazole. It needs only a single tablet. I can only presume the 'extra layer of skin' refers to a reaction from scratching. The vagina is covered with skin which will scar like any other skin. It turns white when oestrogen levels fall, as in the menopause. Not to put too fine a point on it, lack of abrasion will also result in a white layer over the lining of the vagina. This is the basis of the routine test used by GPs to see if you have been eating. A white-coated tongue is the most convincing evidence that not a lot passed this way over the last few days. Alternatively, you have misheard your doctor. He was possibly referring to an extra oilskin for your Volvo.

Sixty-nine reasons for not worrying

> I am a 24-year-old woman and a few years ago I was treated for warts in my vagina. They were very difficult to get rid of and I was very happy when the treatment was over. I recently read in a magazine that vaginal warts can't actually be cured and now I don't know if I am completely healthy or not. If they can't be cured I will be unable to let my boyfriend give me oral sex, which we both love, as I don't want him to get a disease or cold sores. Occasionally, I get cold sores on my lips – is this because I have infected my own mouth? Also does it mean I can never have sex without a condom and am I permanently infectious? I'm very confused and worried that my 'sixty-nine' days are over – please help.
>
> J.E.

Warts are basically the same wherever you find them and are caused by the papilloma virus. Verrucas are exactly the same as warts on your hands except they grow inward from the pressure as you walk. I once knew a man who swore he had contracted verrucas of the mouth from sniffing his wife's shoes. Having said that, every time he opened his mouth he put his foot in it. Vaginal or for that matter penile warts are just a variation on the theme and are not related to cold sores. Herpes I is the virus which causes those irritating sores about the mouth. The genital variety are caused by Herpes II. Before AIDS hit the scene Herpes II caught the imagination of the press. In truth, we are talking about a completely different kettle of fish. Death from herpes is rare, unlike with HIV. Genital warts are contagious and most men will ignore them for years before seeing their doctor. This is a shame as there may be a connection between vaginal warts and cervical cancer. You have been most responsible and obviously love your boyfriend. Relax, there is no need to give up oral sex. While the papilloma virus may remain dormant for years, removal of the warts themselves reduces the risk of infection to almost zero. Mouth infection from genital warts is very rare anyway so go now and adopt the correct position, as they say in all the American cop movies.

Unfair advantage – abuse

Abuse comes in many forms, from simple lack of consideration to physical and mental harm. Sex is such a powerfully emotional physical act, there is always a fine line between what is and is not acceptable. This is further complicated by an overlay of morals which vary from one culture and indeed one person to another. These morals also change with time. Even so, common sense will often dictate what is acceptable. This basically boils down to whether all parties have consented, whether all are of legal age to consent, and whether anybody gets hurt.

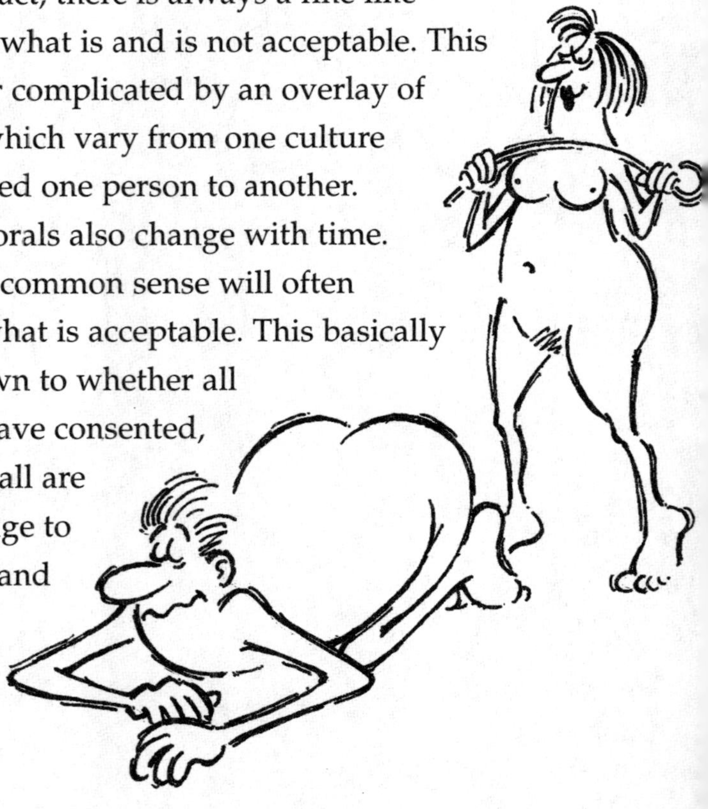

I'll leave you to judge who is being abused, by whom and who is getting hurt. It's not always quite so obvious as we might like to think.

Self-abuse

> Ten years ago I had an operation to remove a tiny cyst on the side of my penis. This provoked a compulsive reaction with me mutilating myself consistently for hours every day over this period, although recently this has stopped. With extreme anxiety and obvious difficulties in having a normal life with someone, I have tried suicide since having an orgasm is frustrating and sexual intercourse is not realistic. Can I get plastic surgery? Please help.
>
> D.K.

Cysts can occur anywhere, even on the penis. More serious conditions such as cancer can also affect the penis. Any operation can arouse a feeling of disgust when it involves some disfigurement of the body. Amputation is a classic example and part of the rehabilitation process involves helping the person come to terms with their body image. When it comes to something as important as your penis it is not surprising that you have reacted badly to surgery. The good news is you have already started to look forward. You really should see your GP and ask for a consultant's opinion if you are badly disfigured. Plastic surgery can be very effective and may be available on the NHS, particularly if your original operation was carried out under its auspices.

Physical and mental violence

Getting beaten up is common, even between 'loving' couples. It can never be condoned from whatever quarter it is delivered. Women come off worse although men are increasingly reporting physical abuse from their female partners. It is not easy to teach self-control, particularly when society is giving mixed messages over what is acceptable when it comes to violence. The portrayal of sexual violence in the media comes perilously close to making such violence 'sexy', in some cases explicitly. Providing real sex education and addressing the problems which give rise to the frustration, such as work, money or the lack of both, are part of the answer.

Third time lucky

> I am a twenty-year-old woman who has had nothing but disastrous relationships. I was fifteen when I had my first serious boyfriend. It was brilliant at first, but then he started taking drugs and beating me up. My next boyfriend used to force himself onto me if I said no to sex. Now I am seeing a very loving and understanding guy whom I love very much and am planning to marry next year. My problem is that I can't bring myself to make love with him. I nearly always pull away and the times I have gone through with it I have been drunk. Please give me some advice on what to do as if I get married with this hanging over me it will probably end in divorce.
>
> S.Y.

You are quite correct. Your marriage probably will end up in divorce unless you get this sorted out before you marry. Marriage itself is no magic cure or quick fix. Any problems you have before taking the plunge will still be there when you surface. Your story is sad but not unique. Many women have had such a terrible time and managed to find happiness at the end. You sound as though a big break is heading your way and you want to grab it with both hands. There is no simple answer but being able to talk to someone who is an expert and can give objective positive advice may make all the difference. More importantly, talk to your boyfriend about what you went through. From what you say of him I doubt if there is any danger of rejection. It will give him an opportunity to understand what you experienced and will explain your need to sort things out so you can be as happy as you obviously are going to be. Keeping all this to yourself will only make the anxiety and fear even worse.

Sad legacy

Without doubt the saddest form of abuse involves children. This grim side of life has traditionally been hushed up and is only now really coming to light. Institutions as well as individuals, often in positions of responsibility, are being exposed for their dreadful legacy to children's lives. Again society has mixed opinion about abuse. Some would say that sending children away from home to boarding schools at infant ages is a form of abuse. We may not be sending our kids down the mines or up chimneys any more but we are prepared to buy goods from countries which perpetrate the equivalent by the use of child labour. Sexual abuse is particularly nasty, as this letter shows.

Abused when young

> I'm a gay man aged twenty-four. Between the ages of four and seven, I was continually and violently raped by another male relative, after which I received no help from my family. I have only had one serious relationship in my life which ended because I won't participate in anal penetrative sex – this idea really frightens me. Now I am worried that I will never settle down in a relationship because of my dread of anal sex.
>
> Please help me, I'm really unhappy.
>
> K.M.

Child abuse, of both sexes, is much more common than we would like to think. Most of the perpetrators of this mangling of childhood are protected by family, figures of authority and even religious organisations. No social class or ethnic group can claim a monopoly of this sad phenomenon. Sexual persuasion is a factor although not in the way many would think. Gay men are actually less likely to abuse children than are heterosexual men. Women are also not immune. Many cases are brought against mothers or relatives of children so mistreated. Thankfully, it is coming out into the open more and institutions are finding it more difficult to protect those people who should be exposed for what they are. Your sad story is unfortunately not a rare occurrence. Heterosexual women and men also find themselves unable to enjoy sex properly after such histories of abuse. Whatever your sexual persuasion you have the right to enjoy sex and counsellors will help you overcome your fears and phobias after your terrible experience.

Lack of consideration

Not all forms of abuse are so horrendous, but there can be a mental scar none the less. At times it can be difficult to sort out sheer lack of thought for the other person from actual intended harm.

A heavy weight on her mind

At the age of fifty-two I had my first sexual experience, which only lasted a few weeks, but now I am living with my first proper partner. The only problems we have are sexual and there's not much fun at all in the bedroom, which is mostly because he is so much taller, heavier (eighteen stone), stronger and more experienced than me. I try to please him but he says he is master of the bedroom and doesn't understand that I am frightened of his weight

> falling on top of me. He rests his hand on my right shoulder to support himself, but it's arthritic and hurts plus I worry his hand is going to slip and go round my throat. This means I am always tense and just want to get sex over with. Frequently, our lovemaking ends in frustration with him shouting and me trying not to cry, which drives him mad. I don't like going on top of him because I've put on lots of weight since I met him. He's such a lovely man in every other way and when sex is good, it's wonderful. I don't want to lose him but it's making me very stressed out and I can't sleep well. Please help.
>
> S.E.

Communication between lovers is not always the best. Your partner's dominance is only acceptable if it is acceptable to you. He can still feel the dominant partner without scaring you half to death but you do need to talk about it to him. Putting on a significant amount of weight is paradoxically a sure sign of being unhappy over something. Eating makes you feel better and able to cope. Unfortunately, overeating only makes things worse, which then makes you eat even more. A vicious circle. You could experiment with different positions such as him behind with you on your side. Once the element of fear is removed, you should be able to enjoy sex again and this will help both of you. At the end of the day you are going to have to think about your future and if things do not improve whether you can live with the fear.

Twenty of the scariest questions I have ever been asked

Some questions can petrify me. A man once asked me whether or not it was safe to have sex if you rubbed your penis with lemon juice before intercourse. As his eyes were watering at the time I suspected he had put this novel, innovative and totally insane theory to the test. Sure enough, when I examined him, the helmet of his uncircumcised member resembled a Belisha beacon.

'I've had a bit of trouble pulling my foreskin back into place,' he told me, which was not altogether surprising as his glans was now the size of a small, hot football. Men do tend to underestimate the sensitivity of the glans and wonder why they are walking like John Wayne after a night's indulgence. Ironically, women once used a cut lemon as a form of contraception, which explains that enigmatic smile on the Mona Lisa's face. 'Some poor sod is going to get a surprise after this painting is finished,' she was probably thinking. I always wondered why Leonardo da Vinci had such a pained expression.

Can you get pregnant while you are breastfeeding?

This question is usually asked by the father of twelve children. Although there may be a prolonged delay in the resumption of periods and thus ovulation, there is no way of knowing just when it is going to start. Obviously, an egg has to be released for a period to follow. If unprotected intercourse takes place at this time there will be an even more prolonged delay. Getting pregnant is another excellent way of stopping periods.

Does the pill prevent you catching VD?

A patient once told me he had caught a dose of vernacular disease. As he swore blind it was the truth he was obviously correct. Venereal disease is an old term for sexually transmitted diseases. The pill most definitely does not stop you picking up fellow travellers. Condoms on the other hand will protect you from almost all nether region nasties *and* prevent unwanted pregnancies. Unfortunately, men will often leave contraception entirely up to the woman. Vaginal condoms are now available which really do protect a woman from a fate worse than death, in fact just death.

Does masturbation make you deaf?

Given the horrendous hours junior doctors work, asking any casualty officer this question will prompt a reply of

'Pardon?' In truth, masturbation doesn't affect your hearing. Worse still, it has no such effect on your mother's hearing either, who invariably rushed into your bedroom thinking you were being attacked by a Dobermann pinscher with a stutter.

Is there something wrong with masturbating when you are having regular sex?

Masturbation is subtly different from sex. First, it is almost 100 per cent safe except when performed in zero gravity. Most men and women in stable, happy relationships also masturbate. This is where fantasy plays its part. Many people masturbate after sex to prolong the pleasure. This is particularly noted in couples where one of them falls fast asleep with the final gasp with little time to ask the other whether the earth moved for them also.

Can you reuse a condom by turning it inside out?

Desperation is truly a terrible thing. The short answer to this question is yes, but your choice of sexual acquaintances may be severely restricted afterwards. You could also be a daddy as sperm can survive for a short space of time in the air. Additionally, you may also

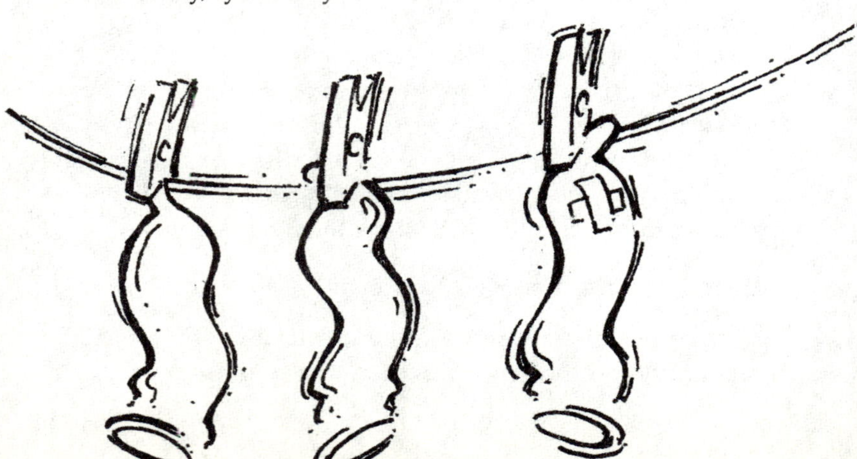

contract just about any sexually transmitted disease going. But yes, you can reuse a condom by turning it inside out just as you can wear three-day-old socks by using the same manoeuvre. On the other hand, it is probably better to shell out for another packet or have a cold shower. Both are a good deal cheaper in the long run.

Is it possible to get stuck when making love?

Cramp is a dreadful invention. It always affects your calf just when you really don't want it to happen. Simply wiggling your little toe causes intense pain. Vaginismus is the spasm which contracts the vagina. It is not so painful but it can be embarrassing. Some women even experience it when having a cervical smear performed. It can also occur during intercourse but the chances of endlessly doing the Lambada with your trapped partner round and round the kitchen are extremely low. More important is the discomfort it can cause for both of you. Extended foreplay, which does not mean asking, 'Are you awake, Sheila?', can do the trick, that and a sense of humour, along with a relaxed atmosphere. Not too relaxed though, you don't want to fall asleep, Sheila.

Can you can catch sexually transmitted diseases off a toilet seat?

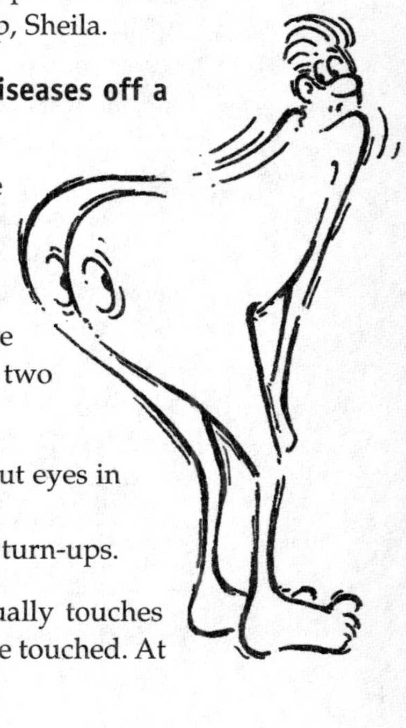

This is the standard question from people who treat British bogs like some of those you find in French campsites. For the enlightenment of those of you who always caravan instead, you stand over a small hole while attending to nature. This teaches you two things:

1 If God was French he would have put eyes in our bums.
2 French men prefer trousers without turn-ups.

On the plus side, your rear end never actually touches those parts that other people's rear ends have touched. At least not until you pull the chain and it flushes the entire loo area before you have a chance to get out of the door, slipping in the process. Even so, sexually transmitted diseases are called sexually transmitted diseases because that is how they are transmitted. Otherwise they would be called 'toilet-transmitted diseases' and there would be no such thing as turn-ups. Viruses such as the one which causes HIV cannot survive for any significant amount of time in the open air. Similarly, bacteria and other small organisms responsible for these infections need body fluids to survive. This immunity does not extend to larger creepy-crawlies like lice or crabs which can survive for a while, particularly their eggs, which are laid on the pubic hairs. Mind you, telling your doctor that you picked up your itchy little hitch-hikers from a public loo may raise an eyebrow but the treatment will be the same. (See 'Hangers-on – STDs'.)

Can you only catch HIV if you are gay?

So far as scary questions go, this has to be the mother of them all. The virus which causes HIV is not politically correct. It has no preferences for either sex or the way they choose to make love. It is true that in the UK more gay than straight men have developed the disease but things are changing. We have had a breathing space of a sort because the 'UK' virus strain is not as virulent as we first thought. There has not been the major epidemic once predicted. Enter a nasty variation on a theme. Some parts of the world have been devastated by the HIV virus, with it hitting both women and gay or straight men. Once this virus gets going in the UK there will be no second chances. Even with our present variety, unprotected casual sex, gay or straight, is near-suicidal. A condom provides almost 100 per cent protection and beats the hell out of half a lemon. Some of them even taste better too, so I am told.

Is petroleum jelly the best lubricant?

Yes is the answer if you are talking about a baby's bum but

for use with a condom you would be wiser using sandpaper. At least you would feel the condom falling to pieces. Petroleum-based lubricants will dissolve most condoms, particularly the ultra-thin varieties. Always use water-based lubricants such as KY Jelly; they are also less of a fire risk during burning passion.

Can you use a tampon to protect you from getting pregnant?

There is a doctor in England who uses tampons to stop severe nosebleeds, though walking around with one up your nose has not yet hit the television advertisements. Tampons are a marvellous invention for soaking up blood such as the menses, or a nosebleed for that matter. Unfortunately, they are not quite so good at stopping little genetic torpedoes hell-bent on being the first successful headbanger. Not only will they not prevent pregnancy, they provide even less protection against sexually transmitted diseases. Part of a casualty officer's life is taken up by removing these machines after they have been rammed home in a fashion not unlike loading a cannon. Worse still, they can be forgotten and fresh tampons used for the rest of the period. Removing them can then be hazardous as the tampon becomes saturated with offensive bugs a lot worse than headbangers. Septic shock is no joke and lives have been lost so de-tampon before the fun with your ramrod, if you follow my drift.

If the man does not actually ejaculate is the woman still safe?

This is part of the 'You can trust me, I'm in complete control' approach favoured by men who mistakenly put their money into the chewing gum machine instead of the condom dispenser. As this fundamental error was caused by fifteen pints of lager, you have some idea of exactly how much control he will have over his bodily functions. If you like a bit of a flutter on the Grand National you might want to take your chance on the lager reaching those places three of sand and two of cement cannot reach. It will not, however, make any difference to your risk of picking up a nasty sexually transmitted disease such as HIV. In terms of 'fates worse than death', men produce a pre-ejaculatory fluid designed to smooth the troubled waters for the following sperm. Even without ejaculation this fluid may contain sperm sitting in the pipeline from an earlier, more successful mission. If any man asks you to accept this 'guarantee', you should first check whether he can chew the gum he bought and walk at the same time.

Is it safe to have only one testicle?

This is a trick question. Yes, it is safe if you actually had the other one removed for whatever reason. An unremoved, undescended testicle increases your chances of cancer by at least four times. In terms of conferring immunity from becoming a father, you are most definitely not safe. Each testis produces more than enough sperm to produce a chip off the old block. Similarly, your levels of testosterone will remain normal. The pituitary, a gland in the brain, controls the circulating amounts of sex hormone and simply prods the testicle into more action should levels fall. Mind you, Hitler thought he was pretty safe and look what happened to him.

Can you get HIV from mouth-to-mouth resuscitation?

As most of the teenage population appear to be performing this life-saving procedure on each other every Friday night, the answer is probably no. There is a theoretical risk from saliva, which may contain infinitely tiny amounts of the virus; this risk is so small as to be non-existent. If the resuscitee is bleeding from the mouth this increases the risk but it is still relatively small. Blowing through a perforated piece of plastic barrier film further reduces the risk. At the end of the day you have to decide whether the small risk is worth it. The chances of meeting someone needing this attention who has HIV out of a population of fifty-two million are extremely low. Personally, I always carry a sprig of parsley in case they have been eating garlic. Most of my patients have green teeth after coming round.

Does having sex on an aeroplane make your testicles blow up?

Fortunately not, otherwise it would give terrorists a whole new angle on plane hijacks. Members of the Mile-high Club, an exclusive group of underweight individuals who loiter around airborne toilets, are particularly happy. 'You are aware of something which doesn't happen on the ground,' I was told by one leading member, who wishes to remain anonymous. 'Perhaps it is the reduced cabin pressure?' More likely the cabin crew adjusting the video camera for the next office party. If you take a plastic mineral water bottle on board it will fizz far more on opening because the cabin pressure is maintained as that at a few thousand feet. This has no effect on the internal organs, or the external ones for that matter. Newton's law states, however, that to every action there is an equal and opposite reaction so you might like to tell your mile-high partner to adopt the brace position.

How long after sex can you take the morning-after pill?

A surprisingly large number of questions come from men. An equally unsurprising number of calls come from men four weeks after sex and a recent phone call. The so-called emergency pill is simply a very high dose of sex hormones. It prevents a fertilised egg from implanting on the uterine wall. One dose is taken immediately, followed twelve hours later by another. After forty-eight hours the chances of preventing pregnancy begin to decline. If left too long there is a theoretical danger of damaging the developing foetus without stopping the pregnancy. You will need a pregnancy test performed three weeks afterwards. The emergency pill is very effective but not in the same league as the oral contraceptive pill itself. You need a doctor's advice if you suffer from high blood pressure or have ever had a problem with blood clots.

Can semen make you fat?

I am always intensely jealous of anyone who asks this question as it implies they are having much more fun than I am. Semen is a mixture of fructose (the same sugar as honey), an acid-neutralising substance, minerals, lubrication fluid and tiny amounts of sperm. It has a calorific value similar to honey from very lazy bees. Absorption in the vagina is poor and contributes little if any in the way of energy. On the other hand, all the effort involved in getting it there is the equivalent of a five-mile jog. On balance, semen most definitely does not make you fat.

Can semen give you cancer?

There is no evidence that semen causes cancer. From an evolutionary point of view, it wouldn't really make much sense if all the females of a species promptly died a horrible death every time they tried to procreate. For many years a battle raged over whether sex with uncircumcised men caused cervical cancer. It was noted that virgin women never contracted cervical cancer and that Jewish women in Israel had a lower incidence than women in, say, the UK. Obviously, the scientists thought, it's all down to the foreskin. When all the statistics are examined more fully, it appears that promiscuity is a greater factor and that the presence or absence of the foreskin is of relatively little consequence. If you, therefore, were one of the countless number of men who laid down their wobbly bit for the sake of womankind, I have a message from the scientists: 'Sorry about the tip-off.'

Is cling film a suitable alternative to a condom in an emergency?

Obviously, the word emergency means different things to

different people. I was once phoned at 4 a.m. to prescribe an emergency 'morning-after pill'. Cling film, or rubber gloves for that matter, are not a suitable alternative to anything except pockets full of tuna and cucumber and smelly fingernails. Despite its name, cling film slips off very easily once wet; likewise rubber gloves unless you choose the fingers very carefully and with a fair degree of prescience. Worse still, phthalates present in plastic food wrappings may make the whole thing an academic exercise through chemical emasculation.

Is butter a good lubricant when using a condom or is it safer to use margarine?

No to both, even if you would never know it wasn't butter. Oil-based lubricants dissolve latex condoms. Petroleum jelly, cooking oil or even WD40 will produce a slippery slope towards a drippy willie, not to mention unwanted fatherhood. Use only water-based lubricants.

Is everything you read about sex in books absolutely true?

No.

Useful addresses and telephone numbers

From 1 June 1999 new telephone numbers for some regions of the UK came into use. The new numbers will run parallel with the old numbers until 22 April 2000. In the list below, where relevant, we give the old number followed by the new number in brackets.

AIDS helpline
TEL 0800 567 123 (National 24-hour freephone)
TEL 0800 282 445 (English, Bengali, Hindi, Punjabi and Urdu) 6 p.m.–10 p.m.
TEL 0800 776600 (Welsh) 11 a.m.–11 p.m.

AIDS helpline Northern Ireland
TEL 01232 249268 (028 90249268)

BHAN (Black HIV and AIDS Network)
111 Devenport Road, London W12 8PB

Body Positive
14 Greek Street, Soho, London W1V 5LE
TEL 0171 287 8010 (0207 287 8010) FAX 0171 287 8020 (0207 2878020)

British Association for Counselling
1 Regent Place, Rugby CV21 2PJ
TEL 01788 578328

British Association for Sexual and Marital Therapy
PO Box 62, Sheffield, Yorkshire S10 3TS

Brook Advisory Clinics
233 Tottenham Court Road, London W1P 9AE
TEL 0171 323 1522 (0207 323 1522)

Northern Ireland Headquarters
29A North Street, Belfast BT1 1NA
TEL 01232 328866 (028 90328866)
FAX 01232 235735 (028 90235735)

Campaign for Homosexual Equality
PO Box 342, London WC1X 0DU
TEL 0402 326151 FAX 0181 743 6252 (0208 743 6252)

Continence Foundation Helpline
2 Doughty Street, London W21N 2PH
TEL 0171 831 9831 (0207 831 9831)

Dublin AIDS Alliance
53 Parnell Square, Dublin 1
TEL 00353 1 873 3480 FAX 003531 8733174

Family Planning Association
2–12 Pentonville Road, London N1 9FP
TEL 0171 837 5432 (0207 837 5432)
FAX 0171 837 3026 (0207 837 3026)

Family Planning Association (NI)
113 University Street, Belfast BT7 1HP
TEL 01232 325488 (028 90325488)
FAX 01232 312212 (028 90312212)

Gender Dysphoria Trust International BM
PO Box 7624, London WC1N 3XX

Health Education Authority
Trevelyan House, 30 Great Peter Street, London SW1P 2HW
TEL 0171 222 5300 (0207 222 5300)

Terrence Higgins Trust
52–54 Gray's Inn Road, London WC1X 8JU
TEL 0171 242 1010 (0207 242 1010) 12 noon–10 p.m.

Impotence Association
PO Box 1130, London W3 0BB
TEL 0181 767 7791 (0208 767 7791)

London Friend Helpline
TEL 0171 837 3337 (0207 837 3337)

Lesbian and Gay Line
TEL 01279 639637

Norm UK
PO Box 71, Stone, Staffordshire ST15 0SF

Prostate Association
Stanley House, 22 Paradise Street, Rugby CV21 3AP

Prostate Help Association
Langworth, Lincoln LN3 5DF

Prostate Research Campaign UK
36 The Drive, Northwood, Middlesex HA6 1HP

Relate Marriage Guidance
Herbert Gray College, Little Church Street, Rugby CV21 3AP
TEL 01788 573241 FAX 01788 535007

Northern Ireland Headquarters
76 Dublin Road, Belfast BT2 7HP
TEL 01232 323454 (028 90323454)
FAX 01232 315298 (028 90315298)

SPOD (Association to Aid the Sexual and Personal Relationships of People with a Disability)
286 Camden Road, London N7 0BJ
TEL 0171 607 8851 (0207 607 8851)

Index